TRUST & MO 232
SCEPTICISM VS AUTHO_____ ____ EUDCOTISE 233
DIFFS POL ORGS VS
POLS = CONTR E____
REVISIT DELIB. D____
IS PM INEVITABL____
'DEMANDS OF TH____
'RIGHT TO A GOOD____
'BEST PEOPLE AT T_P _____   5? ?
PM IMPROVE DEMOCRACY ('RULE?.) 238

The political marketing revolution

IND'L, CONSUMER SOV'GY VS. CIT'SHIP 238
— ECON MAN VS POLS & PHIL 239

POL CONSUMERS NEED TO 'BE ACTIVE TO A DEGREE' 239
ACADEMICS TO GIVE BEST SERVICE 239 [?]

PM 'FOCUSES ATTENTION ON THE PEOPLE, / THE
MARKET, THE CONSUMER, THE CITIZEN; SO IT
MAKES SENSE THAT FOR IT TO REACH IT'S
POTENTIAL' POL CONSUMER AS WELL AS PRODUCER
(MARKET) MAKE IT WORK 239-40

POL CONSUMER → BENEFIT OF IND'L SOC 240
(RESPONSIBILITY)

RISE OF POL CONSUMER 4-5

MOPS IN GOVT (PRESSURE)

CONSEQS OF CHANGING SOC

RISE OF CONSUMERISM & MARKETING IN BUS'S

6 ECON DEFN OF POLS 'ALL IN SCARCE RESOURCES'

Published in our
centenary year
≈ 2004 ≈
MANCHESTER
UNIVERSITY
PRESS

The political marketing revolution

Transforming the government of the UK

Jennifer Lees-Marshment

Manchester University Press

Manchester and New York

distributed exclusively in the USA by Palgrave

Copyright © Jennifer Lees-Marshment 2004

The right of Jennifer Lees-Marshment to be identified as the author of this work has been asserted by her in accordance with the Copyright, Designs and Patents Act 1988.

Published by Manchester University Press
Oxford Road, Manchester M13 9NR, UK
and Room 400, 175 Fifth Avenue, New York, NY 10010, USA
www.manchesteruniversitypress.co.uk

Distributed exclusively in the USA by
Palgrave, 175 Fifth Avenue, New York,
NY 10010, USA

Distributed exclusively in Canada by
UBC Press, University of British Columbia, 2029 West Mall,
Vancouver, BC, Canada V6T 1Z2

British Library Cataloguing-in-Publication Data
A catalogue record for this book is available from the British Library

Library of Congress Cataloging-in-Publication Data applied for

ISBN 0 7190 6306 X *hardback*
0 7190 6307 8 *paperback*

First published 2004

13 12 11 10 09 08 07 06 05 04   10 9 8 7 6 5 4 3 2 1

Typeset in Sabon
by Servis Filmsetting Ltd, Manchester
Printed in Great Britain
by CPI, Bath

To all those in my life – family, friends, colleagues – who have ever encouraged or inspired me to try out new ideas and follow my dreams.

Contents

List of boxes, tables and figures

Boxes

Tables

Figures

Preface

The idea for this book, like most research, was born out of the unanswered questions of previous study. In September 1999 I was in the process of submitting my doctoral thesis on how parties were using political marketing to win elections, and trying to anticipate criticisms. One problem was Stage 8, 'delivery', in the process I envisaged parties going through. This was a big problem, because it was possible to see that parties would go through the rest of the process with no problem, then, reaching delivery, falter because this involved the rest of the political system – the media, parliament, local government, public services etc. Whilst on a work trip to London, I browsed in a book shop and saw a book on public sector management that had a chapter on marketing in it. Scanning it, I realised there was a whole other area of marketing – public sector marketing – which could be explored. I realised then that I could no longer study political marketing just by focusing on parties. Political marketing involved other areas of politics also, and so must the study of this new phenomenon. I added the odd paragraph or two to my thesis saying so and over the next few months played around with the idea that political marketing needed to expand to involve all areas of politics.

During this time, with my ears newly attuned to comments and events beyond the world of party politics, I began to see more evidence for the idea that marketing was permeating other areas of politics. Television programmes, conference papers and conversations all pointed to the need to broaden my research. Moving from politics to management at Aberdeen University, I found the new area of literature within management studies on the marketing of services or non-profit organisations. Interaction with staff at the newly formed Scottish parliament and with other visiting speakers I arranged for my students provided further support for the belief that marketing had indeed permeated all areas of politics. Even the monarchy was not immune. I also glimpsed a link between the use of political marketing in one area of the political system and the other: Labour's market orientation in turn led to greater pressure on the health service to satisfy the public. Not only was marketing affecting non-party areas of politics, it was affecting the system itself, and transforming the governance of the

SALE

255 / 9455   06 FEB 2005 12:30

CASHIER: SJL

9719063078   POLITICAL PARK   16.99

TOTAL   ITEMS   1   16.99

CASH   20.00
CHANGE CASH   3.01

UK. I began plans for my next work the week after I submitted my final manuscript for the PhD, and in spring 2000 I submitted a proposal for a second book to Manchester University Press.

This is the first book to argue that marketing has permeated all areas of politics – not just party politics, but local government, the media, parliaments, health and education services, charities and even the monarchy. As such, it is innovative in thought, utilising a wide range of literature from two disciplines, political science and management, but it does not claim to be an in-depth, tried and tested empirical work. Political marketing is a new and exciting field of study, but blazing a new path in any walk of life is never an easy process. As other cross-disciplinary academics will understand, this book is driven by the desire to make sense of empirical reality, and as such fails to fit perfectly within the constraints of either parent discipline. It has attempted to integrate a wide range of the most pertinent literature, but it was impossible to capture everything out there.

Some of the areas I have touched on have been well researched (e.g. health care marketing) whilst other areas have never been viewed from this angle (such as parliamentary or monarchy marketing). All required critical, challenging thought. This book is therefore a thought piece. In-depth, empirical, quantitative work on political marketing will have to come later. What this book does, however, is to show that political marketing is broad and encompasses all areas of politics, that there are links between the use of political marketing in party politics and the rest of the system, and that therefore a 'political marketing revolution' has taken place in the UK. The book is both prescriptive in indicating how political organisations might use political marketing, and empirically descriptive, acknowledging how in practice the use of political marketing is often extremely limited and difficult. Ideas have been generated by discussions with local government workers, staff in the Scottish parliament, party politicians, educational marketers and staff working at Buckingham Palace.

I therefore offer it to the academic community, expecting criticism but hoping to stimulate debate. In doing so, I acknowledge the support of all the political actors and staff who have taken time out to speak to me about their use of political marketing; to Manchester University Press for being willing to take on a young author; to my undergraduate students at Aberdeen and Keele universities who participated and responded so positively to the courses I based on this book in spring 2002 and 2003; to Richard Harrison for his unstinting support of my interest in political marketing and for giving me the time to explore the idea in teaching and research in my first lectureship in marketing; to all of my colleagues in the Department of Management Studies at Aberdeen who provided the warmest and most welcoming environment in which I have ever worked, especially Lorna McKee, Angus Laing, Nisha de Silva, Clare Guest and Gisela Van Bommel; to my new colleagues in management and higher levels at Keele (particularly Nicholas O'Shaughnessy and Richard Sparks) who supported the establishment of the Centre for Political Marketing; to all those in the political marketing community, especially the PSA Political Marketing Group (particularly Darren Lilleker and David Dunn) and the 2002 Political Marketing Conference delegates and presenters; to my parents, who I have come to realise passed on a double dose of the genes which make one rebellious and questioning of authority; and to family and friends all over the world, particularly those in Aberdeen who helped me learn that maybe work wasn't the only thing in life, so I could survive the stress of the last few years to enable me to get to where I am now and complete this book. Indeed, Scotland was a friendly and open place both socially and professionally; I vividly recall ending up attending a departmental meal in an Aberdonian restaurant and dancing with my academic colleagues on a table to the song *Dancing Queen*. No such thing has happened in England – at least not yet!

The varying pathways of academic life have now taken me full circle and I complete this book back where I started, at Keele University, albeit now based in management rather than politics. I am not entirely sure why I ended up back where I started, but the ten years between now and when I was an undergraduate have been an interesting journey. Hopefully this book will be as interesting a read.

Jennifer Lees-Marshment
Centre for Political Marketing, Keele University

1

Political marketing and the rise of the political consumer

Political marketing is sweeping through the British political system. Not only is it influencing how the political parties behave, but the parties themselves in government are then applying pressure to the health service, education, parliament and even local councils to become more responsive to the citizens these political institutions were created to serve. No longer so deferential, the British people have demanded these changes, with increasingly critical voices ready to offer opinions of their own. They are unwilling always to accept the advice a doctor gives them on how they should be treated, or the verdict of a school teacher on the academic future of their child, or the inefficiency of a local government administrator. They want to have a say in how every area of politics is run – because every area affects their daily life and future happiness. The local school, hospital, doctor's surgery, council, police service and transport system have a significant influence on their quality of life. It is not just a case of the public failing to believe what party politicians promise during election campaigns. Citizens question *every* aspect of elite provision and will no longer accept being told by the elite what is good for them. Education, a more fluent social structure, exposure to different ideas and ever-flowing information through the mass media and the internet mean that Britain's 'political consumers' are as critical as we expect customers to be within an economic marketplace.

Political organisations are therefore responding with political marketing. Staff within the new Scottish parliament and councils up and down the land, at every school, hospital and surgery, have realised that the old ways of operating do not work. Every organisation needs to understand the people it is trying to serve, to design a service that they will want, if it wishes to succeed, even if it is not in the business of making profit. Marketing is being adopted not just by political parties, but by every organisation within the non-profit, political, public or governmental sphere. The UK is experiencing a political marketing revolution that is transforming the way the country is run.

This book provides an overview of this transformation. It explores how marketing has permeated eight significant areas of the political system. It investigates parties, the monarchy, the media, charities, health, education, parliament and local government. It examines the extent to which these areas show signs of using political marketing as well as explaining the forces behind such a change. It provides theoretical concepts of how each area might use political marketing, and draws on primary research and evidence from a wide variety of sources to illustrate them. Each chapter looks at the three different orientations of product, sales and market for the chapter's subject area, with a box outlining the stages of each approach as they apply to that area theoretically, followed by a more detailed empirical examination of the processes and the extent to which the organisations studied follow these stages. Where there is an exception to the development of behaviour through all three orientations, as with parties or the monarchy, the focus is on the dominant approach or approaches used. For example, although the monarchy's behaviour has historically been product oriented, Chapter 3 focuses on the more up-to-date examples of sales- or market-oriented forms of behaviour. The Conservative and Labour parties both tried to follow a market orientation in order to win the 2001 general election, so Chapter 2 focuses on this model rather than on product or sales orientation. The overall aim of the chapters is to stimulate discussion in the present and further research in the future.

This book's main purpose, like that of its predecessor, *Political Marketing and British Political Parties* (Lees-Marshment 2001a), is to show how aspects of the political system are changing and traditional conceptions of how the country is governed are in need of revision. It also aims to show how there are links between changes in one aspect of the political system and another. The change in party behaviour captured by *Political Marketing and British Political Parties* has stimulated the rise of political marketing in other areas of politics. Parties now need to pay greater attention to how policies get through the system so they can be seen to deliver.

Like anything that challenges existing conceptions, this book will no doubt be subject to much criticism, but it is to be hoped that it will nevertheless stimulate further books, articles, papers and debates. It is a thought piece, rather than a review of academic literature or a major empirical positivist test of marketing in politics. It simply aims to stimulate, excite, question, illustrate and observe so that others may follow with their own opinions and analysis. It begins, not ends, the debate.

Political marketing is, in practice, an increasingly exciting and integrated phenomenon that the majority of significant public figures and political staff are vividly aware of. It holds the potential to transform politics as we know it, and exert a tremendous influence on the way everyone's life is run, but we will only ever reach a greater understanding of the existing and potential consequences of political marketing if we acknowledge and accept the breadth and nature of the phenomenon. This book is empirically driven and whilst drawing on a wide range of literature from different discipline areas, it could not cite every potentially relevant academic work, particularly when it deals with so many subsections of politics that could be books in themselves. Furthermore it would not fit the purpose to construct a book driven by existing literature: literature reviews do not make for exciting reading.

The main body of the book begins with an update on party marketing in Chapter 2. This illustrates how the Conservative and Labour parties continued to use political marketing in 1997–2001 but both experienced difficulties. Labour's big question is delivery – hence they put pressure on the health and education systems to become market oriented. The book then moves on to the monarchy, whose political marketing orientation can be affected by that of the party in government. Chapter 3 therefore explores how substantial changes have occurred within the royal family and how it has also succumbed to market forces. Responding to the nature and demands of its market, the monarchy designed a popular product: the palace pop party during the 2002 jubilee.

To do this, the royal family utilised television, which leads us onto the media. Chapter 4 indicates how significant debates are currently taking place within television in particular about how to report politics, given the significant fall in turnout in the 2001 UK general election from around the usual 70 per cent mark to the low 40s. Other developments, helped by the advance of technology, are producing more interactive media in radio and television that increase the participation of consumers. The BBC in particular has had to undergo a massive change from being product oriented and thinking it knew what was best for the public to trying to be market oriented. This nevertheless raises questions about whether the media should be subject to market forces and the need to entertain.

The media is an extremely important force in the political system and the channel through which other organisations and actors communicate their behaviour. Chapter 5 examines how charities have faced increasing competition for financial and active donors, and how the charities' first response was to move to a sales orientation, focusing on dramatic events to gain media coverage and using direct mail and free offers to get money from donors. Recently, however, they have begun to move to a more market-oriented position and to try to create an established relationship with members, realising that some do not simply wish to give money but want to have a role and involvement in the organisation. Market intelligence helps the charities understand their market more effectively, and a market orientation has led some of them to work more co-operatively with related organisations such as health and educational institutions. Chapters 6 and 7 therefore look at the rising pressure on such institutions to become market oriented themselves, and at the barriers to doing so. Analysis of the increasing marketisation of health and education connects as well to the pressure from the governing market-oriented parties, which need to be seen to deliver in these areas. Chapters 8 and 9 consider how this pressure has spread to parliament, contrasting the use of political marketing by the new Scottish parliament with that of the more traditional Westminster, and then examining how local government is also aware of the need to respond to the rise of the political consumer. Throughout the book, an attempt is made to help the reader understand linkages between all the different areas being examined, links which are then further discussed in the final chapter in terms of their implications for UK governance and society.

Before beginning the journey through each area of the political system, however, we need to understand more about why political marketing has developed at all in the UK. To do this, we first examine the rise of the political consumer.

The rise of the political consumer

There are three main causes of the rise of the political consumer: pressure from market-oriented parties in government, which need to deliver; significant changes in society (education, communication, class, geographical and social mobility) that have altered people's attitude towards all political products, organisations and services; and the rise in consumerism in the business sphere that has stimulated changes in public attitudes in the political environment.

Pressure from governing parties to deliver

Political Marketing and British Political Parties illustrated how parties become market oriented in order to win elections, conducting market intelligence to identify voter demands, designing a product to suit, implementing it, communicating it, winning the election and then – Stage 8 of the theory says – needing to deliver. But political delivery means delivering on promises in health care, the education system etc., which means getting legislation through parliament and then implemented right down to the level of the local council. It is not straightforward, and encourages governing parties to look at other parts of the political system and to use political marketing in order to help fulfil the demands on the parties. This is why political marketing needs to move beyond the campaign (Laing and Lees-Marshment 2002). Under the market-oriented Labour government, there has been increasing pressure to deliver or be seen to deliver, especially given the definite pledges the party made for the 1997 election on education and health.

Consequences of a changing society

There are many factors that encourage the rise of the political consumer. The drop in party identification or strength of attachment to one party, falling party membership and growth of alternative means of political participation are just some of the cause. Electoral volatility has also increased, so voters are more likely to decide whom to vote for just before the election and to change their choice from one election to the next. In marketing terms the brand is not working any more; the consumer is more ready to switch brands, or try new products than ever before (see Lees-Marshment 2001a: 14–21 for further details, data and references). Furthermore, the public has always been somewhat critical of government and politicians, but it is also increasingly critical of all public officials (see Mortimore 2003: 107–121). Non-political changes help support the trend towards a new political market: political information comes from a variety of sources and is usually highly critical of all political elites, whether party politicians, doctors or teachers. An increasingly educated public has better skills to criticise and absorb this information; the population is also more socially and geographically mobile, being exposed to many different points of view in their lifetimes. This also means that any failing by, for example, a doctor becomes well known across the country or even the world, rather than remaining an isolated case.

Rise of consumerism and marketing in business

The rise of consumerism within the business sphere has gradually permeated the political arena. Collins and Butler (1998: 3) noted how 'private citizens, used to being treated as discerning customers in other aspects of their lives, are beginning to take a more consumerist view of the public service' (see also Walsh 1994: 63). There is a general move in society against simply accepting political rhetoric, towards a greater demand for demonstrable improvements in performances: better schools, health care, transport, police, parliamentary institutions, more efficient and responsive local government. Even the monarchy is becoming subject to citizen opinion. The UK has seen the rise of the political consumer: no longer are the public so deferential and unwilling to complain. They now understand that they are paying, however indirectly, for political services and believe they have a right to determine the nature and quality of those services as well as question the professionals who run them.

Result: political consumer

Consequently, there is a substantial and growing demand for all political organisations to become responsive to public needs and wants and therefore to use political marketing. The British people are more critical, with voices of their own. The people want results: they want a product geared to suit their needs and wants, and they want it to be delivered in a satisfactory manner. The entire political context in which organisations now operate has been transformed, and with the change has come pressure for the organisations themselves to change their behaviour. Indeed, we now see in Britain citizens acting like political consumers.[1]

The rise of the political consumer represents a transformation in the conditions of the political market in which organisations such as Westminster, the monarchy, the NHS, schools and universities are operating. If parties are to attract votes; hospitals patients; charities donors; schools pupils; local government public support; Scottish parliament visitors; universities students; they need to change their behaviour in response to the demands of those they seek to serve or gain support from. Furthermore, the low turnout in the 2001 UK general election has led many commentators in academia, politics and the media to wonder if voters are so dissatisfied with the political system that they won't even bother to go out and vote any more. Political consumers are as cautious and critical as those in the traditional economic marketplace or shopping centre, leaving politicians to wonder 'who will buy,' like the strawberry seller in the musical *Oliver*. Responding to this is not an easy exercise and organisations are finding that traditional politics no longer works so effectively.

The question for this book is: how can political marketing help? In the next section we will explore the basic nature of politics, the core concepts of marketing, and how they might go together.

The connection between politics and marketing

Politics is about power and conflict, the resolution of different demands: how systems work, how people relate to each other and how people organise. The study of politics examines how conflict is resolved, how the political system meets different demands. Everybody wants something different in life; politics examines how it is decided who gets what, when and how. It therefore includes areas such as:

- political behaviour: voting behaviour, electoral conditions, public opinion, support for institutions and organisations;
- political organisations: parties, interest groups, charities, movements;
- political institutions: parliament, public services, local government, media, monarchy.

Within these areas, politics studies the relationship between the masses and elite, including therefore:

- people and government;
- voters and parties;
- patients and health service;
- pupils and teachers;
- students and academics;
- members and charities;
- audience and media.

Politics explores how these groups interact to allocate scare resources. As Jones and Moran (1994: 6) defined it, politics describes 'the interactions of any group of individuals but in its specific sense it refers to the many and complex relationships which exist between state institutions and the rest of society'. Politics therefore holds the potential to affect every day of our life. Politics has traditionally been viewed as concerned with ideas, belief and ideology, not market pressures or demands.

The rise of the political consumer, and challenges to traditional behaviour by political organisations, however, have left many of the traditional tenets of political science semi-redundant and ill equipped to explain the world as it is now. There is therefore an opportunity for the academic scholarship of political science to be supplemented by that of marketing, from the different discipline of management. Political science, like other fields, emerged from various disciplines – philosophy, history, law, economics, sociology, psychology, geography and statistics – so a link with management studies or marketing in particular should not be so much of a surprise.

Marketing is about how organisations understand the needs of their consumers, design a product to satisfy them and communicate it to achieve their goal. The study of marketing is therefore concerned with:

- the relationship between an organisation's behaviour and its market;
- the product it offers and the response of consumers;
- all influences upon the relationship between the organisation and its market.

Marketing is therefore concerned not just with the selling of a product, but with how it is designed and whether it reflects the demands of those it is produced for. Whilst much of the literature on marketing is suited to business, it can be adapted to study the political world.

Political marketing: a more modern traditional politics?

The reason why marketing can be attached to politics is that in essence they share some common tenets: the aim to understand how political organisations act in relation to their market and vice versa. Furthermore, marketing, being somewhat more prescriptive, provides tools and ideas about how organisations could behave in relation to their market in order to achieve their goals. It can help an organisation understand the demands of its market. The idea of a political system that meets people's needs and demands links back to traditional politics: Jones and Moran (1994: 17) argue that British democracy 'means that the people can decide the government and exercise influence over the decisions governments take'. Political marketing is simply a way of doing this in the twenty-first century with a critical, well-informed and consumerist mass franchise.

Indeed, academics studying pure politics have themselves observed changes within the political system. For example, Peele (1995: 15) noted that beneath the superficial stability of the UK system, 'change was always occurring even if it was not always readily apparent to the naked eye . . . What is less certain is whether the traditional methods of organising the government of the United Kingdom are still sufficiently adaptable and resilient to cope with the wide range of demands on the system.' In Scotland, in particular, the creation of the Scottish parliament changes the nature of the overall political system. McFadden and Lazarowicz (1999: 100) commented that 'The establishment of the Scottish Parliament in 1999 will lead, almost immediately, to major differences in the way Scotland is governed. For the rest of the UK, government is changing in ways that would not have been contemplated less than a decade ago.' Westminster, Holyrood, local councils, every political party, hospitals, universities, schools, surgeries and even the monarchy cannot command public support and acceptance in the way they used to. They are therefore turning to political marketing as the means to understand and service their 'market' or people better.

Difficulties with marketing politics

It is, however, fully acknowledged that there a number of potential difficulties associated with applying marketing to politics. These will be discussed and explored further throughout the book.

First, there are clear differences between politics and business. The primary difference is language. Both in practice and within academic theory, the language of marketing is very different to that of politics. Another difference is goal. As Hannagan (1992: 17) observed, traditionally 'marketing has been linked to the concepts of profitability and of providing a competitive edge', which leads us to ask what role it could play in a political organisation, which is not supposed to be about making a profit. There is also a suggestion that market-oriented political marketing clashes with the traditional ethos of political and public organisations (see Lovelock and Weinberg 1990: 7; also O'Leary and Iredale 1976: 153; Sargeant 1999: 18; Lees-Marshment 2001b). Political organisations also have multiple, conflicting markets, in particular both the wider public and the government. Within the political arena, everyone can be interested in a political organisation because of its potential long-term influence on society. Another difference is the product. Political organisations offer a product to the public, but it is not readily obvious what this is. It is not a physical good. All of these will be taken into account and will be discussed in detail in each area or chapter and then again in the conclusion.

Another issue is that of the normative objections to political marketing. Many objections are voiced to the marketing of politics, which will no doubt be considered and raised by readers and the general academic and political community in the years to come, such as the following:

• Politics does not need to be marketed, and marketing lowers the tone of the institution or its perceived quality.
• Marketing is manipulative.
• Marketing will stop new ideas, innovation and creativity.
• Political marketing will lead to the end of ideology.
• Marketing focuses on short-term benefit.

There are also a number of more practical problems, such as:

• difficulty in implementing marketing in organisations;
• threat to professional expertise and political leadership;
• too much pressure to deliver.

Nevertheless, at the 2002 Political Marketing Conference held in Aberdeen, the party politicians and practitioners who attended and spoke were all aware of the phenomenon, if also concerned about the difficulties and complexities in marketing politics.

Political marketing

Scope of political marketing

One of the problems with discussing and researching political marketing is that the conventional view of political marketing is narrow and therefore does not reflect political practice. Ask a person on the street what political marketing is about – in fact, go one better than that, and ask the average academic at a conference – and they will say 'spin-doctoring and sound-bites'. This is not political marketing. This is behaviour that has developed alongside the domination of political communication by television. A party or any political organisation can engage in political marketing without spin-doctoring or producing sound-bites. Similarly, just because a party adopts effective media management does not mean it becomes market oriented or uses political marketing.

Political marketing is not just about spin-doctors or election campaigns: it represents the application of marketing to a wide range of political areas. Political marketing is about political organisations adapting techniques (such as market research) and concepts (such as a market orientation to satisfy user demands) originally used in the business world to help the organisations achieve their goals. This is in addition to the use of techniques to identify public demands and sell the political product on offer. In terms of application, political marketing can be applied to and is used by a wide range of political organisations and actors, including:

- political parties;
- health organisations;
- universities and schools;
- parliaments, e.g. Westminster and the Scottish parliament;
- local government and councils;
- newspapers and television;
- charities and interest groups;
- the monarchy;
- government departments, e.g. social security;
- the police;
- the civil service;
- employment offices and job centres.

Such organisations are turning to marketing to determine their behaviour, and so political marketing is no longer conceived as being simply about spin or snappy slogans in election campaigns. It is much more about *behaviour*, as well as organisation, policy design and leadership; it is more concerned with the design of the political product than how it is sold.

Definition of political marketing

Political marketing is, quite simply, the use of marketing by political organisations. Viewed more comprehensively (Lees-Marshment 2001a):

Political marketing is about political organisations adapting techniques and concepts originally used in the business world to help them achieve their goals. It studies the relationship between a political organisation or individual and its market, its use of marketing activities (market intelligence, product design, communication and delivery), its product, and its overall attitude (product, sales or market-oriented). Such political organisations include parliaments, political parties, charities, bureaucracies and television channels; their product legislation, policies or meetings; their market is the public, electorate, members, financial donors, tax-payers, benefit receivers or viewers; their goals are passing legislation, winning elections, campaigning for better rights for a section of society, and providing entertainment.

Comprehensive political marketing (CPM) (Lees-Marshment 2001a, 2001c, 2001d, 2003a, 2003b) is a term used to indicate how political marketing should be studied broadly. This approach will be taken throughout the book, so it is worthwhile highlighting the main aspects. CPM research has five principles: see Box 1.1. The most important point for this book is that political marketing involves the marketing of all areas of politics, which is why it considers other areas of politics, not just party behaviour.

Box 1.1 Comprehensive political marketing (CPM) principles

1 CPM applies marketing to the whole behaviour of a political organisation, not just communication.
2 CPM uses marketing concepts, not just techniques: the product, sales and market orientation as well as direct mail, target marketing and market intelligence.
3 CPM integrates political science literature into the analysis.
4 CPM adapts marketing theory to suit the differing nature of politics.
5 CPM applies marketing to all political organisational behaviour: interest groups, policy, the public sector, the media, parliament and local government as well as parties and elections.

Each area of politics has a different product, markets and goals, and these all need to be taken into account, whether in a party, interest group or public service. Throughout the book we will take certain steps or ask particular questions when studying each political organisation. It will then be possible to create an appropriate process for each organisation. Political marketing uses three main conceptual orientations to explain behaviour: product, sales and market orientations:

- A *product-oriented* political organisation would determine how to behave from its own skills, expertise and beliefs. It would then expect its users to respond.
- A *sales-oriented* political organisation would focus on presenting itself in the most positive light in order to achieve positive evaluations from users. It would concentrate on communicating the benefits of its behaviour and why it is better than any other competing organisation.

• In contrast, a *market-oriented* political organisation would have the creation of user satisfaction as its goal. It would attempt to understand those it seeks to serve and deliver a product that reflects their needs and wants. It would be open to changing the way it behaves in order to obtain more support.

In the political arena many organisations are now attempting to move towards a market orientation, but for a long whole the general approach of public institutions was more product oriented, and only when consumers became more critical did the institutions begin to think about becoming sales oriented. A political organisation may still succeed with a product orientation, however, because it has a 'niche' in the market, or no competition, or simply because it offers what people want. Over time, users can change their demands, or competitors can adopt the new idea (e.g. a political party may adopt the new policy first introduced or raised by a third party). However, if the organisation continues to hold a product orientation, it will not be able to adapt or respond to these. Political organisations are perhaps unlikely to adopt different orientations without stimulation from the market: without a decline in public satisfaction or a rise in criticism. However, even if an organisation becomes highly responsive, adopting a market orientation, it can end up slipping back to sales or product approaches. This has, for example, been observed amongst political parties once they get into power: they become remote from the people, or arrogant because of their success, and stop conducting basic political marketing activities such as market intelligence, or ignore the results.

The academic perspective: relationship between political marketing and the disciplines of management studies and political science

This book is not written only for academia: the intended aim is a wider spread than that. Nevertheless, obviously academics and students will be amongst the readership and so it is important to discuss the relationship between this book and the two main disciplines that feed it. As noted at the beginning of this chapter, this book cannot provide an exhaustive literature review, and this is not its purpose. The aim is to bring two disciplines together: to integrate them. To make the 'literature situation' clearer, Figure 1.1 is a diagram of the different aspects of political science and management science which can potentially feed into political marketing.

Doubtless other disciplines and areas could also contribute, such as communications itself, philosophy, sociology, psychology and economics. Every area has something to offer, but they cannot by definition all be 'right'. And political marketing, as an emerging field (or discipline), has the duty to pick out what works best from these literatures, even if it means going against some strictures of other disciplines. There are therefore many such issues and barriers to overcome, and this book attempts to make a start on doing so by overriding disciplinary objections and creating new theoretical frameworks that seem most appropriate to a study of the real world.

Figure 1.1 Political marketing literature umbrella

In doing so, it follows the current trend of the most recent political market-ing research. Although political marketing used to be confined to election cam-paigns, new research has developed, which takes it beyond the campaign and includes not only party behaviour but also education, health, government com-munication and local government. The 2002 Political Marketing Conference in Aberdeen had papers on all these areas. There is much enthusiasm amongst the political marketing community. The field will develop and grow tremendously over the coming years and doubtless will return to this book to criticise, update and improve the rudimentary cross-disciplinary theories written here – but if that happens this book will actually have succeeded in its intentions.

Until such development takes place, however, it is time to get on with this book. Political marketing is sweeping through the British political system. The rise of the political consumer has stimulated political parties to utilise political marketing, but also affects other institutions. Political parties were the first to use marketing, being more directly affected by the increase in consumerist behaviour because their survival depends on success in elections every four to five years, whilst the monarchy, on the other hand, has no such direct 'buying' mechanism. Marketed parties in turn put extra pressure on the health service, education, parliament, even local councils to become more responsive to the citizens these political institutions were created to serve. Tony Blair was re-elected prime minister in 2001 with a 'mandate to deliver'. There is pressure on the public services, such as the NHS and education, to become market oriented themselves: to identify the needs of users and develop a service that responds to this. The structures of delivery are increasingly important: parliament, the civil service, local government and devolved government all need to work effectively if the market-oriented parties are to achieve success in delivery. Charities are using direct mail to recruit donors. The health service is conducting market intelligence to design a plan of action. Academics have to think about the quality of their teaching and whether it meets student demands rather than simply do what they think is best. Teachers are subject to continual inspection and evaluation. The Scottish parliament is currently responding to results from market intelligence indicating that it has not established a public profile. Even the monarchy can think about what it offers to the public and study the results of polls and focus groups on its public standing. First, though, we start with the familiar, marketing major UK parties. Representation through elections is extremely important; it is the first step in the democratic process of governmhent being run for the people. Not only that, but, as we will see, it has the potential to influence every other area of the political system and so transform how the UK is governed, taking the ideas of political marketing with it as it goes.

Notes

1 Literature on postmodern consumerism moving beyond the high street into other areas of life such as politics could be incorporated within a discussion on this aspect.

Bibliography

Collins, N. and P. Butler (1998), 'Public Services in Ireland: A Marketing Perspective', Working Paper VII, Department of Public Administration, National University of Ireland, Cork, August.

Hamel, G. and C.K. Prahalad (1996), *Competing for the Future*, Harvard Business School Press, Boston.

Hannagan, T. (1992), *Marketing for the Non-profit Sector*, Macmillan, London.

Jones, B. and D. Kavanagh (1994), 'Pressure Groups', in B. Jones (ed.), *Politics UK*, Harvester Wheatsheaf, London. pp. 220–237.

Jones, B. and M. Moran (1994), 'Introduction: Explaining Politics', in B. Jones (ed.), *Politics UK*, Harvester Wheatsheaf, London. pp. 1–24.

Kotler, P. and S. Levy (1969), 'Broadening the Concept of Marketing', *Journal of Marketing* 33(1): 10–15.

Laing, A. and J. Lees-Marshment (2002), 'Time to Deliver: Why Political Marketing Needs to Move Beyond the Campaign', paper presented at the PSA conference, Aberdeen, April.

Lees-Marshment, J. (2001a), *Political Marketing and British Political Parties: The Party's Just Begun*, Manchester University Press, Manchester.

Lees-Marshment, J. (2001b), 'The Marriage of Politics and Marketing', *Political Studies* 49(4): 692–713.

Lees-Marshment, J. (2001c), 'The Product, Sales and Market-Oriented Party and How Labour Learnt to Market the Product, Not Just the Presentation', special issue on political marketing, *European Journal of Marketing* 35(9/10): 1074–1084.

Lees-Marshment, J. (2001d), 'Marketing the British Conservatives 1997–2001', special issue on *The Marketing Campaign: The British General Election of 2001*, eds P. Harris and D. Wring, *Journal of Marketing Management* 17: 929–941.

Lees-Marshment, J. (2001e), 'The World's Most Unpopular Populist, a Poorly Sold Product, or Just Mission Impossible? A Political Marketing Analysis of Hague's Conservatives 1997–2001', paper presented at EPOP conference, University of Sussex.

Lees-Marshment, J. (2003a), 'Marketing Political Institutions: Good in Theory but Problematic in Practice?', *Academy of Marketing Conference Proceedings*, University of Aston, 8–10 July.

Lees-Marshment, J. (2003b), 'Political Marketing: How to Reach that Pot of Gold', *Journal of Political Marketing* 2(1):1–32.

Lees-Marshment, J. (2003c), 'Marketing Good Works: New Trends in How Interest Groups Recruit Supporters', *Journal of Public Affairs* 3(3).

Lees-Marshment, J. and A. Laing (2002), 'Time to Deliver: Why Political Marketing Needs to Move Beyond the Campaign', *Political Marketing Conference Proceedings*, September 19–21.

Lovelock, C.H. and C.B. Weinberg, eds (1990), *Public and Nonprofit Marketing: Readings and Cases*, Scientific Press, San Francisco.

McFadden, J. and M. Lazarowicz (1999), *The Scottish Parliament: An Introduction*, T. and T. Clark, Edinburgh.

Mortimore, R. (2003), 'Why Politics Needs Marketing', International Journal of Non-profit and Voluntary Sector Marketing, special issue on *Broadening the Concept of Political Marketing*, ed. J. Lees-Marshment, 8(2): 107–121.

O'Fairchellaigh, P. and P. Graham (1991), 'Introduction', in C. O'Faircheallaigh, P. Graham and J. Warburton (eds), *Service Delivery and Public Sector Marketing*, Macmillan, Sydney. pp ix–xiii.

O'Leary, R. and I. Iredale (1976), 'The Marketing Concept: Quo Vadis?', *European Journal of Marketing* 10(3): 146–157.

Pagan, L. (1994), 'Testing out Support', *Marketing* 12 May: 43.

Parsuraman, A., V.A. Zeithaml and L.L. Berry (1988), 'SERVQUAL: A Multiple Item Scale for Measuring Consumer Perceptions of Service Quality', *Journal of Retailing*, 64(1): 12–40.

Peele, G. (1995), *Governing the UK*, Blackwell, Oxford.

Pirie, M. and R. Worcester (2001), *The Wrong Package*, report on a MORI poll, Adam Smith Institute, London. Also at www.mori.com/polls/2001/asi.shtml or www.adam-smith.org.uk.

Sargeant, A. (1999), *Marketing Management for Non-Profit Organisations*, Oxford University Press, New York.

Walsh, K. (1994), 'Marketing and Public Sector Management', *European Journal of Marketing* 28(3): 63–71.

2

Marketing representation: parties and elections

The era of producer politics has gone. (Philip Gould, New Labour advisor, at the 1999 Political Marketing Conference held in Bournemouth)

Parties win elections by formulating 'a product that is attractive'. (Sir Archie Norman, the former chief executive of the Conservative party, 2001)

The idea that we as politicians can sit in our ivory towers and people come to us I think is generally accepted that it is gone now. There are too many competing factors . . . in the political system . . . we have to go out to them. (Director of development, Conservative party, 2001)

In the Scottish Conservative party we are certainly using polling and focus groups in the run up to the Scottish and local elections. It is just that marketing techniques have to be used properly. (David McLetchie, MSP, leader of the Scottish Conservatives, 2002)

The election of the British national government is at the heart of the political system. It can influence all other areas of the political system, by granting power to one dominant party. Political marketing, therefore, starts here: with the use of political marketing by political parties to determine their policies, organisation, communication and, ultimately, potential delivery in government. Political parties were traditionally perceived as bastions of ideology, dogma, idealism and rhetoric. In the twenty-first century, however, most if not all political parties in the UK of varying ideologies, histories, sizes and fortunes are aware of political marketing. The extent to which they choose to use it, the form they adopt, and their success at adopting a market orientation may vary, but all understand the pressure from the political market to respond to public demands.

This chapter explains the theory behind party marketing. It analyses how Britain's major parties attempted to use marketing to win the 2001 general election, and explores all aspects of their behaviour during the four years from the election of the Labour government in 1997 through to the voting in 2001, noting the difficulties of putting theory into practice. It also explores how smaller parties in the UK might use political marketing, discussing the difference party size and goals can make. Noting the importance of party marketing, the chapter concludes by highlighting the link between the marketing of political parties and other areas of the political system.[1]

Political parties are generally ahead in their adoption of marketing strategies. Major parties in particular have moved towards the market-oriented model, as shown in Lees-Marshment (2001a), and both the Conservative and Labour parties tried to follow this orientation between 1997 and 2001. This chapter, unlike all others, therefore focuses on this model rather than the product or sales orientation.

Marketing political parties: the options for UK parties

Political parties can use political marketing in various ways, depending on their own nature. Parties differ in their size and goals. Major parties are large, established organisations whose dominant goal is to win control of government, therefore to win a general (or devolved) election. The Conservative and Labour parties in the UK are major parties and so try to use political marketing to win an election. Their market consists of the electorate, in addition to anyone else who has influence on voters, although the parties do not need to win support from everyone to gain power. Their product includes all aspects of their behaviour. Although a major party generally asks political consumers to vote for it on the basis of what it promises to do in government – its policy promises or manifesto – voters also take into account other aspects of party behaviour such as leadership, party unity, organisation and the behaviour of members, because these may affect the ability of the party to deliver on policy promises.

Major parties need to adopt an orientation – an attitude towards how they behave in relation to the electorate. There are three main political marketing orientations (Lees-Marshment 2001a, 2001b). Market-oriented parties (MOPs) design their product, including policies, leadership and organisation, to suit what political consumers demand, in order to achieve their goal of winning a general election. This does not mean they simply follow what everyone wants – this would be impossible anyway, because demands are complex and competing. Instead, they need to go through a complex process of stages, represented in Box 2.1.

Other parties with different goals may not choose to use political marketing in this way, however. If the dominant goal of a party is to advance a particular policy, rather than win an election, it may be more product oriented. Product-oriented parties (POPs) decide their behaviour or product themselves without much care for the opinions of political consumers – or, rather, they assume that voters will realise that it is right and vote for it accordingly. Their process is quite simple: see Box 2.2.

A product-oriented party refuses to change its ideas or product even if it fails to gain electoral or membership support. If a party is a small or minor party, with the main goal being not to win a general election but to put ideas on the agenda, this may be the most appropriate political marketing orientation.

Box 2.1 The process for a market-oriented party

Stage 1: Market intelligence
Party finds out what voters need and want by:

- 'keeping an ear to the ground', talking to activists, meeting the public;
- using quantitative research (electoral results, public opinion polls and privately commissioned studies) and qualitative research such as a focus group.

Stage 2: Product design
Party designs behaviour (including leadership, members, policies, staff, constitution and symbols) according to voters' demands.

Stage 3: Product adjustment
Party designs product to suit the electorate at large and then needs to make sure it considers other factors:

- *achievability* – determine whether the product design is achievable;
- *internal reaction analysis* – alter design to ensure it will obtain the support of enough MPs and members to ensure its implementation;
- *competition analysis* – promote opposition weaknesses and highlight own strengths;
- *support analysis* – focuses on winning the support of voters it does not have but needs to win power.

Stage 4: Implementation

The findings from Stages 1–3 must be implemented. The majority must accept the new behaviour broadly. This requires effective and considerate organisation and management.

Stage 5: Communication
This includes the so-called near-term or long-term campaign but also ongoing behaviour. The party ensures that communication helps it achieve electoral success; attempts to influence others in the communication process, such as journalists and opposition parties; and uses selling techniques such as direct mail and targeted communications.

Stage 6: Campaign
The final chance to communicate with the voters.

Stage 7: Election
The party goes through the election.

Stage 8: Delivery
The party carries out promises made once in government.

Box 2.2 The process for a product-oriented party

Stage 1: Product design
The party designs its behaviour according to what it thinks best.

Stage 2: Communication
This includes the so-called near-term or long-term campaign but also ongoing behaviour. Not just the leader, but all MPs and members, send a message to the electorate. The organisation is clear and effective; it is designed to advance arguments.

Stage 3: Campaign
The official election campaign period leading up to the election.

Stage 4: Election
The general election.

Stage 5: Delivery
The party will deliver its product in government.

However, most parties, over time, grow to be concerned about their performance. They may then move to a sales orientation – retaining the same product or behaviour, but using political marketing communications to try and persuade voters to support it. Sales-oriented parties aim to sell what they decide is best for the people, utilising effective political marketing communication techniques: see Box 2.3. Market intelligence is used not to inform the product design, but to help the party persuade voters it is right. Sales-oriented parties are often perceived as the more manipulative, because they use marketing to persuade or change public opinion.

Previous research has indicated that the trend in the UK, at least amongst major parties, is towards the market-oriented approach (Lees-Marshment 2001a). The trend is to evolve from product through to sales and then finally a market orientation, responding to the gradual rise of the political consumer. Major parties can, however, win power using a market orientation and then switch back to sales or product once in power. Parties often find it harder to remain in touch with the public and responsive to the demands of political consumers once they are in government. As will be discussed towards the end of the chapter, other smaller UK parties adopt any one of the three orientations, although some such as the Scottish National Party have also moved through the classic product–sales–market-oriented cycle.

Marketing political parties is not as easy as the theory suggests. The latest research in political party marketing indicates that despite the desire of both the Conservative and Labour parties to adopt and maintain a market orientation, many obstacles get in the way, as will be seen in the next section, which will discuss the behaviour of both the major parties between 1997 and 2001.

Box 2.3 The process for a sales-oriented party

Stage 1: Product design
The party designs its behaviour according to what it thinks best.

Stage 2: Market intelligence
The party aims to discover voters' response to the product, especially voters who do not support the party but might, so that communications can be targeted on them. Informally it 'keeps an ear to the ground', talks to party members, creates policy groups and meets with the public. Formally it uses quantitative research (electoral results, public opinion polls and privately commissioned studies) and qualitative research such as a focus group.

Stage 3: Communication
This includes the so-called near-term or long-term campaign but also ongoing behaviour. Not just the leader, but all MPs and members send a message to the electorate. Attempts are made to ensure all communication helps achieve electoral success, and to influence others in the communication process. The organisation is clear and effective; designed to advance arguments. It also makes use of selling techniques such as direct mail and targeted communications to persuade voters to agree with the party.

Stage 4: Campaign
The official election campaign period leading up to the election. The party continues to communicate effectively as in Stage 3.

Stage 5: Election
The general election.

Stage 6: Delivery
The party will deliver its promised product in government.

Labour use of political marketing, 1997–2001

The Labour Party is one of political marketing's success stories – at least on the surface. Using political marketing to become more in touch with the public, reduce any unwanted historical baggage, and even relabel itself as 'New' Labour, it first became market oriented in order to win the previous election in 1997. It remains the fullest example of a market-oriented party, following the model to the greatest degree of any party before or since. However, after obtaining control of government, the party met many obstacles to delivering on its 1997 election promises. This is a major potential weakness: Labour's support is very much based on promised outputs, so it needs to be seen to deliver. It is in this context that Labour attempted to maintain a market orientation and retain its electoral support during 1997–2001.

Table 2.1 The Labour government and delivery, February 2000

'There is a lot of talk at the moment about whether the present government is or is not "delivering". From what you know, do you think that it is or is not delivering on each of the following?'

	Yes (%)	No (%)	Don't know/ not answered (%)
Getting people back to work	60	36	4
Improving the National Health Service	28	71	1
Improving the quality of education in schools	48	44	8
Putting an end to the old stop-and-go, boom-bust economic cycle	40	43	17
Improving the quality of public transport	27	68	5
Being tough on crime and tough on the causes of crime	36	61	3

Source: Gallup Political Index

Delivery in government on the 1997 election promises

Delivering the political product is not easy: it is one of the unanswered potential conundrums at the heart of political marketing (see Laing and Lees-Marshment 2002). Labour at least understood this. The party talked constantly about the need to deliver. It copied business and started to issue an annual report on its delivery of its promises (see Labour Party 1999: 3–7, 2000). Labour undoubtedly succeeded in some areas, such as constitutional reform, with the introduction of devolution in Scotland and Wales and the removal of hereditary peers from the House of Lords. However, Labour failed to convince many voters that it had made real improvement to standards in the public services – the core part of the 1997 product. Public resentment about Labour's failures to deliver grew: for example, see Table 2.1.

There was also underlying dissatisfaction. A report from the Labour party itself based on its private polls leaked in the *Independent* warned that 'the Party's huge lead in the opinion polls masks the fact that people are turning against the Government because they believe it is failing to deliver its 1997 general election promises'. In July 2000 a MORI survey indicated that 57 per cent of respondents did not think Tony Blair had kept his promises: see Table 2.2. Labour therefore still needed to utilise political marketing, but this time to maintain rather than win support.

Stage 1: Market intelligence

The Labour Party conducted substantial market intelligence. Philip Gould conducted focus group work for the party; Greg Crook ran a rolling programme of opinion polling (Cook 2002); the party's advertising agency, TVWA London, also conducted research (Lawther 2002). Labour also analysed results of

Table 2.2 Perceived performance of prime minister, July 2000

	'Since becoming prime minister in May 1997, do you think Tony Blair has or has not . . . ?'		
	Has (%)	*Has not (%)*	*Don't know (%)*
Kept his promises	36	57	7
Kept taxes down	29	62	9
Improved the NHS	30	64	6
Improved education	42	42	16
Stood up for Britain in Europe	49	40	11
Introduced policies to support the family	45	43	12

Source: MORI telephone survey 20–22 July 2000
Notes: n = 610

elections to local authorities, the devolved institutions, the European parliament and parliamentary by-elections (Cook 2002). It took account of negative criticism despite the overall positive polls and continued to monitor the performance of the opposition. During 1997–2001 Labour continually discussed voters' needs.

Stage 2: Product design
The New Labour product offered to the electorate in 2001 was extremely similar to that offered in 1997, with greater determination to deliver in the second term.

Policy   In terms of policy, the focus remained on raising standards in the public services, such as health and education. The party retained its commitment to low income tax and competent economic management. There were slight changes in terms of greater investment in public services in order to improve them, but such moves were made without a call to increase tax. Stephen Lawther, polling co-ordinator for the Scottish Labour party, argued that Labour put forward a strong product:

* minimum wage;
* 1 million new jobs;
* lowest unemployment in 25 years;
* lowest inflation in 30 years;
* winter fuel allowance;
* record investment in schools in hospitals;
* small class sizes;
* a nursery place for every 4-year-old;
* 10,000 more nurses in the NHS;
* working families' tax credit;
* Scottish parliament. (Lawther 2002)

Leadership   As leader, Tony Blair continued to exercise strong and determined control over his party and the senior leadership and cabinet in particular. Blair enjoyed extremely high popularity scores in public opinion polls until the end of the 1997–2001 period, when he began to attract criticism for being smarmy, arrogant and out of touch. In June 2000 Blair was even slow-hand-clapped by the Women's Institute.

Internal membership   Changes were made within the party with the aim of making members more involved (see Seyd 1999: 390–391). Members-only sessions were introduced at the annual party conference, to ensure members had a chance to air their views without damaging the party externally. *Partnership in Power*, a series of proposals to change certain organisational structures within the party, devolved policy-making to the National Policy Forum to provide greater consultation with the membership. Nevertheless, party membership slumped from 420,000 after the 1997 election to just 320,000 by mid-1999. Many of those who remained were 'de-energised' (Seyd and Whiteley 1999). This reflects the limited application of marketing to the membership (Lees-Marshment 2001a). The foundations of Labour's support have been eroded, making it even more crucial that the party satisfy voters through delivery on public services.

Party unity   The leadership exerted significant control over the party's participation within the new devolved institutions in the selection of the leadership candidate for the Welsh assembly, which aroused significant discontent among Labour party activists. Another case was the election for the London mayor. After failing to be selected as the Labour candidate, an old left-winger, Ken Livingstone, stood as an independent after calls from the public to do so, and won. This was an indication of the discontent at the grassroots: an issue that Labour continues to struggle with due to its use of political marketing.

Stage 3: Product Adjustment

Achievability   Learning in government that 'delivering' on the 1997 pledges, particularly those about the quality of public services, was extremely difficult, the party made promises for the next term of office in terms of inputs rather than outputs, such as '*x* number of nurses or police' rather than 'reduce waiting lists' or 'lower levels of crime'. Inputs are easier to deliver because they are easier to control (see Lees-Marshment and Laing 2002). The 2001 pledges were:

- mortgages to be as low as possible, low inflation and sound public finances;
- 10,000 extra teachers and higher standards in secondary schools;
- 20,000 extra nurses and 10,000 extra doctors in a reformed NHS;
- 6,000 extra recruits to raise police numbers to their highest ever level;
- pensioners' winter fuel payment retained, minimum wage rising to £4.20 an hour.

Internal reaction analysis   The decline in membership that Labour experienced after 1997 suggests a failure of internal reaction analysis. The new system of policy-making was criticised for restricting the opportunity for debate at conference and ignoring the work of the policy forums (Seyd 2002). The selection processes used for the Scottish parliament, Welsh assembly and London mayor also indicated a lack of internal reaction analysis and generated further discontent.

Competition analysis   Labour engaged in significant competition analysis in terms of its planning for the campaign. It was keen that voters would see the election as a choice between the parties rather than a referendum on Labour's mixed record of delivery (Gould 2002; Lawther 2002). Posters reassured voters about the party, saying 'Thanks for voting Labour', but also reminding them of the potential problems the Conservatives might bring, with posters headed 'Economic Disaster II' (Lawther 2002).

Support analysis   Labour analysed voters who were former Conservatives and had defected to the party in 1997, and found that this group would stay with the party. Attention then shifted to mobilising people to vote, as the party feared it could lose support due to a low turnout. Labour played on the emotion of fear at a prospective Tory victory, commissioning the famous 'wiggy' poster of William Hague with Thatcher's hair, warning 'Get out and vote or they get in' (see Lawther 2002). It tried to put forward the vision that 'the work goes on' and voters needed to give the party more time (Lawther 2002).

Stage 4: Implementation
Blair insisted on strict party unity: all ministers had to agree any interaction with the media with the No. 10 press office, to ensure unified communication from government. The Parliamentary Labour Party was generally extremely quiescent. Blair had few difficulties passing legislation, and ambitious MPs knew they had to keep in line with the leadership if they wished to advance their careers. Blair followed the market-oriented party model to fine detail (see Lees-Marshment 2001a: 38), promoting those who followed the product design and sidelining those who voiced dissent. Nevertheless Labour was criticised for 'control freakery'.

Stage 5: Communication
Labour continued to control communication from the party and also central government. The Government Information Service was used to communicate the government's message and delivery (Scammell 2001). Government spending on advertising increased massively in the four years between 1997 and 2001 (Grice 2001). Party communication was also focused on delivery: party political broadcasts during the elections to the European parliament, for example, focused on the government's achievements, rather than European issues. Communication did not succeed in convincing voters that the government had delivered, however.

Stage 6: Campaign

Labour's campaign was determined by the character of the party's product and its delivery performance in office. It focused on the need to deliver, asking for more time to do its job. Labour used target marketing and campaigned most heavily in marginal seats where it was assumed that its efforts would have greatest effect (Cook 2002). In Scotland Labour sent out targeted direct mail in the form of a letter from Tony Blair or John Prescott to segments of the market such as Scottish National Party (SNP) floaters, and Labour also ran health rallies and a pledge day to reinforce key themes (Lawther 2002). The campaign was extremely closely co-ordinated from the party's Millbank headquarters, with an integrated marketing communications structure (Lawther 2002). Responding to market intelligence, significant effort went into getting the vote out, through 'Operation Turnout'. This assessed the party identification and voting history of electors in target seats and sent a direct marketing (personalised) message to them to get them to vote (Lawther 2002).

Nevertheless, the underlying public dissatisfaction with public services was brought to the fore when Blair was accosted by the partner of a patient complaining about the poor standards of care in the NHS in a directly personal, but also televised and therefore highly public, manner. This indicated the significant voter dissatisfaction with Labour's performance. Labour, though, was lucky: the Conservatives experienced substantial difficulty in trying to use political marketing, and faced with little alternative the Labour product seemed the best one voters could buy.

Stage 7, 'election', will be covered only after exploring the behaviour of the Conservative party through Stages 1–6, so that the election results and other indicators of support can be dealt with for Labour and the Conservatives together. Since Stage 8, 'delivery', clearly cannot be discussed for the Tories, I then give sections on developments in both parties since 2001.

Conservative use of political marketing, 1997–2001

The Conservative party undoubtedly tried to use political marketing during 1997–2001. After the party lost so badly in 1997, William Hague took over as leader. A management consultant by background, he set about reforming the party organisation and culture, and adopted key marketing principles, initiating a major market intelligence exercise to connect with the people. At the beginning of his leadership he declared (1998a): 'The Conservative Party is changing. Changing our institutions and our structures; changing the way we involve our members and changing our culture . . . We are turning our greatest defeat into our greatest opportunity. We are changing the way we do business.' However, he proved unable to implement such change.

Stage 1: Market intelligence

The Conservative party gathered market intelligence throughout the 1997–2001 period. Nick Sparrow of ICM gathered formal intelligence on voters' attitudes towards the Party, its leader and the government (Sparrow and Turner 2001). During the formal campaign the Party conducted two focus groups per night among possible 'switchers'. In the autumn of 1997 they also launched an exercise called *Listening to Britain*, designed to reach out to voters (Lansley 1999). This consisted of a long series of meetings across the country where MPs listened to discussions on a wide range of topics (see Lansley 2001b; Dykes 2001; Francis 2000). A resulting report entitled *Listening to Britain* (Conservative Party 1999b), identified key voter concerns and fed into early policy design.

Stage 2: Product design

Leadership   Between 1997 and 1999 William Hague set the party on a path to produce market-oriented policies and organisation in response to the results from market intelligence. As leader, however, he was an electoral liability. He lacked public standing and continually polled low ratings in relation to the Labour prime minister Tony Blair. Hague's leadership was also beset by continual criticism, defections, challenges and disunity.

Internal organisation and constitution   Hague reformed the Conservative organisational structure to reflect the concerns of members and voters. The party's rules over funding were also revised, responding to voters' concerns about this issue. Market intelligence on the membership led to the introduction of voting rights for individual members, and the membership was also balloted during 1997–2001 on several occasions. The organisation part of the product was therefore market oriented, and laid the foundations for the emergence of a market orientation in other aspects of the product (see Lees-Marshment and Quayle 2001).

Membership   The party adopted direct marketing mail techniques associated with business, using the company Archibald Ingall Stretton (Chambers 2001). It profiled existing members and then bought membership lists of names for wine clubs, garden centres, rugby or cricket clubs for a direct mail recruitment drive. A Conservative Network was launched to offer a social and political programme to attract young professionals, and provided training in skills needed for candidates (Dykes 2001). *Conservative Future* was created for those members aged 30 and under (Pugh 2001). However, the membership dropped from the alleged 350,000 in 1997 to the official number of just 300,000 by the time of the election in 2001. The Tory party seemed to be in a chicken-and-egg situation: it needed new members to change its product, but it also needed to change the product in order to attract new members. Organisational changes take years to have an affect: as Christina Dykes, head of development at Conservative Central Office, observed, 'there is no quick delivery on what I'm doing' (Dykes 2001).

Candidates   The internal culture of the party also proved a barrier to Hague's intended changes. The leadership attempted to attract candidates more representative of the population: it encouraged associations to select women and ethnic minority candidates. Women candidates were offered help with a 'mentoring' programme (Dykes 2001) and guidelines on interviewing candidates were widely circulated. Both these initiatives appear to have had little impact, however: one applicant recalled being asked what would happen if she went into labour when there was a three-line whip (*Daily Telegraph*, 2 September 2000). Hague also set up a new Cultural Unit to encourage the participation of ethnic minority communities and established a 'listening link' with ethnic communities and organisations (Mannan 2001; Norris 2001). However, the increasingly 'populist' tone of the Tories' campaign from mid-1999 onwards ensured, in the words of Steven Norris (2001), that Hague 'inadvertently had managed to create the impression . . . that the Tory Party was full of people who were vaguely xenophobic and vaguely homophobic'.

Policy   Responding to market intelligence, Hague initially attempted to take the party in a new direction on policy, arguing that the party should focus on improving state provision of public services rather than looking to the market and simply reducing taxes. In April 1999, just as the party met to celebrate the twentieth anniversary of Mrs Thatcher's first election victory, the then deputy party leader Peter Lilley delivered the R.A. Butler Memorial Lecture, arguing that, 'Conservatism is not, never has been and never will be solely about the free market.' The speech was designed to mark the beginning of a new 'compassionate' Conservatism. However, the speech led to internal rows and Hague began to doubt his market-oriented strategy. In October 1999, the party launched the Common Sense Revolution, with a number of guarantees, responding to market intelligence and the need for achievable promises:

- A parents' guarantee giving them the power to change school management that fails to provide adequate standards.
- A patients' guarantee giving a fixed waiting time based on the need for treatment.
- A tax guarantee ensuring that taxes would fall as a share of the nation's income over the term of the next parliament under a Conservative government.
- A 'can work, must work' guarantee ensuring that benefit claimants who can work would lose their dole if they did not.
- A sterling guarantee that the Tories would oppose entry into the euro at the next election as part of their manifesto.

These promises responded to the results from market intelligence. They could have built the party's overall reputation for honesty and believability. They were also focused on areas of prime importance to voters. When they were first communicated, press coverage was potentially positive: it was seen as a break with the past, a new way forward. It was even likened to Tony Blair's abandonment of Clause IV, when Labour had removed its previous commitment to the workers' owning the means of production, a change away from an ideology-based state-ment to one that followed the opinion of the electoral market.

By the time of the election, however, the guarantees had all but disappeared, following a period of statements from senior party figures. For example, in February 2000, Hague suggested that the tax guarantee was an aspiration, not a definite promise to reduce tax, and in June 2000, he admitted that many medical conditions would not be covered by the patients' guarantee at first. This under-mined the party's credibility. Voters were left to wonder where the guarantees had gone. This also undermined Hague's strength and he lost the will to continue to pursue the focus on public services. As Archie Norman (2001) observed, 'we lost confidence in the reform programme'. Thereafter the party focused more on its core vote and issues such as asylum. As Kenneth Clarke later commented, 'from about half-way through the parliament we stopped trying to broadening our appeal, we narrowed it' (BBC 1 *Question Time*, 5 July 2001). Indeed, Lansley (2001a) argues that 'it would have been a damn site better if we'd stuck closely to the Listening to Britain outcome and to the Common Sense Revolution policy document rather than allow ourselves to be drawn onto other things'.

The final general election manifesto was called *Time for Common Sense* (Conservative Party 2001). The main policies emphasised were those on families, pensions, Europe, immigration and crime. Although it contained policies on edu-cation and health, they did not receive the prominence desired by voters. Furthermore, there was a pledge for £8 billion tax cuts, which led voters to question the Conservatives' real commitment to public services. The Conservative party then made matters worse as it went through the rest of the political marketing process.

Stage 3: Product adjustment

Achievability analysis The Conservative party was handicapped throughout the 1997–2001 period by its reputation for failed delivery when it was last in government. It then found its new promises, the guarantees, were thought to be unachievable. It tried to water the guarantees down but this only served to gen-erate confusion over just what the Conservative product was.

Internal reaction analysis Organisational reforms were subject to widespread consultation in the Conservative party and carried through with few problems, Lilley's speech was heavily criticised internally. A senior campaign official (Senior Conservative Official 2001) later admitted that there had been an 'inter-nal failure of policy clearance'. As the party row ultimately led to the abandon-ment of a strategy focused on public services, it represented a major barrier to the effective use of political marketing.

Competition analysis One major criticism of the Tories in 2001 was that they neglected the issues voters most cared about: health and education. However, the Tories were themselves tarred with the same brush from the pre-1997 period. John

Crawford, planner for Yellow M, the Tories' advertising agency, noted that 'even though Labour were seen to not be as good on health as people thought they might have been pre-1997 – I saw a poll on the day, 81 per cent of people thought Labour weren't delivering on health – even then I don't think that the [Conservative] party felt quite as comfortable as they might have done criticising them about it because our record on health wasn't fantastic either' (Crawford 2001). Simon Turner, director of the Scottish Conservative party, also said that 'I just think if we'd gone on health and education we'd have got no coverage on them and been ripped apart by Labour' (Turner 2001). However, simply ignoring the issues that voters cared most about and hoping it would not matter was not an effective strategy. It did matter; it made the party seem unresponsive and out of touch.

Support analysis The Tories took this into account, but unfortunately it encouraged the abandonment of a market-oriented approach. Discussions with internal party staff and figures suggest that Hague lost his bottle when the party made no progress in the polls. He then changed to a less ambitious strategy of 'getting core supporters to turn out' (Senior Conservative Official 2001; see also Turner 2001).

Stage 4: Implementation
Implementation is the stage where Hague really fell down. He faced one battle after another in trying to introduce the initial, market-oriented product design. The *idea* of a market orientation was fully accepted by the central leadership (Peele 1998: 141–143) but was never fully accepted throughout the party. The initial design to focus on public services was heavily criticised internally by staff and politicians. Hague's official reaction at first was to say he would not change this strategy: 'I will go thorough any number of arguments, take on anyone in debate, endure any criticisms, do whatever it takes to get across this position on health and education' (quoted in the *Daily Telegraph*, 29 April 1999). Over time, however, declarations focusing on improving the public services were replaced by communications about popular positions on minority issues such as the asylum and the euro. The party had not sufficiently adopted a market orientation that would ensure implementation and communication of a product and set of policies designed to suit voter demands.

This can also be seen in the amount of disunity and the number of defections and disunity even at the top levels of the Tory party, such as those of Shaun Woodward in December 1999 and Ivan Masow in August 2000. Ken Clarke reopened divisions over Europe, appearing on a shared platform with Labour (and Tony Blair) to launch the 'Britain in Europe' campaign and even stating 'I'm in favour of joining the single currency in principle. I don't agree with the party's policy' (*Guardian*, 5 July 1999). This gave the impression that Hague was not in control and publicly demonstrated the disunity that damaged the product. Additionally, Hague's leadership was criticised by senior Tories including John Major and Kenneth Clark from 1999 to 2001. There was always talk of potential challengers to the leader, such as Ken Clarke and Michael Portillo, even extremely close to the general election. Overall, disunity, change of direction, defections and lack of cultural change at lower levels of the party prevented implementation, making communication very difficult.

Stage 5: Communication

Communication became more professional but focused on non-mainstream issues: in his New Year message for 2001 Hague identified tax cuts, crime and Europe as the main political battlegrounds. Furthermore, his speeches on asylum were perceived and portrayed as attacks on refugees, and could be interpreted as racist. The Conservatives also failed to communicate an alternative product to Labour. Criticism of the government was not enough to encourage voters to return to the Tories. The party appointed a little-known Scottish advertising agency, Yellow M, to design its advertising, but communication was generally negative. The party began a 'Keep the £' old-fashioned mini-campaign, more suited to patriotic Conservatives who would vote for the party anyway. In the summer and autumn of 2000 the party launched one policy initiative after another, but lacked a big idea or theme that would hold them all together. As a senior Conservative official (2001) involved in the campaign noted, 'we were not devising messages and then crafting them in ways that would appeal to the media'. However, the Tories' failure to persuade journalists and voters had one core cause: the unappealing product that it was trying to sell.

Stage 6: Campaign

As Lansley (2002) noted, the 2001 campaign 'illustrated forcibly the truth that elections are won and lost over four years, not four weeks'. It was quickly marred by division due to failed implementation. The Tories focused on law and order, tax and Europe (Crawford 2001): not issues voters cared about. This gave the impression of a party that was out of touch. The Conservative party ended the campaign with the same share of the vote as when they had started. It was their behaviour – their product – that was the problem.

Stage 7: Election, for both Conservative and Labour

The overall election result reflected the way both parties behaved between 1997 and 2001. Labour won a second full term and although its share of the vote fell two points to 42 per cent, it lost only seven seats and managed to gain two more. Its second consecutive victory was a landslide, with the party winning 412 seats, giving a majority of 165. Labour gained significant electoral dividends by continuing to use political marketing in office. The Conservatives, however, gained only 32.7 per cent of the vote and one net seat.

More detailed analysis of the electoral support provides quantitative evidence that Labour responded to voter concerns. When voters were asked to decide which major party had the better policy on each issue, Labour had the lead in the majority: see Table 2.3.

Table 2.3 Best party policy on key issues, 2001

'I am going to read out a list of problems facing Britain today. I would like you to tell me whether you think the Conservative party, the Labour party or the Liberal Democrats has the best policies on each problem.'

	Labour or Conservative better policy (% lead over the other) 2001
Health care	Labour (35)
Public transport	Labour (21)
Unemployment	Labour (53)
Housing	Labour (29)
Pensions	Labour (30)
Education	Labour (34)
Trade unions	Labour (42)
Protecting the natural environment	Labour (7)
Animal welfare	Labour (6)
Law and order	Labour (2)
Taxation	Conservatives (3)
Europe	Conservatives (16)
Constitution/devolution	Labour (2)
Managing the economy	Labour (34)
Northern Ireland	Labour (15)
Defence	Conservative (20)

Source: MORI polls
Notes: n = c.1,000 or 2,000, surveys based on GB residents aged 18+. Poll taken 8 April 1997; for 2001, n = 1,846; poll taken 17 May 2001

The results also reflected the failure of the Conservatives to implement a market-oriented strategy. The British election study (BES) found that a majority of voters did not think that the party would handle the most important issues of health and education well. All polls showed Hague in a poor position when voters were asked who would make the best prime minister, ranging from only 17 to 20 per cent in his support. The Conservatives also lacked governing and delivery competence. Only between 30 and 32 per cent of voters believed they were the best party to handle the economy (Gallup/*Daily Telegraph* poll, 6 June 2001) and only 9 per cent thought the party was the most clear and united about what its policies should be (MORI poll, 15 May 2001, for *The Times*).

Although it is tempting to claim (and indeed the common view in 2001 was) that Hague lost because he followed right-wing populist policies, data does not suggest this was the main problem. An ICM exit poll indicated that former Tory voters failed to return in 2001 not because the party was too extreme or right wing, but more because they felt that the Tories would not improve public services. The Conservatives simply did not offer a viable product that voters wanted to buy. People were dissatisfied with Labour. They were open to the possibility of the Tories: the hostility present in 1997 had gone, but the party failed to produce clear and popular policy responses to the enduring issues of health and education. The party had not adopted a market orientation throughout its organisation and had failed to respond to voters' needs and desires.

Implications for political marketing

Both cases therefore suggest issues for political marketing. The Tory case indicates that it is not enough for a leader to want to use political marketing. Internal aspects got in the way. When interviewed about this, Archie Norman (2001) admitted that his role within the Tory party was difficult; 'it was a big change coming to this world' and, he said, 'had I known I'd have been much more cautious'. Similarly, Andrew Lansley (2001b) noted said there was always a sense that the party should be focusing on issues voters were most interested in, but 'the difficulty was translating it into practice' (Lansley 2001a). Indeed, both the Labour and Conservative cases suggest that parties need to pay greater attention to Stage 3, 'product adjustment', to avoid such problems: the internal party democracy and marketing aspects are more important than might first appear (see Lees-Marshment and Quayle 2001). It can be argued that Labour have also neglected their internal supporters and product adjustment, which is an issue for them. Blair's neglect of this stage between 1994 and 1997 may have laid the foundations for some of Labour's problems post-2001. New Labour's support is weak and conditional. This will also make delivery in its second term of office even more crucial. Political marketing – the market-oriented approach – at first seems at odds with internal democracy, membership, tradition and ideology, but in fact they may be an important component of the strategy if it is to really be effective. The market-oriented party model purposefully sought to integrate insights from political science literature within the political marketing approach, acknowledging that the inherent nature of the political party organisation needs to be considered when trying to use political marketing. More general management literature, particularly the organisational behaviour and organisational change areas, might provide greater assistance in resolving issues that have puzzled political scientists (Lees-Marshment 2003a).

Political marketing is used by political parties, but not without difficulty, and scholars need to engage in further critical evaluation of the theories and the model to advise parties how to implement the strategy more effectively. This advice is, after all, very much needed: as we speak, the new Tory leader attempts yet again to follow a market-oriented approach and the Labour government grapples with the question of delivery to a sceptical public.

Conservatives since 2001

Indeed, the Tories have failed to make much progress since 2001 and the election of a new leader (see Lees-Marshment and Rudd 2003). Further interviews with Conservative party staff suggest that although they are very aware of the party's weaknesses, it is not easy to find a workable solution to correct them.

William Hague was replaced by Iain Duncan-Smith (or IDS as he likes to be called). IDS was not as popular with the public and youth as other leader contenders such as Michael Portillo. Portillo would have been a much more market-oriented choice: he had already made moves to reach out to the wider public, but he had enemies internally. He lost by one vote in the second round. As one MP said after Portillo was deselected, 'The Tory Party? That's it. We're out of business' (*Daily Telegraph*, 18 July 2001). Iain Duncan-Smith has indicated signs of attempting to reconnect with them. He has spoken of the need to get back in touch with voters, appointed the Party's first female chairman, Teresa May, and initiated a policy review. Market intelligence has been conducted – the party currently uses the polling company YouGov, for example (Tait 2003). As John Tait from the policy unit explained, they have also sought intelligence from think tanks, businesses, relevant professionals and the Conservative Policy Forum (Tait 2003).

IDS made the 'strategic choice when [he] took over as leader of the Party to concentrate on the public services' (Tait 2003). A Senior Conservative Official (2003) involved in communication said that the party had focused more on the public services since 2001 than it ever had in its history. To address past weakness and 'find new and counter-intuitive ways to present Conservatism' (Tait 2003), the Tories adopted the theme of protecting the vulnerable in order to encourage caring voters amidst the middle class to support the party once again (Tait 2003; Senior Conservative Official 2003; informal conversation with senior figure in the Scottish party leadership, autumn 2002). IDS made several high-profile visits to a rundown council-house estate, Easterhouse, in Glasgow. This approach has filtered through to speeches by other senior party figures and in November 2002 the party launched a campaign to tackle domestic violence, working with Women's Aid, the NSPCC and the Police Federation. In October 2002, the party launched a document entitled *Leadership with a Purpose: A Better Society* (Conservative Party 2002), which set out five goals that represent all sections of society, not just the middle class, or traditional Tory voters.

In terms of communication, the images of IDS and David McLetchie, leader of the Scottish conservatives, in Glasgow hit headlines and grabbed media attention, completely challenging the stereotypical view of Tory agendas. They have used slogans such as 'No child left behind' to convey the new approach, borrowed from the US Republican party (Tait 2003). New technologies are being explored, with the 2003 New Year message from the leader sent out by DVD to constituency associations. The idea that the party can both help the vulnerable and not increase tax on those well paid, though, as staff themselves pointed out, is 'harder to explain' (Tait 2003) and therefore presents a communication challenge.

Qualitative research inside the Conservative party has identified crucial awareness of the need to change, of the public's viewpoints, but despite this, the external public image continues to be a negative one. Political consumers are sceptical of the 'vulnerable' strategy, which is designed to focus on the less well-off, such as single parents, the ill and the elderly. Very few of the candidates selected for the next general election so far are women. The party changed the first stage of assessment to a more professional one that tests a matrix of skills, favours women and men equally and indicates what skills candidates have (Dykes 2003; see also Silvester 2003). This could be a selling point for the party, a differentiating factor to offset its previous weaknesses. However, communication and policy staff seemed not to appreciate this (Senior Conservative Official 2003; Tait 2003) and the wider public is unaware of this change. Meanwhile, women are still put off from coming forward because of the constituency selection stage, whilst informal qualitative research suggested that even single young men felt fed up with the process, which ranked them lower because they had not yet acquired the wife and children necessary to obtain selection in the Tory party. Given the importance of delivery competence in winning elections, a professionally selected candidate list could help offer a superior product, but as Dykes (2003) observed, some still think 'political parties offer policies, full stop. The idea they have to offer a shape of a party is new.'

The parliamentary party and leader need to ensure the party offers a popular, visible product at the top level to win votes, which will see the new people get into power. There is a blue-glass ceiling in the Conservative party, which, whilst enabling new talent to be seen every now and again if one looks closely through the Tory-blue haze, prevents it from reaching the higher and public levels within the organisation, and so from exerting its potential electoral appeal. Communication of the new policies and approach has also not been very effective. Although, as noted by staff, 'most of the opinion-formers have heard' of the vulnerable strategy, 'people are sceptical of it' (Senior Conservative Official 2003). When interviewing staff about this, there seemed to be acknowledgement and understanding of the obstacles but little idea as to how to overcome them. In terms of public support, a poll published in October 2002 (YouGov, *Daily Telegraph*, 6 October 2002) indicated that only 10 per cent of voters thought the Conservatives looked like a government in waiting. The strategy to reposition the party does not appear to have worked, with 70 per cent still regarding the Tories as the party of the rich.

Furthermore, IDS himself is not a very popular leader. Although some respect comes for a quiet, serious approach to politics he continues to attract poor roll ratings, and not just amongst the public but among Conservative voters (see www.mori.com/digest/2002/c021101.shtml for further details). Once again, a leader elected to change the party and make it more electable is thwarted by its own inability to be popular. IDS also suffered from internal criticism and threats to his leadership in the autumn and winter of 2002. Marketing the Conservatives seems fraught with difficulties.

Labour since 2001: return to traditional politics with the war?

Developments in the Labour party since 2001 have only increased the problem with delivery. Upon winning in 2001, Tony Blair declared that the result was 'very clearly an instruction to deliver' (*Independent*, 9 June 2001). As Laing and Lees-Marshment (2002) noted, 'after the election, Labour established the Downing Street Delivery Unit under the leadership of a former chief executive of a major media company'. Its goal was to ensure the delivery of electoral pledges on public service reform. Voters' expectations in terms of delivery are significantly higher in Labour's second term. Labour has continued to enjoy a relatively weak opposition and this has limited the impact from perceived non-delivery. Another distraction was the Iraq war, begun by Tony Blair and US president George Bush in autumn 2002; but this also suggested a change of political marketing approach that raises issues for the analysis in this book. In going to war with the US against Iraq, Tony Blair adopted a traditional, product-oriented approach: the policy was such because it was what he believed in, and was against the opinions of the public and his own parliamentary party. This is a complete reversal of the New Labour market-oriented approach to politics that Blair became famous for. Now the war is over, the leader continues to suffer criticism for it, whilst attacks on the party's performance on delivery in the public services are renewed.

The whole political marketing, or market-oriented, approach is also questioned, at least under the surface. For example, Newcastle-under-Lyme MP Paul Farrelley (2003) said that political marketing was 'a term I would never dream of using' and that politics is different to a Big Mac or a Mars bar: 'parties should have principles that preclude some policies'. Farrelley (2003) also argued that 'in politics you have to lead and make hard choices that won't appeal to people', and 'if you reduce politics to two rival sales teams you will turn people off' (Farrelley 2003). These issues will be discussed further in the concluding chapter of this book.

Nevertheless, whatever difficulties or issues there may be, the political marketing approach does not seem to be abating. UK politicians broadly accept the need for a market-oriented strategy, as is evident in politicians' own descriptions of what they do, given in the quotations at the beginning of this chapter. Andrew Lansley, former vice-chairman of the Tory party, drew an analogy between its situation and that of another established institution in need of rejuvenation, Marks and Spencer:

> without stretching the analogy too far, perhaps we are like Marks and Spencer's: a declining number of loyal customers; some products seen as worth buying, but overall perceived as out-of-date, out-of-touch, with products which just won't sell ... the act of buying into our brand is not seen as a positive, forward-looking, exciting statement of who you are. (Lansley 2001a)

Additionally, as the next section will note, it is not just major parties in the UK which use political marketing, but most if not all are aware of, and perhaps using, marketing in order to achieve their goals.

Marketing smaller parties in the UK

There is not the space here for a detailed analysis, but new research on party marketing is beginning to examine the use of political marketing by smaller parties, which, with different goals, may be more likely to be product-oriented. For example, the Scottish Socialist Party (SSP) (studied by Mochrie 2003) is driven by the desire to influence policy and represent particular sections of the political market, and is much more ideological than a party such as New Labour. The product is more visionary, with a set of principles rather than policies developed to suit the changing demands of the electorate. The SSP is able to adopt a product-oriented, ideologically focused approach because the party's market is smaller. The product is already geared to suit those the party seeks to represent, so it does not need to convince the entire political market. Tommy Sheridan is the party's leader and famous spokesman, now an MSP in the Scottish parliament. His speeches gain significant media attention, as do his actions, some of which lead him to jail, as he fights for what he believes in. Indeed, an article in the *Herald* newspaper in 2001 noted how Sheridan was 'a politician of some principle; a rare commodity in an age of spin when presentation seems more important than substance'. Arguably there is a role for such product-oriented parties in society, even while market-oriented parties dominate the electoral market. There is also the possibility that different electoral systems, such as the proportional representation (PR) introduced in the devolved Scottish political system, by fostering the development of minor parties may enable a wider range of political marketing orientations, thereby preventing the overall mass trend towards the market-oriented party as the means to success. The forthcoming edited collection *Political Marketing in Comparative Perspective* (Lilleker and Lees-Marshment) which includes analysis of party marketing around the world, will explore these trends and correlations in greater detail. The overall point remains, however, that parties throughout the UK are using political marketing, albeit in different ways and with varying consequences.

Political marketing and the big question: delivery

Although political parties are aware of political marketing, marketing political parties is not easy. Even if parties use it successfully and win control of government, this then leads to the question: what do they do next? The last stage of the process is delivery – but delivery is far from straightforward. Indeed, it is the other big question for the Labour party. This involves other areas of the political system, such as health and education, and the structures of delivery are increasingly important: parliament, the civil service, local government and devolved government all need to work effectively if the market-oriented parties are to achieve success in delivery. There are a lot of intermediaries involved in political delivery. Policy first designed within a market-oriented party then needs to go through:

- Westminster or devolved parliaments, where it is subject to influence by interest groups and charities, other parties, and lawyers developing it into legislation;

- the civil service, to be implemented;
- local government, to be delivered at the local level.

Such channels provide clear potential for change or blockage; they involve different groups of political opinion and staff, all with their own structures and organisation that may impede implementation, over which national government has little effective control.

Perhaps because of this, there is increasing pressure from government for the other political institutions to become market oriented. Not only is marketing informing political parties how to behave, but they in turn are putting pressure on the health service, education, parliament and even local councils to become more responsive to the citizens these political institutions were created to serve. Furthermore, the rise of the political citizen affects these organisations as well as parties. No institution is immune. Professionals working in education and health care organisations are increasingly subject to criticism from their students or patients. Those who donate to charities do not give unquestioningly: supporters increasingly ask the organisation to involve them in the organisation and inform them of campaign process – and they want to know what their money is being spent on. Even the monarchy is subject to public pressure.

This is the reason for the rest of this book. Political marketing used to be about campaigns, then it was broadened to include the whole area of party behaviour. Now we begin to see marketing permeating all other areas of the political system. Furthermore, there are links between them, as the rest of the book will show. Indeed, there may even be a link between the emergence of a market orientation in Labour, its acquisition of government, and the increasing responsiveness of the monarchy to how the public views it. As such, we now move onto discussing marketing one of the areas one might least expect to turn to: the monarchy.

Notes

1 In doing so it draws on discussion with Labour and Conservative party staff, particularly significant qualitative research in the Conservative party in both central London and Scotland. The majority of primary research was funded by the Carnegie Trust as part of a project 'Marketing the Conservatives 1997–2001'. The support from Carnegie is gratefully acknowledged here. The author would also like to thank the MPs and staff who agreed to be interviewed. The results of this research were developed and presented in conference papers. This chapter builds upon first Lees-Marshment (2001d), followed by Lees-Marshment and Bartle (2002) and Lees-Marshment and Rudd (2003). It was updated and incorporates further primary empirical research conducted in 2003. Attempts were made to interview Michael Portillo and William Hague but failed.

Bibliography

Butler, P. and N. Collins (1996), 'Strategic Analysis in Political Markets', *European Journal of Marketing* 30(10/11): 32–44.

Chambers, P. (2001), Interview by J. Lees-Marshment with P Chambers, head of direct marketing, Conservative Central Office, London, 18 October.

Conservative Party (1997), *Our Party: Blueprint for Change*, Conservative Party, London.

Conservative Party (1998a), *The Fresh Future: White Paper on Organisational Reform*, Conservative Party, London, February.

Conservative Party (1998b), *Listening to Britain Constituency Manual*, Conservative Party, London, July.

Conservative Party (1998–9), "Listening to Britain: List of Events", correspondence with J. Lees-Marshment from Conservative Central Office, London, July–May.

Conservative Party (1999a), *Speak Out: Your Say on Tomorrow's Challenges: Listening to Britain*, Conservative Party leaflet, London.

Conservative Party (1999b), *Heartland: The Conservative Party Magazine*, Conservative Party, London, October.

Conservative Party (1999c), *Listening to Britain: A Report by the Conservative Party*, Conservative Party, London, Autumn.

Conservative Party (1999d), *The Common Sense Revolution*, The Conservative Party, London, Autumn.

Conservative Party (2000), *Believing in Britain*, Conservative Party, London.

Conservative Party (2001), *Time for Common Sense*, Conservative Party, London, May.

Conservative Party (2002), *Leadership with a Purpose: A Better Society*, Conservative Party, London, October.

Cook, G. (2002), 'The Labour Campaign', in J. Bartle, S. Atkinson and R. Mortimore (eds), *Political Communications: The General Election Campaign of 2001*, Frank Cass, London, pp. 87–97.

Crawford, J. (2001), Interview by J. Lees-Marshment with John Crawford, planner at Yellow M (Conservative Party's advertising agency), Tuesday 7 August.

Duncan-Smith, I. (2003), 'A Fair Deal for Everyone', speech to Conservative Spring Conference, 16 March.

Dykes, C. (2001), Interview by J. Lees-Marshment with C. Dykes, head of development, Conservative Central Office, London, 18 October.

Dykes, C. (2003), Interview by J. Lees-Marshment with C. Dykes, head of Development and candidates, Conservative Central Office, London, 19 February.

Farrelly, P. (2003), Labour MP talk to Keele students, Keele University, 10 February.

Foley, M. (2002), *John Major, Tony Blair and a Conflict of Leadership*, Manchester University Press, Manchester.

Francis, R. (1999), Letter to J. Lees-Marshment about 'Listening to Britain', 18 May.

Francis, R. (2000), Interview by J. Lees-Marshment with Rachel Francis, 'Listening to Britain' officer, Conservative Party, 11 April.

Gould, P. (2002), 'Labour Strategy', in J. Bartle, S. Atkinson and R. Mortimore (eds), *Political Communications: The General Election Campaign of 2001*, Frank Cass, London. pp. 57–68.

Grice, A. (2001) 'Call for Inquiry into Labour's £192 Million Advertising "Splurge"', *Independent* (26 July).

Hague, W. (1998a), 'The Fresh Future', statement provided by Conservative Central Office, 16 February.

Hague, W. (1998b), 'The Fresh Future', speech at '*The Fresh Future*' Launch Conference, information from the Conservative Party, 28 March.

Hague, W. (1998c), Opening speech, Conservative Party Conference, 6 October.

Hague, W. (1999a), 'Common Sense Conservatism', speech given at the Albany Club, Toronto, information from the Conservative Party, 15 February.

Hague, W. (1999b), Interview, *On the Record*, BBC, 14 March.

Harrop, M. (1990), 'Political Marketing', *Parliamentary Affairs* 43(3): 277–291.

Hennessy, P. (2000), *The Prime Minister: The Office and its Office Holders Since 1945*, Penguin, London.

Hogue, S. (2000), Interview by J. Lees-Marshment with Stuart Hogue, campaign officer, 'The Common Sense Revolution', Conservative Party, 11 April.

Houston, F. (1986), 'The Marketing Concept: What It Is and What It Is Not', *Journal of Marketing* 50: 81–87.

Keith, R. (1960), 'The Marketing Revolution', *Journal of Marketing* January: 35–38.

Kohli, A. and B. Jaworski (1990), 'Market Orientation: The Construct, Research Propositions, and Managerial Implications', *Journal of Marketing* 54: 1–18.

Kotler, P. (1972), 'A Generic Concept of Marketing', *Journal of Marketing* 36: 46–54.

Kotler, P. (1979), 'Strategies for Introducing Marketing into Non-profit Organisations', *Journal of Marketing* 43: 37–44.

Kotler, P. and A. Andreasen (1991), *Strategic Marketing for Non-profit Organisations*, Prentice-Hall, Englewood Cliffs, NJ.

Kotler, P. and S. Levy (1969), 'Broadening the Concept of Marketing', *Journal of Marketing* 33(1): 10–15.

Labour Party (1997), *Partnership in Power*, Labour Party, London.

Labour Party (1999), *The Government's Annual Report 1998/1999*, Stationery Office, London.

Labour Party (2000), *The Government's Annual Report 99/00*, Stationery Office, London.

Labour Party (2001), *Ambitions for Britain*, Labour Party, London.

Laing, A. and J. Lees-Marshment (2002), 'Time to Deliver: Why Political Marketing Needs to Move Beyond the Campaign', paper presented at the PSA conference, Aberdeen, April.

Lansley, A. (1997), 'The Future of the Conservative Party', presentation at the Elections, Parties and Opinion Polls Conference, Essex University, September.

Lansley, A. (1998), 'Statement: A Unique Event in Conservative Party Policy-Making', information from the Conservative Party, 1 October.

Lansley, A. (1999), Letter to J. Lees-Marshment about 'Listening to Britain', 9 June.

Lansley, A. (2001a), 'Image, Values and Policy: From Here to the Next Election', address to the Bow Group, Conservative Party Conference, 9 October.

Lansley, A. (2001b), Interview by J. Lees-Marshment with Andrew Lansley, Porticullis House, 18 October.

Lansley, A. (2002), 'Conservative Strategy', in J. Bartle, S. Atkinson and R. Mortimore (eds), *Political Communications: The General Election Campaign of 2001*, Frank Cass, London.

Lawther, S. (2002), 'The 2001 Campaign: An Insider's View', presentation by the Scottish Labour Party polling co-ordinator, Political Marketing Conference, Aberdeen University, September.

Lees-Marshment, J. (2001a), *Political Marketing and British Political Parties: The Party's Just Begun*, Manchester University Press, Manchester.

Lees-Marshment, J. (2001b), 'The Marriage of Politics and Marketing', *Political Studies* 49(4): 692–713.

Lees-Marshment, J. (2001c), 'Comprehensive Political Marketing: What, How and Why', *Proceedings of the Academy of Marketing Conference*, Cardiff University, 2–4 July.

Lees-Marshment, J. (2001d), 'The World's Most Unpopular Populist, a Poorly Sold Product, or Just Mission Impossible? A Political Marketing Analysis of Hague's Conservatives 1997–2001', paper presented at the EPOP conference, University of Sussex.

Lees-Marshment, J. (2001e), 'Marketing the British Conservatives 1997–2001', special issue on *The Marketing Campaign: The British General Election of 2001*, eds P. Harris and D. Wring, *Journal of Marketing Management* 17: 929–41.

Lees-Marshment, J. (2001f), 'The Product, Sales and Market-Oriented Party and How Labour Learnt to Market the Product, Not Just the Presentation', special Issue on political marketing, *European Journal of Marketing* 35(9/10): 1074–1084.

Lees-Marshment, J. (2003a), 'Marketing Political Institutions: Good in Theory but Problematic in Practice?', *Academy of Marketing Conference Proceedings*, University of Aston, 8–10 July.

Lees-Marshment, J. (2003b), 'Political Marketing: How to Reach that Pot of Gold', *Journal of Political Marketing* 2(1): 1–32.

Lees-Marshment, J. and J. Bartle (2002), 'Marketing British Political Parties in 2001: An Impossible Challenge?', *Political Marketing Conference Proceedings*, University of Aberdeen.

Lees-Marshment, J. and A. Laing (2002), 'Time to Deliver: Why Political Marketing Needs to Move Beyond the Campaign', *Political Marketing Conference Proceedings*, September 19–21.

Lees-Marshment, J. and D. Lilleker (2001), 'Political Marketing and Traditional Values: "Old Labour" for New Times?', *Contemporary Politics* 7(3): 205–16.

Lees-Marshment, J. and S. Quayle (2001), 'Empowering the Members or Marketing the Party? The Conservative Reforms of 1998', *Political Quarterly* 72(2): 204–212.

Lees-Marshment, J. and C. Rudd (2003), 'Political Marketing and Party Leadership', paper presented at the PSA Conference, Political Marketing Group panels, April.

Lilleker, D. (2003), 'Is there an Emergent Democratic Deficit in Britain? And is Political Marketing the Cause?', paper presented at the PSA conference, Political Marketing Group panels, April.

Lilleker, D. and J. Lees-Marshment, eds (forthcoming), *Political Marketing in Comparative Perspective*, Manchester University Press, Manchester.

Lilley, P. (1998), Statement on 'Listening to Britain', information from the Conservative Party, 14 July.

Lilley, P. (1999), 'Rab Butler Memorial Lecture', presented to the Conservative Party, 20 May.

Lock, A. and P. Harris (1996), 'Political Marketing: Vive la Difference!', *European Journal of Marketing* 30(10–11): 21–31.

Luck, D. (1969), 'Broadening the Concept of Marketing – Too Far', *Journal of Marketing* 33: 53–55.

MacDonald, M. (2001), Interview by J. Lees-Marshment with Moray MacDonald, head of research, Scottish Conservative Party, Central Office Edinburgh, Thursday 2 August.

Mannan, S. (2001), Interview by J. Lees-Marshment with Sabeeha Mannan, head of the Cultural Unit, Conservative Central Office, London, Thursday 9 August.

Mochrie, R. (2003), 'Niche Marketing as an Entry Strategy: Formation and Growth of the Scottish Socialist Party', paper presented at the PSA conference, Leicester.

Newman, B.I. (1994), *The Marketing of the President: Political Marketing as Campaign Strategy*, Sage, Beverley Hills.

Newman, B.I. (1999a), *The Mass Marketing of Politics: Democracy in an Age of Manufactured Images*, Sage, London.

Newman, B.I., ed. (1999b), *The Handbook of Political Marketing*, Sage, London.

Niffenegger, P.B. (1989), 'Strategies for Success from the Political Marketers', *Journal of Consumer Marketing* 6(1): 45–61.

Norman, A. (1998), 'Power to Party Members', *House Magazine* (30 March).

Norman, A. (1999a), Letter to J. Lees-Marshment about the Conservative Party, 20 May.

Norman, A. (1999b), Letter to J. Lees-Marshment about Conservative Central Office Staff, 23 June.

Norman, A. (2001), Interview by J. Lees-Marshment with Sir Archie Norman, Porticullis House, 18 October.

Norris, S. (2001), Interview by J. Lees-Marshment with Steven Norris, Citigate Public Affairs, 19 October.

O'Shaughnessy, N.J. (1990), *The Phenomenon of Political Marketing*, Macmillan, London.

Peele, G. (1998), 'Towards "New Conservatives"? Organisational Reform and the Conservative Party', *Political Quarterly* 69(2): 141–147.

Pugh, D. (2001), Interview by J. Lees-Marshment with David Pugh, Conservative Future, 28 November.

Scammell, M. (1999), 'Political Marketing: Lessons for Political Science', *Political Studies* 47(4): 718–739.

Scammell, M. (2001), 'The Media and Media Management', in A. Seldon (ed.), *The Blair Effect: The Blair Government 1997–2001*, Little, Brown, London.

Senior Conservative Official (2001), Interview by J. Lees-Marshment with a senior official involved in the Conservative campaign, Conservative Central Office, London, 19 October.

Senior Conservative Official (2003), Interview by J. Lees-Marshment with a senior official involved in the Conservative campaign, Conservative Central Office, London, April.

Seyd, P. (1999), 'New Parties/New Politics? A Case Study of the British Labour Party', *Party Politics* 5(3): 383–406.

Seyd, P. (2002), 'Labour Government–Party Relationships: Maturity or Marginalization?', in A. King (ed.), *Britain at the Polls, 2001*, Chatham House, Chatham, NJ. pp. 95–116.

Seyd, P. and P. Whiteley (1992), *Labour's Grass Roots: The Politics of Party Membership*, Clarendon Press, Oxford.

Seyd, P. and P. Whiteley (1999), 'Middle Class Activists', *Guardian* 20 September.

Shama, A. (1976), 'The Marketing of Political Candidates', *Journal of the Academy of Marketing Science* 4(4): 764–777.

Shapiro, B. (1973), 'Marketing for Non-profit Organisations', *Harvard Business Review* 51: 123–132.

Silvester, J. (2003), 'Occupational Psychology and Political Selection: A Diversity Challenge', *People Management* (9 January).

Smith, G. and J. Saunders (1990), 'The Application of Marketing to British Politics', *Journal of Marketing Management* 5(3): 295–306.

Sparrow, N. and J. Turner (2001), 'The Permanent Campaign: The Integration of Market Research Techniques in Developing Strategies in a More Uncertain Political Climate', *European Journal of Marketing* 35(9/10): 984–1002.

Tait, J. (2003), Interview by J. Lees-Marshment with John Tait, Conservative Party policy unit staff, 20 February.

Trustrum, L. (1989), 'Marketing Concept: Concept and Function', *European Journal of Marketing* 23(3): 48–56.

Tucker, W.T. (1974), 'Future Directions in Marketing Theory', *Journal of Marketing* 38(2): 30–35.

Turner, S. (2001), Interview by J. Lees-Marshment with Simon Turner, director of the Scottish Conservative Party, Thursday 2 August.

Whiteley, P., P. Seyd and J. Richardson (1994), *True Blues: The Politics of Conservative Party Membership*, Clarendon Press, Oxford.

Wring, D. (1994–5), 'Political Marketing and Organisational Development: The Case of the Labour Party in Britain', Research Paper in Management Studies 12, Judge Institute of Management Studies, University of Cambridge.

Wring, D. (1996), 'Political Marketing and Party Development in Britain: A "Secret" History', *European Journal of Marketing* 30: (10–11) 100–11.

3

Marketing the monarchy

No institution, city, monarchy, whatever, should expect to be free from the scrutiny of those who give it their loyalty and support. Not to mention those who don't. (HM The Queen, 1992 Speech to the City of London, four days after the fire at Windsor)

One reason why Windsor plc has hung on to the monarchy contract is that it has always tried to reinvent the product, tailoring it to meet changing demand. (Hamilton 2002)

It's just a brilliantly managed public relations campaign. St James' Palace and Mark Bowland have used a number of tools to help judge the climate of public opinion including focus groups so beloved of New Labour. (Editor of *PR Week*, interviewed in BBC1 2002c)

The marketing of our future King William V . . . has such a weight of reverse spin applied to it that you might think he was just plain Bill. An heir without airs; a young man miraculously blessed with ordinariness. The campaign is so subtle that it hardly looks like a campaign at all, but it is utterly consistent. Give or take the odd tooled-up detective, Prince William is 'just like any other university student in a flat-share'. (Girling 2003)

It's all about helping people . . . the monarchy is something that needs to be there. Modernisation is quite a strong word to use with the monarchy because it's some-thing that's been around for many hundreds of years. But I think it's important that people feel the monarchy can keep up with them and is relevant to their lives. (Wales 2003)

The monarchy is one of the oldest and most established parts of Britain's polit-ical system. It continues to attract substantial attention from the public both in the UK and abroad. Marketing the monarchy presents interesting intellectual and practical dilemmas, requiring conceptual leaps for myself as an academic but also challenges for those working to maintain citizen support for an elite, aristocratic institution. As one assistant press secretary commented, 'marketing the monarchy is an interesting challenge as it is an unique institution that is con-stantly evolving' (Cohen 2002). Yet, as I made my way to Buckingham Palace to conduct the first set of interviews for this chapter, moving through crowds of tourists from all over the world, and passed through the police-guarded gates, attracting looks of curiosity as I walked 'the other side' of the royal–public exchange, the linkage between elite and masses, between queen and country, seemed as strong as ever and it seemed that here, too, marketing might play a role.

Conventional analysis would lead most of us to think the monarchy might be the one area marketing could never reach. Inside the gates, it became clear that the monarchy has recruited new professional staff, uses market intelligence, and has altered its behaviour to try to respond to a changing and increasingly critical public. It has gone on-line and hosted a pop concert in its garden. But marketing the monarchy is not a straightforward exercise. It raises many questions: what is the royal family's product? Can you market princes like popcorn?

This chapter explores whether market-oriented behaviour can reinvigorate an ancient institution to ensure its survival in the twenty-first century. The chapter sets out the nature of the monarchy and explores how the royal family has evolved over time, before discussing the complexities of marketing the monarchy. In doing so, the chapter draws on television documentaries, public documents, websites and interviews with current and former staff at Buckingham Palace and the BBC.[1]

Marketing the monarchy: background and basic theory

The monarchy is one of the oldest parts of the UK political system (Norton 1994a: 295). Today, the monarch rarely uses its political powers; its importance lies more in its symbolism and a non-partisan, apolitical representation of the people. The Queen serves as head of state, albeit an unelected one.

Product
The monarchical product in formal, historical terms consists of its official functions, which you can find in any standard textbook on UK politics (see, for example, Norton 1994a: 301–303), such as opening parliament each year, saluting the troops and giving honours and knighthoods. However, the product includes much more than this:

- the royal family – individual people such as the Queen and Prince Charles;
- staff;
- finances;
- all activities, including charity work, giving speeches, opening new buildings or events, hosting garden parties, planting trees, meeting the public;
- buildings – palaces and castles;
- boosting the UK economy through tourism;
- representing the nation and public of the UK above the level of partisan politics;

- providing a focus in times of crisis such as war or death;
- providing a symbol of national unity and stability;
- providing a 'dream' or 'fairytale' for the public to use to escape ordinary life.

As with any organisation, aspects of the royal family product change over time. Like a company that finds its product performance falls, and launches a different if related product to compensate, so the royal family product can develop. In the 1970–90s one of the royal family activities was to portray a model of a happy family life. When this fell into disrepute, the royal family began to drop trying to present this ideal.

There is also a highly significant but intangible aspect of the royal product. As Nairn (1988: 19) noted, its 'unique place and appeal depend upon a strong popular support going far beyond . . . the cool calculation of benefits which academic supporters of the Crown have so often relished'. Leadbeater (2000: 18) argued that 'the British Royal Family has no output other than symbolism', but the monarchy takes people away from their ordinary lives, as do celebrity lives and movies, although the royals remain distinct from celebrities because, as Nairn (1988: 27) noted, 'they posses in addition a "secret": an element of mystique'. Arguably the most important part of the product is the people in the royal family, which makes marketing the monarchy extremely complex and unusual.

Market

In terms of market, the monarchy's principle market is the UK people, as well as the Commonwealth. Penny Russell-Smith, press secretary to the queen, noted that although the queen may not be elected she 'represents everybody' and aims to be 'as inclusive as possible' (Russell-Smith 2003). The monarchy needs to pay attention to the media, which provides a central means of communication from and to the people, and the elected government, which can influence the monarchy's funding, behaviour and rights.

Goals

The ultimate goal of the monarchy is to maintain public support. Without broad support for its existence, the government will not be able to fund the civil list with tax-payers' money. If no one turned up to see them when they undertook public duties, their *raison d'être* would vanish. The monarchy is in an apparently fortunate position in that, unlike parties, it has no formal competition (Nairn 1988: 34). Nevertheless the monarchy's position, as an organisation where power is determined by birth within a meritocratic, liberal democratic society, can never be taken for granted.

The monarchy has been one of the last organisations to adopt marketing concepts and naturally began with a more product-oriented, traditional approach before moving through to a sales orientation and then finally attempting to become market oriented.

History of the monarchy: product oriented?

> The Royal Family has an old-fashioned relationship with its consumers. We get what they choose to give us, as and when they choose to give it to us. (Leadbeater 2000: 25)

The monarchy is concerned with elitism at the highest level, predicated on birth and wealth rather than ability, and the very antithesis of market-oriented forms of behaviour. It is not supposed to conduct focus groups into how common people want royals to rule. The reign of Queen Elizabeth II was typical of a product-oriented institution, driven by tradition and precedent much more than public fashion. As Leadbeater (2000: 22) observed, 'the Royal Family was a national industry, trapped by its dependence upon a safe local market'. Its staff was also elitist, recruited from the social elite or armed services, and the public was highly deferential to the royal family. In this context, the royal family exhibited behaviour that typifies a product orientation.

As a *product-oriented monarchy*, it designed its behaviour according to what it thought best, assuming the public would support this because of deference to the royal status. Communication with the public was on royal terms, with information only provided if the monarchy thought it wise to do so.

In terms of marketing activities, a product-oriented monarchy goes through three basic activities: product design, communication, and monitoring public support. The behaviour of Queen Elizabeth in the 1950s and 1960s was driven by tradition, due to the nature of society as a whole. Communication was limited. In 1944, a special film, *Heir to the Throne*, was made to mark the occasion of Elizabeth's eighteenth birthday, but little personal information was made available about her (ITV 2002a). A relationship between the monarchy and the media gathered momentum with the filming of the 1953 coronation. The BBC managed to persuade the palace to allow televising it only after agreeing to make various changes to suit the royal family (BBC2 2002a). The filming ended with the music 'Land of Hope and Glory': it was presented almost as a piece of theatre and helped to maintain the magic surrounding the monarchy. The queen's Christmas message was first broadcast in 1957, but as the Queen herself conceded, 'it is inevitable that I should seem a rather remote figure to many of you. A successor to the kings and queens of history. Someone whose face may be familiar in newspapers and films, but who never really touches your personal lives.'

Reflecting the product-oriented era overall, media reporting was unquestioning and reverent towards the monarchy. The Queen was treated as if she was divine; microphones were not allowed near her; she was a silent figure, protected from too much exposure. In 1952, Commander Colville, who ran Buckingham Palace's press office, took the approach that 'journalists had no business writing anything about the royal family apart from information contained in official hand-outs' (Walker 2002). Indeed, a *Panaroma* programme broadcast in 1966 commented 'Buckingham Palace stands aloof, its intimate workings, a dark unknown. A barricade of silent formality keeps the onlooker at a distance, (reported by BBC2 2002a).

The problem was, as Leadbeater (2000: 22) observed, 'the Royal Family found that the protocol designed to entrench its power left it marooned, out of touch, unable to learn about the world around it'. No one was allowed to make suggestions or criticise the monarchy, leaving it bereft of feedback and ideas. In 1957 John Grigg (later Lord Altrincham) criticised the Queen's speeches for, as he later recalled, being 'the speeches of a elderly high priest, and she was talking down from a great height' (BBC1 2002a), but he was publicly vilified. Communication at this time was too product oriented: designed to suit the rulers, not those ruled.

As the public was much more deferential, support was broadly maintained. As UK society changed, the monarchy began to think more about how it ran its communications, even engineering events to gain support and attention from the public, culminating most particularly in the fairytale weddings of the 1980s.

Razzmatazz royalty: the sales-oriented era

> Princess Diana was a creature of the modern communications revolution. (Leadbeater 2000: 20)

> I must say that I am in the pro-Diana camp, and always have been, as a phenomenon. As somebody interested in public relations, you can't write down what she had in a manual: some people have that empathy with mass audiences which others do not – and she had it in spades. (Lord McNally, quoted in Strober and Strober 2002: 462)

Communication in the 1980s was of a glamorous, happy-family, fairytale-type product created through the media. The focus was on creating the impression of something the people wanted by effective communication.

A *sales-oriented monarchy* focuses on selling its product to the public, responding to market intelligence by communication strategies and techniques that promote what the public want, without necessarily really changing the product at all. Such behaviour is depicted in Box 3.1.

Stage 1: Existing product; Stage 2: Market intelligence

In many ways, as with many sales-oriented organisations, the basic product remained the same from the 1960s through to the 1980s. First, a new press secretary, William Heseltine, was appointed in 1967 and appreciated the problem that lack of communication had caused: 'the royal family has become what you might call one-dimensional cardboard cut-out figures. I thought it could only do good if the public were able to see them (as people who had rather more direct access to them could) as three-dimensional and very human' (BBC2 2002a). Secondly, Prince Charles, the young heir to the throne, was alleged to have a new girlfriend every week but, as he grew older, he came increasingly under pressure to respond to public demand for an appropriate bride to produce the next line of succession.

Box 3.1 The process for a sales-oriented monarchy

Stage 1: Existing product
Determined by tradition, history, desire of the queen, advisors, elites etc.

Stage 2: Market intelligence
Monitor public support; find out weaknesses, strengths etc.

Stage 3: Product redesign
Without altering the product too much, try to appear to be what the public want, make promises.

Stage 4: Communication
Communicate most positive aspects; give the public what they want.

Stage 5: Delivery
The difficult bit: need to deliver redesigned product.

Stage 6: Monitor public support
Ensure product redesign works and make changes, especially using communication, if needed.

Stage 3: Product redesign: appearing to be what the people wanted
Prince Charles chose Diana Spencer to be his bride. Their wedding – 'the stuff of which fairytales are made' – appeared to be everything that people wanted. The future of the monarchy seemed secure. As a journalist who witnessed the wedding said, 'we were a very innocent and uncynical nation then . . . we saw the images, we believed them implicitly' (BBC1 2001a). The 'fairytale princess product' continued after the wedding as Diana's image projected happiness, glamour, youth and 'a touch of magic' (Imagicians/Visual 1997), and captured media attention wherever she went. The product, albeit a possibly media-created rather than royally designed one, was sold to the public.

Stage 4: Communication
Proactive communication began under events initiated by William Heseltine, such as a BBC documentary called *The Royal Family* in 1969 (BBC2 2002a) and the first public walkabout in March 1970 in Wellington, New Zealand. The Investiture of the Prince of Wales was also created in response to the public desire for greater communication about the royal family. It was designed by Lord Snowden to attract a modern television audience. In the 1980s other programmes were made: Princess Anne was accompanied on Safari by *Blue Peter* presenter Val Singleton and there was a documentary on Prince Charles learning to be a naval pilot (BBC2 2002a). Media coverage lost some of its reverence: Prince Andrew was depicted as 'Randy Andy', for example, in the tabloids and the satirical puppet show *Spitting Image*. The spectacle *It's a Royal Knockout*, organised by

Prince Edward, was criticised and some advisors thought it reduced respect for the royal family. However, the introduction of Diana into the royal family led to a fresh media interest. The wedding was extremely effectively communicated: people all around the world watched it and Princess Diana captured substantial coverage, increasing the attention paid to the royal family. The problem was that, after the wedding, they had to 'deliver' on the promise of love and happy families.

Stage 5: Delivery

This problem with marketing the royal family aspect of the monarchy product is that delivery is about someone's relationship, normally an entirely personal concern. On the surface, the Charles–Diana marriage delivered: two male heirs, the appearance of happiness and a very glamorous princess. However, the authenticity of the product would come to be questioned: simply promising the public what they want, regardless of whether it can be delivered, is classic sales-oriented behaviour, but is fraught with problematic consequences in the long term. Even Charles's earlier investiture was somewhat false; as a contemporary broadcaster remarked, it portrayed 'an invented crown on an invented throne in an invented situation' (BBC2 2002a). As became known over time, the marriage between Charles and Diana was in many ways a sham and stories of infidelity, bulimia and attempted suicides began to emerge from the royal palaces.

Stage 6: Monitoring public support

In 1984, a report edited by R. Jowell and C. Airey on British social attitudes said the popularity of the monarchy was so secure and unlikely to change that 'this question clearly need not be repeated annually' (quoted and noted by Nairn 1988: 19). The editors were unfortunately incorrect in their predictions: attitudes did indeed change. Furthermore, Diana's way of operating attracted more support for the monarchy than the more traditional styles, but the breakdown of the marriage pushed her outside of the institution, creating competition between her royal product and that of her husband or mother-in-law.

Public support for the monarchy reached a new low, exemplified by the reluctance of the public to foot the bill when Windsor Castle caught fire. Conservative politicians were partly to blame for assuming the public would be happy to pay, sparking public dissent (see Daley 2002). This is an example of the way the orientation of other parts of the political system – the product-oriented Conservative government – has an impact on the rest. John Major did later concede that he 'completely misjudged the way people would react' (BBC1 2002a). The fire acted as a catalyst for a debate about the role and future of the monarchy that continues to this day. Overall, the 1970s–90s represented behaviour typical of a sales orientation: as a former member of the royal family staff observed, the 1980s and 1990s are often referred to as the 'celebrity era'. However, whilst this achieved a certain success inasmuch as it drew substantial public attention to the royal family, it also created certain problems, which in the long term resulted in the need to revise the royal product and behaviour significantly.

The monarchy today: marketing the royal product?

> Sound-bites and spin-doctors will not be enough for the monarchy to thrive in the next century. The monarchy must commit itself to real change, and put itself in touch with its people priorities, hopes and fears. (Leonard, www.demos.co.uk/catalogue/modernisingthemonarchy_page135.aspx, accessed February 2003)

> It is a complete misconception to imagine that the monarchy exists in the interest of the monarch. It doesn't. It exists in the interests of the people. (Bodganor 1995: 302)

> They've been forced to adapt to changes in modern society . . . the institution has had to change [and they are] more approachable now. (Cohen 2003)

The monarchy today is an institution that is very much aware of the potential danger of being perceived as out of touch. Whilst an element of tradition and regality doubtless remains, it is being blended into the product design in a way to serve rather than rule the public. The institution is slowly but surely moving towards a market orientation.

The more market-oriented behaviour of Princess Diana was a major contributor to such a change. She seemed to understand what the nation needed and wanted; she challenged royal protocol and spoke about 'hidden' issues such as bulimia and adultery. As the journalist Nicholas Owen commented, 'she had been a royal, but not a remote one. She had more of the common touch than the rest of the House of Windsor' (ITN 1998). Leadbeater (2000: 22) commented that she used a form of direct marketing:

> Diana was Royalty Direct . . . Her lack of traditional assets allowed her to be quicker than the Royal Family to respond to public opinion . . . In the weightless economy where intangible assets are critical, new competitors can spring from unexpected sources. Supermarkets can challenge banks, television companies can challenge building societies, biotech companies can challenge giant pharmaceuticals groups and divorced single mothers can launch a challenge to the Crown. (Leadbeater 2000: 23)

Diana's death in 1997 ironically and sadly served to increase her effect on the institution. The nation went into mourning and then criticised the royal family's initial response. Having listened to current and former palace staff, the problem seems that it was both a public and private event and the royal family placed immediate priority on their private need to grieve, and in particular to protect the two young princes who had lost their mother at a very young age. The difficulty with having a head of state on the basis of family and birth is that there is a mix of public and private, formal role and individual human being, which when it works provides effective representation for society but when it goes wrong can have extremely problematic consequences for the monarchy.

The royal family did not make a formal statement of the need for private grief immediately. They seemed distant: the public could not know what was going on behind the castle walls. In the week that followed the death, apparent monarchy behaviour and public reaction contrasted sharply. There was no public lying in state, although the public used the palace gates to lay flowers as a focus of mass grief; there was no official week of mourning, but it happened anyway; when the queen returned to Buckingham Palace the royal flag was hoisted upright, whilst crowds outside the palace cried out in disappointment that it was not flown at half-mast for Diana. The situation was unprecedented and complicated. The public had a right to feel grief but so did the 12- and 15-year-old boys for whom Diana was not just a princess but a mother. In response to criticism, the Queen's own press secretary appeared for the first time on television to give a statement, the Queen made an unprecedented public live address to the nation about Diana's life and death, and the royal flag was flown at half mast on the funeral day. As one commentator said, 'belatedly the Palace complied with public demand' (BBC1 2002a), providing powerful testimony to the basic idea that it is the consumer that is king – not the Queen. When the procession moved in front of the palace, the Queen and other members of the royal family stood in front of the gates, and the Queen even bowed her head to the cortège.

There was an overall impact from Diana's death. As one assistant press secretary to the Queen commented:

> After the death of Diana, Princess of Wales, the institution examined the way it had communicated with the public. The media has accused the institution of being 'out of touch' with ordinary people. A number of reforms or changes resulted, including the Way Ahead Group and the appointment of an external Communications adviser from the private sector. Meanwhile, more of The Queen's work was opened up to the cameras (e.g. Receptions, Audiences, Garden Parties and Investitures). (Cohen 2002)

It shook all traditions and led to more open, new thinking on the monarchy. The queen herself said in her public address, 'I for one believe there are lessons to be drawn from her life and from the extraordinary and moving reaction to her death.'

A *market-oriented monarchy* seeks to understand the desires and dreams of its public, and to determine its product carefully – including events, public duties, buildings and overall style – in response to this. Communication is used not to sell the monarchy, but to connect with the public; intelligence is used to understand what the public needs from the monarchy. The monarchy can use marketing activities in the same way as political parties, but it is a more delicate process, see Box 3.2.

Stage 1: Market intelligence
Like any market-oriented organisation, the royal family, to be able to respond to public demands, needs to understand what the public want from it. It can use all the normal methods: internal discussions, drawing on think tanks, intuition or gut feeling and professional research. The royal family engaged in significant debate about its role and potential modernisation during the 1990s. In the late

---

Box 3.2 The process for a market-oriented monarchy

Stage 1: Market intelligence
To identify and discuss the needs, demands and changing nature of the public.

Stage 2: Delicate product design
Continual development of the royal family product, with care, combining tradition and future, noting that marketing individuals is not straightforward.

Stage 3: Communication
Working with the media, but also communicating directly with the public where possible; pursuing campaigns where needed; being proactive, not just reactive; and also protecting the privacy of individuals where appropriate.

Stage 4: Delivery
Delivering the promised product.

Stage 5: Monitoring public support
Continually ensuring the product broadly satisfies the public; responding to any loss of support where possible and appropriate.

1990s, after the death of Princess Diana (Cohen 2002, 2003; Walker 2003), the royal family formed the Way Ahead Group: a committee under the direction of the queen which meets twice a year to discuss the future of the monarchy. Lewis (2001) noted that 'what the royal family do, where they go, the organisations they are involved in, the physical side of the monarchy, have been examined to ensure a much better reflection of contemporary Britain, (see also Walker 2001; Pilkington 1998: 176; Wighton 1996).

Stuart Neil, assistant press secretary to the queen, noted how Buckingham Palace also draws upon lord lieutenancies round the country to provide an informal link with the country. Lord lieutenants are nominated locally, and are people who have given service in a local community, such as the chair of a health trust. They 'provide us with some feedback' and are the monarchy's 'eyes and ears on the ground' (Neil 2003a). The monarchy recently began to collect its own formal market intelligence: as Walker (2003) said, 'it's no secret that Buckingham Palace does polling' (see also Neil 2003a; Lewis 2001). Interestingly, the queen's press secretary, Penny Russell-Smith (2003), said that they 'deliberately don't do polling after significant events' but prefer to use regular, routine polling to provide overall data less subject to short-term fluctuation.

Stage 2: Delicate product design

Staff The whole area of staff in terms of recruitment and management has been reviewed (Lewis 2001; Walker 2001). Recruitment is open, from the private and public sector. There is 'recruitment on merit . . . not who you know' (Russell-Smith 2003). In 1998, it selected Simon Lewis from British Gas to be the queen's communications secretary between 1998 and 2000 (Lewis 2001). Simon Walker took over from him in September 2000, also on secondment, from British Airways. Walker formerly worked as a media director with the New Zealand Labour party and the John Major policy unit (Walker 2003). Prince Charles employed a new public relations officer, Mark Bowland. There is, of course, benefit in introducing new staff with completely different backgrounds and experience. Lewis remarked how he 'was able to look at a lot of the issues that were germane to the monarchy with a degree of objectivity which is difficult if you're there as a long-term permanent member of staff' (Lewis 2001). The average stay within the press office in particular is now two to three years, with an average staff age in the late twenties, and the office includes staff seconded from consultancy firms, which provides a 'constant reinvigoration of new ideas' (Russell-Smith 2003).

The royal family members   *The Queen* brings people together in Britain, as something above politics. She continues to offer stability to the royal family product, and remains overall broadly popular with the public. John Major, the former prime minister, noted that the Queen is:

> Someone who is dedicated to service and dedicated to the country as a whole. I think that communicates itself to people. They have seen the queen for a very long period – there isn't a sudden outburst, there isn't a sound-bite here, a sound-bite there. There's something constant and enduring that they know is there to serve the country as a whole. (ITV 2002a)

However, some suggest that the queen is a barrier to change: Bentley and Wilsdon (2002: 15) said her record of one of 'reactive, rather than proactive, reform' (see also Campbell 2002). It is impossible to confirm this without extensive and complete access to the workings inside Buckingham Palace: an empirical data collection process that is in all reality extremely unlikely ever to take place. As discussion will show, the Queen has responded to suggestions from her aides, government and other members of the royal family.

As *Prince of Wales,* Prince Charles has carved out a significant role, through charity work and speaking out on controversial issues. The issues he focuses on are young people, environment, architecture, spiritualism and organic farming. His website states that he 'has spoken of his pride in being heir to the throne in a multi-racial society'. In many ways, his views indicate an understanding of the changes in society (see Bogdanor 1995: 308), as he supports multiculturalism, wishes to be defender of faith rather than of one faith, and put forward arguments for organic farming before it became accepted. He is willing to say what politicians are sometimes prevented from talking about because of the need for moderation, party unity and appeal to the majority rather than new ideas; for example, he spoke out against genetic crops and against modern architecture, risking the wrath of establishment groups in doing so. The Prince's Trust is the Prince of Wales's main charity. This has proved to be a highly successful organisation: it has a turnover of £32 million, has helped over half a million young people, and continues to expand. Charles has also attempted to ensure that he is seen by the public as more caring since Diana's death. He has his own office, with press officers and advisors. As I was not granted direct access, I cannot comment much further.

Prince William, currently in his twenties, is fast becoming a potentially highly significant part of the royal family 'product'. Although he has been protected from royal duties and the press, whilst of student age, on the few visits and appearances he has made he has attracted positive coverage and eager crowds. He is in a prime position to add much value to the royal family, despite his inevitable wealth, upper-class background and Eton education. In an interview to mark his twenty-first birthday, he highlighted the opportunity to live like a typical student at St Andrew's university: 'people here treat me like everyone else . . . I'm able to live a near-normal life' (St James's Palace 2003).

Activities   The royal family has broadened the nature of public duties it engages in, responding to market intelligence (Cohen 2003: Lewis 2001). Walker (2002) noted that 'when The Queen visits a shelter for disadvantaged youngsters she meets them and goes into their rooms. If there's a further special emphasis it will be on staff and volunteers. Before the 1970s any Monarch on a similar visits would have met only the chief executive, his wife and the board of trustees.' Russell-Smith (2003) also noted how visits are conducted to mark any improvement, rather than an established success; examples are improvement in schools, a reskilling project in an area of high unemployment, and a mobile drugs rehabilitation bus.

In 2002 the nation celebrated the Queen's Golden Jubilee, the fiftieth anniversary of her coronation and accession to the throne. The design was developed over a long period of time, and involved discussion by committees and groups made up of civil servants, royal advisors, the BBC and government figures (Walker 2003; Neil 2003a; Russell-Smith 2003). Buckingham Palace worked with the BBC and Golden Jubilee Office (GJO) in particular; the GJO dealt with the government infrastructure (Russell-Smith 2003) whilst the BBC organised the concerts (Vaughan-Barratt 2003). They key themes for the jubilee reflected a change in approach; for example, one was 'Giving thanks: The Queen has said that she sees her Golden Jubilee as an opportunity to express her thanks for the support and loyalty she has enjoyed during her reign' (www.goldenjubilee.gov.uk/Jubilee_Celebrations).

The Palace tried to make the Jubilee as representative as possible, consulting the different religions 'to make sure the programme reflected multi-cultural Britain today' (Russell-Smith 2003). The Queen toured the poorer eastern suburbs of London, visited a mosque, and opened a football stand at West Ham. The Palace tried to ensure that everyone in the country was within 50 minutes' drive of the queen's visit (Neil 2003a). In particular, there was a jubilee weekend and for the first time public concerts were held in the gardens of Buckingham Palace. Nick Vaughan-Barratt (2003), BBC events editor, commented that the aim was to provide 'lots of different things for different people' and that 'we basically moulded it to work for people on the streets and at home' via the television. The overall aim was to 'create something that people would want' (Neil 2003a). Nevertheless, the Palace just 'wanted people to celebrate the Jubilee in their own way' (Walker 2003). It was 'more enabling rather than creating something for people to buy into' (Neil 2003a).

The 'Party at the Palace' did not completely remove all elements of royalty, but used them to provide a market-oriented form of entertainment. At each side of the stage was a royal lion holding an electric guitar. During the fireworks, the palace was swathed in extraordinary light effects, including pink and purple. The most poignant moment that symbolised the transformation of the monarchy was the opening of the concert, when legendary rock star Brian May performed the national anthem on an electric guitar on the roof of Buckingham Palace. You still had the palace, but with a pop star playing on its roof; you still had the anthem, but it could be played on an electric guitar to mark the beginning of the pop concert. It was royalty, but market-oriented royalty. Vaughan-Barratt (2003) recalled how the BBC was 'given the most extraordinary freedom to book who we wanted for the shows . . . The big dramatic change in the Palace during the jubilee was they decided to just let go of it, they trusted people, they broke all their own rules . . . they just opened the gates and it paid off.' As Borkowski (2002) commented, 'this was the rawest possible illustration of what the market wanted, and what the brand was uniquely able to deliver'.

Finances   A big cause of criticism of the monarchy is the cost. Since the 1990s, there have been several changes in the Queen's finances in response to public opinion. In 1971 the Select Committee on the civil list had considered that 'ten yearly, rather than annual, reports to Parliament were considered more consistent with the honour and dignity of the Crown'; but in 2001 the monarchy adopted a different approach and began to publish annual reports on travel and civil list expenditure (Royal Household 2001). Publication of a detailed breakdown of civil list expenditure in June 2002 showed that the monarchy was attempting to cut costs (Bates 2002). Sir Michael Peat from city accountants KPMG became royal finance director and 'went through the palace like a whirlwind, demanding savings in every corner' (Hamilton 2002: 46). The Queen volunteered to pay tax, and the number of the royal family on the civil list was cut. The Queen also announced she would fund repairs to Windsor Castle by opening Buckingham Palace to the public. The Prince of Wales has the annual net resources of the Duchy of Cornwall, which he uses to meet the costs of all aspects of his public, private and family commitments. The Duchy is a crown body, and so is tax exempt, but the Prince voluntarily pays income tax on his income from it (www.royal.gov.uk).

Stage 3: Communication

> I have to say I was also pleased to discover the techniques of modern communica-
> tions can make contributions even in our most historic institutions. (Lewis 2001)

General approach   The monarchy has three press offices engaged in communication; at Buckingham Palace, St James's and the Royal Collection
(www.royalinsight.gov.uk/output/page1729.asp). The Palace has attempted to
adopt a more strategic, forward-looking approach to communications. Simon
Lewis (2001) recalled that his appointment was designed to 'move away from a
purely reactive approach . . . to be much more proactive and embrace contemporary communications techniques'. He was granted an extra budget of £500,000
to change the way the palace communicated (Lewis 2001). When Walker took up
Lewis's job he had a 'strong desire to reach out to journalists' (Walker 2003).

Websites   The monarchy has gone on-line: the official royal family site,
www.royal.gov.uk, was launched in March 1997. As Samantha Cohen, assistant
press secretary, commented, it 'is now considered a key communications tool . . .
[and] with its ability to offer 24-hour availability to the media and public alike,
the Royal website has increased the Monarchy's accessibility, particularly during
high-profile events such as the Golden Jubilee and Royal deaths' (Cohen 2003).
Plans at the time of writing included launching an educational website in late
2003 to reflect the changing school curriculum (Cohen 2003). There was also a
website for the Golden Jubilee (www.goldenjubilee.gov.uk), which received 28
million hits in a six-month period (Buckingham Palace Press Office 2002) and
hosted a 'virtual media centre' to provide greater resources for the media (Neil
2003a). The Prince of Wales's website (www.princeofwales.gov.uk) is stated on-
line to be 'a new platform for his Royal Highness to communicate directly with
the public'. One section of the site contains an Online Forum through which the
prince seeks to focus on particular issues and invite others to contribute opinions via email links. Increasingly, it holds regularly updated information on his
sons, Princes William and Harry, including information, pictures and interview
material from Prince William's gap year and twenty-first birthday and Harry's
eighteenth. As Tuck (2000) argued, the websites are seen as 'integral parts of our
information and presentational strategies'.

The Queen's Christmas broadcast   The monarchy has attempted to respond to
falling audience figures for the queen's Christmas broadcast. Figures show a
marked decline since the 1980s: see Table 3.1.
    Although such a decline is in line with the fall in general television viewing as
competition increases with digital and satellite options (Neil 2003b; Vaughan-
Barratt 2003), in 2002 a trailer was run for the first time, as 'a continuation of the
Buckingham Palace policy of moving with the times, when appropriate', and
viewing figures increased by 600,000 (Neil 2003b). Nick Vaughan-Barratt looked

Table 3.1 Audience figures for the Queen's christmas broadcast, 1957–2001

	Audience (millions)
1957	27.0
1987	28.0
1992	17.9
2001	8.7

Source: ITV news, 3 December 2002

through previous messages broadcast many years ago and noticed that they had included exclusive televised material which had not been broadcast before, and he is in discussions with the palace to try to 'find one important and unique piece of footage and advertise in advance' (Vaughan-Barratt 2003) to give the public a reason to watch it.

PR campaigns   Mark Bowland ran a mini-campaign called Operation CPB to improve public opinion of Camilla Parker-Bowles, Charles's companion (BBC1 2002c). Camilla was introduced to the public very gradually, with each extra exposure of her and Charles planned carefully. First there were pictures of them together in January 1999 at the Ritz; then a platonic kiss in June 2001; in June 2002 Camilla was present in the royal box at the Pop Party; and in August 2002 Camilla and Charles attended their first official public event together. This led to a gradual, if qualified, acceptance of Camilla by the public. Bowland won an award for this work in 2001 from *PR Week* magazine for 'the public rehabilitation of the couple' (BBC1 2002c). However, it remains to be seen how truly successful this attempt to 'sell' Camilla to the public will be. As a former royal press secretary, Dickie Arbiter, said, 'you can promote a product so far, but at the end to the day – it's a bit like a new breakfast cereal – at the end of the day it's the consumer who decides when they pull it off the shelf whether it is going to be successful or not. Now we have the same thing with Mrs Parker-Bowles. Mark Bowland has set the scene, has to all intents and purposes, he's outed her' (BBC1 2002c). Now we will see if the public actually accept her.

Communication about the young princes   Communication about the two young princes has been handled carefully, with the royal family trying to create a positive but respectful relationship with the press. Lord Wakeham, chairman of the Press Complaints Commission, set out guidelines for self-regulation amongst the press in the reporting on the two princes whilst they were growing up and when William went to university. Whilst welcoming this, the monarchy has been careful to supply certain information actively to help satisfy the press. New photographs of William at 18 were released, and a reporter and photographer from Press Association and an ITN cameraman were invited to spend a few days with William during his time in Chile to produce a special television programme.

Nevertheless, at the time of writing the final draft of this chapter in June 2003, media attention to the two princes was increasing as Harry left school and William turned 21. At the same time, the monarchy's exposure of them was also increasing. Several communication pieces were created. William gave two interviews to the Press Association: one to mark his two years at university on 30 May 2003 (St James's Palace 2003), then another to mark his twenty-first birthday, with new pictures, which was released in two parts around 21 June 2003, and included comments about his thoughts on the monarchy, his parents and the queen (Wales 2003). A 'fly-on-the-wall'-style piece of television footage of William, Harry and Charles playing polo and chatting was released 20 June and made available to all news media. Similarly, photos of Harry's last days at school were also released in June 2003.

Tabloid stories about the princes also began to emerge. On 15 June St James's Palace took the unprecedented step of formally denying a relationship between William and one girl when the story took hold the week before his twenty-first birthday. It is difficult to predict the best strategy for handling such stories. Prince William appealed for the respect for privacy that he had so far enjoyed with the media whilst at school and university to continue. He argued that 'I don't think either side wants to return to the free-for-all of the old days. It's a really fine balance and it could be quite volatile if things get out of hand. So I don't want to go back to that' (Wales 2003).

The jubilee   The Palace held a reception on 28 October 2001 for the broadcasting industry, and then another on 28 April 2002 at Windsor castle for 700 journalists prior to the jubilee concerts (Walker 2003; Neil 2003a; Sumerskill, 2002). However, there was a difference here between a sales- and a market-oriented approach: as Neil (2003a) commented, whilst the Palace co-operated with and facilitated media interest, 'we weren't creating things for the media', merely 'facilitating their needs.'

There was also a strong focus at regional level. Simon Walker and Helen Bayne (a civil servant from the jubilee office) conducted briefings around the country, targeting people who might want to put on a local event, such as a neighbourhood watch meeting in Nottingham (Walker 2003; see also Neil 2003a). The national press argued that no one cared about the jubilee and people would not turn up. The Palace did not argue back; it was 'not for us to tell people'; 'it was bottom-up not top-down'; the attitude was 'you do what you want' (Neil 2003a). 'We didn't just create something that people would buy . . . we're policy-driven not PR-driven' (Neil 2003a). Russell-Smith (2003) also argued 'we're not in the business of doing hype'. The jubilee celebrations were advertised by the BBC to the public in modern, snappy broadcasts with the actor-comedian Rowan Atkinson introducing them from the palace. The role of television in communicating the party at the palace to the mass public cannot be overestimated. Vaughan-Barratt (2003) noted how the Palace 'absolutely understood that . . . a large proportion of people in the world would only experience the jubilee on television'.

Table 3.2 Public views about the monarchy, May 2002

	Yes (%)	No (%)	Don't know (%)	Total votes
Is the monarchy out of date?	41	57	2	58,996
Does the royal family cost too much money?	44	54	2	51,332

Source: www.news.bcc.co.uk/hi/english/audiovid . . . ammes/monarchy/newsid_2040000/2040773.stm

Table 3.3 Public views about the monarchy, June 2002

'Should we retain, reform, or abolish the monarchy?'	
	In favour (%)
Retain	40
Reform	41
Abolish	18

Targeting the opposition The Palace now tries to communicate with and involve its critics. The reception at Windsor Castle for the media included hostile journalists: Walker recalled that 'we deliberately asked everyone including a lot of people who were anti-Monarchy' and even the tabloid newspapers such as the *Sun* and the *Mirror* came (Walker 2003; see also Daley 2002). Rather than simply ignore anyone who criticised the royal family, as once might have been the case, the institution has tried to appease them and, to a certain extent, accept their right to voice an alternative opinion.

Stage 4: Delivery; Stage 5: Monitoring public support
In 2002, the monarchy enjoyed an increase in support – even if it was against all predictions. The Party at the Palace was watched by around 200 million viewers all over the world (Buckingham Palace Press Office 2002). As Cohen (2002) noted, the jubilee 'was considered a high point in "marketing" terms' and 'a great success for its inclusivity and the sense of nationalism it evoked'. Russell-Smith said it was for others to judge; we're 'very careful not to sound complacent'.

At the time of writing, public support for the monarchy remains strong, and the 'monarchy remains an important institution in British political life' (Norton 1994a: 322), although there are plenty who criticise its existence. The BBC held a television and on-line debate hosted by David Dimbleby, *Our Monarchy: The Next 50 Years* (bbc.co.uk/monarchy; BBC1 2002b), which gave the public the opportunity to express their views about the monarchy. Voting took place via the telephone and internet, and digital satellite viewers were also able to vote via their remote control handsets: see Table 3.2 for the results. ITV held a similar programme, a question time, on the monarchy on 2 June 2002, hosted by Jonathan Dimbleby. The programme also displayed results from yougov.com: see Table 3.3.

On the whole, polls indicate broad support for the monarchy, if somewhat qualified by the potential need to reform. There will always be those critical of the monarchy. Pictures of the Mall on 4 June 2002, last day of the jubilee weekend, showed it teaming with more than a million people waving Union Jacks and singing the national anthem. Nevertheless, months later in the autumn of 2002 the royal family was brought into disrepute by the collapse of a trial against Princess Diana's former butler, Paul Burrell, and other allegations of misdoing by palace staff. The royal family is subject to public scrutiny on every aspect of its conduct – such is the strength of the rise of the political marketing consumer and the revolution occurring throughout the UK political system.

Indeed, after interviewing staff at Buckingham Palace, I returned to my friend's flat in London and met her landlord, who had been to the Palace that week because his wife had been awarded an MBE. One of his most abiding memories was that they had been there for two hours but were never even offered a cup of tea or a glass of water. As he said, you would get better service at your local church. Marketing the monarchy clearly involves many challenges and there is always room for improvement.

Political marketing gone too far: can we market princes like popcorn?

The monarchy is using market intelligence, being advised by government and public relations experts, and like other parts of the political system may finally be moving away from its traditional product orientation towards a more responsive institution aiming to meet the demands of the public. As Peters (2002) commented, 'the royal family has made a start in embracing the branding and marketing principles that will bring it up to date with modern culture, and back in touch'. However, because the royal family product is so different to a business it needs to be marketed somewhat carefully, as it raises many questions.

The monarchy is not a business
That the monarchical product is different to a business was raised by all staff I interviewed, who noted various differences between marketing business and the monarchy:

- 'We don't market' members of the royal family.
- 'It's not a product, it's part of the structure of government.'
- It is 'not appropriate to use the word "marketing"'.
- The monarchy is 'not something susceptible to marketing techniques'.
- 'It's not marketing in the conventional sense.'
- 'There is no financial incentive; the institution is not making money.'
- 'It's a unique model.'
- 'Staff are working for a family; there are no common workplace practices.'
- 'There's no competition, but lots of accountability.'
- There is 'no margin for error – cannot recall the product once it is out there'.

- There is 'a lot of public demand and high expectation of performance.'
- 'It's a very traditional institution in a modern changing world.'

Indeed, the family cannot be run like a business; there is no clear chief executive, and the junior members of the family, unlike subsidiaries, cannot be discarded if they do not perform. You cannot close them down, because they're people, even if with a company one would.

The product is long term

> This is for life. (Neil 2003a).

> You don't adjust it to public opinion . . . That's a very tough decision to hold in this world, when public opinion appears to guide everything. (Raymond G.H. Seitz, quoted in Strober and Strober 2002: 532)

> A heavily spun approach to media relations based on likes and dislikes might win short-term enthusiasm, but would mean that in years to come individual Members of the Royal Family would be as forgotten as Billie Piper or Brad Pitt will be in years to come. (Walker 2002)

As Neil (2003a) cautioned, the monarchy cannot be marketed like parties in an election cycle: it cannot simply 'do a focus-group appeal to a C2 audience'; it has to do what is 'right for the country, not a particular market sector'. This is an important theme, not just for what the monarchy offers in product terms, but in terms of communication because the monarchy is mostly conveyed through the national media. However, different generations of the royal family may target different groups – for example, Prince William can appeal to 15–35-year-olds – as long as the sum of the monarchy's activities represents everybody.

The monarchy is also concerned with continuity and tradition – that is a fundamental part of the product – and therefore not amenable to constant change. Russell-Smith (2003) noted that what the queen 'does now is the product of constant shifting and planning' over the years. Floella Benjamin, broadcaster, commented that 'the monarchy is serving all people, whether they're old or they're young. They can't be seen as some sort of trendy item that's going to change with the fashion' (BBC1 2002b).

Linking the mass market and the elite monarchy

> Much depends on presenting a certain mystique. I myself dislike anything that seems to make the monarchy trendy, or going too far towards putting it in the hands of spin doctors . . . the Queen has to be somewhat on a pedestal, otherwise the institution doesn't work. (Lord Powell, quoted in Strober and Strober 2002: 542)

> It would be much better if the monarchy still remained rather mysterious. All the time that I was there we were not trying, particularly, to promote the Monarch as a person. We were trying, in arranging what she did in her speeches and in her visits, to bring her more closely to the people. (Sir Edward Ford, quoted in Strober and Strober 2002: 542)

Political marketing is generally concerned with bringing organisation and people together, elite and masses relating to each other, but by the monarchy is something set apart. As Norton (1994a: 309) explains, 'it is, by definition, impossible for the royal family to be socially typical – since they would cease to be the royal family'. Marketing can be used and helps a remote institution without the check of elections to receive feedback and connect with the people.

The product is people: you can't design people

> The Queen, after all, has been very much unspun . . . She has done as she said she would do for fifty years, in a consistent and unspectacular way. It is that which seems to have earned her respect and affection – not presentational skill and the ability to meet media needs. (Walker 2002)

One issue is that the 'product' can arguably never be designed strictly according to what the public want, because the product is people – individuals. It seems rather strange to market people: can we really treat Prince William like a product? Can't he be free to fall in love with whomever he wants? The royal product cannot be designed or delivered by mail order, strictly according to what the public want, because the product is people with their own ideas, desires and feelings. It would be a bit like creating a stage play or a soap opera – except for them it is their real life. Walker (2003) cautioned against false behaviour: 'the Queen is not an actress'. William-Hague-type baseball caps are not a good strategy for monarchy (or arguably not for political parties!). Additionally there seems a desire at the palace not to be driven by the media. Russell-Smith (2003) noted how once the Iraq War broke out various members of the royal family made visits to families whose relatives were involved in the war, and how 'the important thing is that they were there – the media thing is incidental'; it is important for individual members of the public to meet them because 'for them it shows the royal family is in touch'.

Meeting different needs and demands: personal lives, public interest and individual privacy

> How to keep the balance? That question strikes right to the heart of the paradox of the British monarchy: it is at the same time a remote, or just impersonal, institution that has all these constitutional significances and it is a person with whom one can identify and feel personally. And the balance between these two things – the personal and the impersonal, which could be seen as the remoteness or the revelation of everything – is a matter of judgment at any one time. (Robert Lacey, quoted in Strober and Strober 2002: 544)

Another issue is the need to balance the public demand for information and the individual need for privacy. The public want to know what goes on in the personal lives of the royal family. The advantage is that it is another bridge to the people: weddings and births make everyone feel part of something (Russell-

Smith 2003; see also Nairn 1988: 22). But the insatiable demand for information is problematic. As Bentley and Wilsdon (2002: 13) commented, 'a lifetime in the public gaze – the 60-year ordeal which William and Harry now face – is profoundly unsustainable'. There has to be some limit to information given to the public. The political marketing relationship between elite and mass is a two-way street in some respects, or requires a degree of responsibility on the public's part. There are significant implications if we want to know every detail of what goes on in their lives – who would have wanted their sons to parade in public after their mother died? There is plenty of harrowing coverage of photographers chasing Princess Diana through airports and streets like a hunted animal: is that really what the public want?

Concluding remarks: time to rebalance and renegotiate the political marketing relationship?

The monarchy is one of the most established parts of Britain's political system. It continues to attract substantial attention from the public both in the UK and abroad. Marketing the monarchy presents interesting dilemmas. As noted, there are complexities with the product. The market is also complex: the Queen has to represent everybody, not just enough target markets to win an election. The other aspect is that the monarchy is, almost by definition, naturally an institution immune to market forces. Predicated on non-merit, birth and wealth, it is the very antithesis of market-oriented forms of behaviour. It is not supposed to be designed according to public opinion, or to conduct focus groups into how common people want royals to rule.

Nevertheless, marketing can help ensure the organisation's continued survival and success. Management is not so far removed from the royals as might first be assumed. The royal family needs to be market oriented in order to develop continually in response to a changing society if it is to survive in an ever-altering world. As the Queen herself said, 'change has become a constant: managing it has become an expanding discipline' (HM Queen Elizabeth II, 29 April 2002, quoted in Bentley and Wilsdon 2002). When rock legend Brian May performed the national anthem on an electric guitar on the roof of Buckingham Palace for the pop party, it really seemed as if the monarchy had changed. Although discussions with those involved in organising the event (see Russell-Smith 2003; Walker 2003; Neil 2003a; and Vaughan-Barratt 2003) suggest that the emergence of this idea was more by accident than anything, no one would have dared to *think* let alone *do* this twenty years ago.

Writing at the beginning of the twenty-first century, completing this chapter in the month of Prince William's twenty-first birthday celebrations amidst growing tabloid stories of his private life, I would argue that there is still more development to occur, both inside and outside the palace walls. There is concern for the rights of an individual to a private life, but also naturally growing interest from a public keen to see a more youthful third generation of the 'family firm', which could potentially reconnect with an age-group currently feeling removed from the monarchy.

There needs to be a renegotiation or rebalancing of the relationship between monarchy and the masses; between a young prince and the people. Both sides have different needs and demands of their own. The monarchy has had to make a huge leap to bring it out of the product-oriented 1950s to the twenty-first century, and it will need to go further; but equally, the public needs to be responsible too. Marketing can be used and helps a remote institution without the check of elections to receive feedback and connect with the people, but needs to be used with care because it involves people's lives – you can't market it in quite the same way as a video camera or computer.

An additional complexity within this political marketing relationship is that it isn't simply two-way. There is a political marketing revolution going on through all institutions and organisations and it is very much at play here. With regard to the monarchy, the media is the big other player. The media – whether it is television, radio or newspaper – is a crucial organisation that plays an important role in communication between the royals and the mass market. In July 2002 the BBC dedicated an entire programme to discussing the relationship between two of the most powerful institutions in the UK: the monarchy and the media (BBC2 2002a). The impact of Diana's death on the monarchy was in part enabled by the mass media that reported the event and everything surrounding it to the entire world. The BBC played a hugely significant role in the jubilee concerts, one of the most popular activities carried out by the monarchy.

The media can help the monarchy remain in touch with the public. However, the media is an independent political organisation in its own right and does not always work in favour of the royal family. Vaughan-Barratt (2003) noted that although 'we treat people with respect . . . that doesn't mean we don't criticise them'. Media behaviour is also linked to the problem of balancing privacy, and the public need to know what the royals are doing. Scandal stories about the royals sell newspapers. The media has its own interests, its own goals, its own markets to serve. Yet it is a crucial aspect of the political system, influencing the political marketing success of not just the monarchy, or parties, but all other political systems, being one of the vehicles through which communication between organisation and public flows. The next chapter will therefore explore marketing the media, its markets, goals and products, questioning the utility of a market- or sales-oriented media, with all the associated ethical and normative implications.

Notes

1 Correspondence was sent to the main offices in both palaces; any response was incorporated in and used in this analysis. I received written responses from various staff at Buckingham Palace. Interviews with key staff were carried out, including one of the current press secretaries, two of the Queen's current assistant press secretaries at

Buckingham Palace, a former press secretary (1990–7); and the queen's communications secretary (2000–2). I also interviewed the executive editor of events at the BBC who was in charge of the Jubilee. Repeated attempts were made to interview staff at St James's Palace, but they unfortunately proved unsuccessful: the Palace gave 'a number of staff changes and dealing with several ongoing projects' (Partridge 2003) as the reason. I tried to interview Mark Bowland but was told he could not co-operate due to confidentiality clauses. I also contacted government civil servants who worked in the Golden Jubilee Office, but they kindly redirected me to Buckingham Palace again. I would like to thank all staff who replied so promptly and positively and gave up their time to be interviewed. I am particularly grateful to Simon Walker for putting me in touch with other staff, and to Hugo Manson, who put me in touch with Simon in the first place. Academic literature on this topic is scarce: the only exception I know of is that by Speed (1991), which was relayed to me via another academic two weeks before submission of the manuscript of this book. Other analysis is generally conducted by historians.

Bibliography

Primary sources

Anson, C. (2003), Interview by J. Lees-Marshment with Charles Anson, former press secretary to the Queen, 24 April.
British Monarchy (2002), Official website, www.royal.gov.uk.
Buckingham Palace Press Office (2002), '50 Facts on the Queen's Golden Jubilee Year 2002', press release, 7 August.
Cohen, S. (2002), Letter to J. Lees-Marshment from the Queen's assistant press secretary, 5 December.
Cohen, S. (2003), Interview by J. Lees-Marshment with Samantha Cohen, assistant press secretary to the Queen, Buckingham Palace, 20 February.
Hamilton, A. (2002), 'House of Windsor PLC', *Business Life* April: 44–48.
Havill, P. (2003), Letter to J. Lees-Marshment from the special assistant to the private secretary, 2 December.
Historic Royal Palaces (2002), Official site of Historic Royal Palaces, www.hrp.org.uk.
Lewis, S. (2001), 'Communicating the modern monarchy', Rolls-Royce Lecture, www.cf.ac.uk/jomec/reporters2001/lewismain.html.
Neil, S. (2003a), Interview by J. Lees-Marshment with Stuart Neil, assistant press secretary to the Queen, Buckingham Palace, 20 February.
Neil, S.(2003b), Letter to J. Lees-Marshment from the assistant press secretary to the Queen, 24 February.
Partridge, H. (2003), Letters to J. Lees-Marshment from press officer to HRH The Prince of Wales, 6 March and 1 April.
Prince of Wales (2002), The Prince of Wales website, www.princeofwales.gov.uk/.
Prince's Trust (2002), The Prince's Trust website, www.princes-trust.org.uk.
Queen's Golden Jubilee (2002a), Official Souvenir Programme.
Queen's Golden Jubilee (2002b), Official website, www.goldenjubileeweekend-trust.co.uk.
Royal Household (2001), *The Civil List: Annual Report 2001*. London.

Royal Insight (2002), On-line magazine/monthly guide to the life and work of Britain's Royal Family, www.royalinsight.gov.uk/current/front.html.

Russell-Smith, P. (2003), Interview by J. Lees-Marshment with Penny Russell-Smith, press secretary to the Queen, Buckingham Palace, 23 April.

St James's Palace (2000), 'The Media and the Young Princes', www.princeofwales.gov.uk/about/biography/media/html.

St James's Palace (2001), Interview by S. Greenhill of the Press Association with Prince William, www.princeofwales.gov.uk/about/biography/will-uni.html.

St James's Palace (2002), 'About the Prince: Prince Harry at 18', www.princeof-wales.gov.uk/about/biography/harry18-two.html.

St James's Palace (2003), Interview by the Press Association with Prince William, to mark his two years at university, 30 May, www.princeofwales.gov.uk/news/news/php.

Summerskill, B. (2002), 'The Royal Restoration', *Observer* 5 May. Also at www.learn.co.uk/citizenship/topicallessons/jubilee/article3.asp.

Tuck, D. (2000), 'Site for Royal Eyes', letter, *BA HighLife* November: 9.

Vaughan-Barratt, N. (2003), Interview by J. Lees-Marshment with Nick Vaughan-Barratt, executive editor of events, BBC, by phone, 23 April.

Wales, William (Prince) (2003), Interview by P. Archer, Court Correspondent PA News, with Prince William given to the Press Association to mark his 21st birthday, Part I and II, available on www.princeofwales.gov.uk/news/news.php or www.princeof-wales.gov.uk/news/william21intII.php.

Walker, S. (2001), 'Prinz Speech', presented at Christchurch, April.

Walker, S. (2002), Speech presented to the PR Forum, London, March.

Walker, S. (2003), Interview by J. Lees-Marchment with Simon Walker, former communications secretary to the Queen, 19 February.

Wighton, D. (1996), 'Royals Consider Radical Changes to Monarchy', *Financial Times* 20 August.

Secondary sources

Bates, S. (2002), 'Queen's Budget Revealed for First Time', *Guardian* 28 June 28.

BBC1 (2001a), *You Had To Be There: Royal Wedding 1981*, 29 July.

BBC1 (2002a), *Queen and County*, series by William Shawcross, May.

BBC1 (2002b), *Our Monarchy: The New 50 Years*, debate hosted by David Dimbleby. Also at http://news.bbc.co.uk/hi/english/audiovideo/progammes/monarchy.

BBC1 (2002c), *Panaroma: Queen Camilla*, October.

BBC2 (2002a), *Cue the Queen*, narrated by Fi Glover, Sunday 28 July.

BBC2 (2002b), *Great Britons: Diana*, reported by Rosie Boycott, October.

Bentley, T. and J. Wilsdon (2002), 'The New Monarchists', *Monarchies: What are Kings and Queens For?* 17: 7–16. Demos Collection, London, and www.demos.co.uk.

Bogdanor, V. (1995), *The Monarchy and the Constitution*, Clarendon Press, Oxford.

Borkowski, M. (2002), 'PR Victorious', *Guardian*, 10 June.

Campbell, B. (2002), 'Sex and the Royals', on BBC website section 'Our Monarchy: The Next 50 Years', www.news.bbc.co.uk/hi/english/audiovid . . . ammes/monarchy/newsid_2014000/2014766.stm.

Daley, J. (2002), 'The Windsors Have Come a Long Way Since the Fire', *Daily Telegraph* 5 June.

Davies, C. (2002), 'A Jubilee Sea of Red, White and Blue', *Daily Telegraph* 5 June.

Fletcher, K. (2002), 'When Old Rockers and Young Royals Came Together', *Daily Telegraph* 5 June.

Girling, R. (2003). 'Split Heir', *Sunday Times Magazine*, 15 June: 40–48.

Hames, T. and M. Leonard (1998), *Modernising the Monarchy*, Demos, London.

Hoey, B. (2001), *Her Majesty Queen Elizabeth II 50 Years: The Pitkin Guide*, Jarrold, London.

Imagicians/Visual (1997), *Diana, A Tribute: Queen of Hearts 1961–1997*, visual corporation video.

ITN (1998), *Diana: The Week the World Stood Still*, narrated by Nicholas Owen, Carlton Television production, September.

ITV (2002a), *The Queen's Story*, narrated by Art Malik.

ITV (2002b), *Question Time on the Monarchy*, hosted by Jonathan Dimbleby, 2 June.

Leadbeater, C. (2000), 'Dianomics', in C. Leadbetter, *Living on Thin Air: The New Economy*, Penguin, London.

Lees-Marshment, J. (2003), 'Marketing Political Institutions: Good in Theory but Problematic in Practice?', *Academy of Marketing Conference Proceedings*, University of Aston, 8–10 July.

Mortimore, R. (2003), 'Why Politics Needs Marketing', *International Journal of Non-profit and Voluntary Sector Marketing,* special issue on *Broadening the Concept of Political Marketing*, ed. J. Lees-Marshment, 8(2): 107–121.

Nairn, T. (1988), *The Enchanted Glass: Britain and its Monarchy*, Radius, Derby.

Norton, P. (1994a), 'The Crown', in B. Jones (ed.), *Politics UK*, Harvester Wheatsheaf, London. pp. 295–313.

Peters, M. (2002), 'The Royals are Rocking', *Guardian* 18 May.

Pilkington, C. (1998), *Issues in British Politics*, Macmillan, London.

Speed, R. (1991), 'Marketing the Firm: the Royal Family, Popularity and Perceived Attributes', paper presented to Academy of Marketing Conference.

Strober, D. and G. Strober (2002), *The Monarchy: An Oral History of Elizabeth II*, Hutchinson, London.

Summerskill, B. (2002), 'The Royal Restoration', *Observer* 5 May. Also at www.learn.co.uk/citizenship/topicallessons/jubilee/article3.asp.

4

Marketing the media: the case of the BBC

It cannot be said too often that there is a thoroughly bad analogy between competition in industry and competition in broadcasting. (Ian Jacob, director general, 1958; quoted in Paulu 1961: 25)

From an artistic point of view the great advantage of public service broadcasting is that it doesn't have to live up to equations of audience size, programme popularity and cultural address. (Frith 1993: 102)

In the long run, faced by an inevitable loss of position, the success of the BBC or any other broadcasting institution will depend on its relationship with citizens and audiences, on its legitimacy with them and the extent to which it meets their needs. (Mulgan 1993: 96)

The media is a fundamentally important and influential organisation within the political market. It has previously been viewed more as a mechanism to be used by other political organisations adopting marketing. Most commonly, it is seen as a part of the process of political marketing by parties – spin-doctoring and sound-bites. The media is key to communication by all political organisations and actors. However, the media can also be studied as a separate political entity. Like political parties and the monarchy, it has markets, goals, demands to meet and products to design, and most recently has faced increasingly diversified and expanding competition. It can also use techniques such as market intelligence and target marketing. This chapter therefore analyses the media in its own right, examining the BBC and its response to changes in its market and new competition. It raises questions as to whether the BBC and other television channels are run in the public interest or to make profit by attracting high audiences. For example, is the BBC more product oriented because it has a monopolistic position and is state funded, or has it changed as it has faced greater competition from other TV channels, and now satellite and cable?

The chapter will focus on BBC television and its website because the BBC currently remains one of the majority providers of information to the UK political market. In addition, its development through history illustrates most closely the evolving nature of the media and raises debates about the marketisation of media versus more traditional public service broadcasting. Obviously the BBC as a state-funded institution is in a unique position, but it nevertheless raises generic questions about the provision of media. Analysis also considers the current context of elite concern over a loss of interest in politics, after the low turnout in the 2001 general election and technological advances which enable greater audience participation.

Sources used include the policy documents and government committee reports for the most recent developments, alongside the usual academic books.[1] Obviously, as with every chapter, further research needs to be conducted on both the BBC and other media outlets, including newspapers, on this issue. This chapter has been written within the usual limitations in order to provide a starting point for debate that might then lead to more extensive research at a later stage. Political marketing has never been applied to the media before. In discussions about its behaviour, funding and regulations, there has been increasing talk of consumer sovereignty, of audience research, by government committees and reports, but there has never been an attempt to apply marketing theory to the media. Scammell (2000: 170) predicted that research on the media would more than likely 'increasingly seek evidence of influence on the political system as a whole, broadening considerably from the current emphasis on individual effects upon voters', and this chapter does indeed take that approach.

The media: basic principles and application of political marketing

The role of communication in the political system is profound. In the past, political parties could use interpersonal forms of communication such as meetings and rallies, or rely on partisan-controlled newspapers. However, in the twentieth century the electorate expanded and became more complex and geographically dispersed, and a mass media system was needed to facilitate communication between the masses and the elites (Budge et al. 1998: 322). The role of the media, particularly television, is crucial. Everyone is a consumer of the media. Furthermore, the media is the channel between political organisation and users. The way the media behaves is therefore of great concern to all other political actors and institutions. Indeed, 'the mass media form a web of communications across institutions . . . and their relationships to each other . . . and they contribute . . . to the relationships between institutions and groups in the political system' (Negrine 1994: 5). For citizens to make an informed judgement they need reliable information. The mass media is the means by which they obtain the majority of their information. How responsive the media is to its markets, how effectively it carries out its role, is therefore of great importance to every aspect of the political system.

In applying marketing to the media, we need to consider ways in which it is different to business in order to understand how political marketing might be used, as well as debate the potential difficulties. Some might argue that the BBC in particular is not amenable to such analysis. As Barnett (1993: 1) argued, 'it is the very fact that the BBC is not a business which raises a number of fundamental questions about the nature of its funding and its relationship with those it serves. A business presupposes a market-place where there is direct contact between the service providers and purchases', but with the BBC 'the benefits are deemed to be societal and the service is itself intangible and profoundly influential'.

Nature of the media: the context

There are several types of media, including radio, newspapers, television and internet. Television has become the main source of political information for political consumers. There has been a huge expansion of television stations, especially digital and satellite. The BBC is a public service broadcasting service. Additional terrestrial stations have been funded on different lines, by advertising rather than state/tax-payer funding. Television holds many potential advantages for political marketing. It can bring politics closer. As Budge et al. (1998: 322) explain, it 'brings political leaders and events from around the world into our own living rooms where we see and hear them for ourselves, and form our own judgements'. Television helps politicians reach people, many more than they ever could face to face. There are, however, certain issues of concern: it encourages short speeches and phrases; it requires visuals rather than complex, technical discussion, and can therefore militate against effective discussion of complex political issues. This and the funding of television can profoundly influence the type of political marketing approach the media takes.

Media product

The television product can include:

- programmes, ranging in type from entertainment to informative and educational including dramas, soaps, game shows, documentaries, the news and chat shows;
- staff, including top executives and leadership, presenters, technical staff including camera people, research staff and communication staff;
- technology;
- buildings, including those in London and regional headquarters;
- annual reports;
- budgets;
- mode of delivery: digital, satellite and terrestrial.

The product for a radio station, internet site or newspaper is not dissimilar. The nature of technology may vary, but technology is still a core component of the product. Staff is also a core part of the product, whether it is presenters in the case of radio, or writers for a newspaper. With a newspaper, the 'top executives' include the top editor and also the private owner. Photographers are a key component of newspapers, especially tabloids, who also employ photos by freelance paparazzi. Research staff may not be as important or even present at all in the newspaper product. Budgets will vary depending on whether the organisation is commercially or state funded.

Media goals

As with political parties, the goals of the media are varied, and generally derived from numerous ideals (see Wheeler 1997: 1–5; Marsh 1993: 333; Jones 1994: 211, for example):

- to ensure 'citizen access to the market-place of ideas' (Wheeler 1997: 5);
- to inform the public;
- to enable citizen participation in the general public discourse;
- to ease communication between politicians and the people;
- to provide unbiased, balanced, critical and independent coverage;
- to act as a watch-dog: an additional, modern-day check and balance in the political system;
- to reveal the hidden: to see what is going on behind scenes, which the average person may not be able to know about but is affected by, through investigative journalism;
- to cover the interesting: what people want to know about;
- to educate;
- to entertain;
- to achieve an audience and/or make a profit.

Varying goals depending on organisation   Media goals vary according to the nature of the outlet: for example, regional radio organisations may have specific goals related to the local community. Goals also depend on the source of funding. Commercial television will have economic and financial goals; it needs to make a profit and avoid a loss (Ang 1991: 26). Although the other goals are important, profit is the overriding one. The BBC is state/tax-payer funded. The BBC's goal, stated in 1999, was to enhance 'citizenship and democracy, guaranteeing access to the full range of information necessary for individuals to make informed choices' (quoted in Scammell 2000: 174, from BBC 1999. Like the monarchy, it has to provide diverse, differentiated products to suit all segments of the market, rather than simply majority, popular audiences. As Patricia Hodgson, then director of policy and planning at the BBC (Hodgson 1993: 67), argued, 'the BBC's role must be to provide a service of programmes which the market will not, or which will be put under pressure in a larger but much more competitive broadcast environment'.

Media market

The market for the media includes various groups:

- the public – viewers and non-viewers, TV and radio, market segments within that with different needs, such as regional, nationalist, ethnic and international;

- government;
- other media vehicles for both competition and co-operation – e.g. newspapers advertise on television, different television channels compete;
- producers of communication technology;
- internal staff;
- other political organisations including political parties, the public sector, the monarchy and charities;
- academic commentators.

The importance of each market vis-à-vis another varies from one outlet to another, and also over time. The demands of the markets may of course conflict: for example, the desire of the public for critical reporting about the government conflicts with the desire of the government to influence the agenda; the need to communicate government policy conflicts with the interests of the opposition parties who want to get their ideas across instead. The BBC has to be careful, because its funding comes from government and it needs its charter to be renewed so its existence is sanctioned by the government. This was extremely apparent during completion of this book when a row broke out between the BBC and the Labour government about BBC reporting of the government's reasons for going to war in Iraq and its use of evidence. As will be discussed, the BBC's response to different markets and different segments has changed over time. Certainly though, for all types of media, serving different markets is not necessarily a straightforward exercise. However, the degree to which they aim to do this depends on the orientation they adopt, which also depends on their goals.

Political marketing orientations the media can adopt

Like any political organisation, the media can – and does – adopt any orientation. A brief theoretical overview of these is below.

Product-oriented media   Product-oriented types of media design their product according to what the producers or designers think is best. The focus is on creating the best product they can, using their own expertise, ideas and professional training. No attempt is made to consider the wants of the market; the producers think they know best what the audience needs. Such an approach leads to a simple, three-stage process: see Box 4.1.

Sales-oriented media   Sales-oriented types of media focus on advertising the popular aspects of their product in order to obtain the maximum audiences. The product is designed according to professional and producer views, but if the audience responds negatively to any aspect then the profile of this is reduced, or the service abandoned completely, and effort is put into delivering the most popular aspect of the product. These types of media focus more on audience numbers and selling or presenting their product in an entertaining way. They therefore go through a four-stage process as depicted in Box 4.2.

Box 4.1 The process for a product-oriented media

Stage 1: Product design
Design the product according to what the producers think the audience needs and should have, using their professional expertise.

Stage 2: Communication
Ensure the audience is aware of the product and has the required information to view, listen to, access or read the product.

Stage 3: Delivery
Deliver the product to the audience as promised.

Box 4.2 The process for a sales-oriented media

Stage 1: Product design
Design the product according to what the producers think the audience needs and should have, using their professional expertise.

Stage 2: Market intelligence
Measure audience ratings to analyse which aspects of the product were best received and which least popular; for example, which shows attract the highest audience figures and which presenters are least popular.

Stage 3: Communication
Advertise the most popular aspects of the product; make them appealing; focus on entertainment aspects; use sensation and stimulate interest where possible. Reduce the profile of programmes which are unpopular, and give more time or space to more popular shows or reports.

Stage 4: Delivery
Deliver the product to the audience as promised.

Market-oriented media   Market-oriented types of media design their product according to the needs and wants of the public. They aim to satisfy all their markets where possible, and respond to the varying demands of different market segments. These types of media conduct market intelligence to inform their product design, develop new aspects of the product, obtain feedback on new products as well as communicating to inform the public about what they provide, and deliver the product to the audience as promised. The focus is on using professional or producer expertise and talent in order to provide the best possible product for the market. Market-oriented types of media will engage in five key marketing activities: see Box 4.3.

The process for market-oriented types of media is continuous. Therefore the media should return to conduct market intelligence in order to monitor public reaction to existing and new products and adjust accordingly.

Box 4.3 The process for a market-oriented media

Stage 1: Market intelligence

Identify, understand and predict audience demands and responses to the media product. This is not just about ratings, but about ensuring a broad understanding of the market and market segments within it. This may involve market segmentation and target marketing. It also includes understanding the overall nature of the market to the media outlet, and analysing the behaviour of the competition. Sources of market intelligence include polls, surveys, focus groups, viewing panels and government committees. Market intelligence includes soliciting viewer feedback on products already delivered, to understand viewer satisfaction with quality as well as future needs and demands. With the BBC, the Jenkins Committee advised that the BBC has a '*duty* to study the reactions, needs and interests of the public they service' (Home Office 1977: 450).

Stage 2: Product design

Design a wide range of programmes or reports in response to market intelligence; ensure that there is a balance in coverage or viewpoints expressed; ensure that the staff, technology, building and other resources within the product design support the production of this design.

Stage 3: Product development

Create new ideas and products, sometimes in response to market intelligence, at other times in order to fill a gap or start a new product. This may respond to analysis of the competition and to new and emerging market segments, and use new talent within a media outlet.

Stage 4: Communication

Ensure that the audience is aware of the products available; advertise new products to increase the chances of audience acceptance. Media institutions such as the BBC need to make viewers aware of new programmes so that they have a chance to win audience support and survive. Communication includes two-way communication between viewers and the media organisation, or, in political programmes, between voters and politicians, and utilises technology such as interactive multimedia. It also includes communication to different markets, such as the press for television, launching of annual reports, programme launches etc.

Stage 5: Delivery

Market-oriented media delivery involves not only ensuring good timing and effective transmission on a practical or technical level, but also delivering viewer, listener or reader satisfaction. Moreover, delivery involves ensuring that the organisation doesn't simply conduct market intelligence, design a good product, promise viewers it will be good in communication, and then not actually deliver a good performance that the viewers enjoy. Delivery includes creating viewer satisfaction and also, therefore, monitoring performance or achievement of that goal, which can then feed into product redesign and redevelopment.

This brief overview provides some indication of the different approaches which the media may take to political marketing. Discussion will now cover in greater detail how the BBC has evolved to move through the three orientations, providing empirical application of the theory before exploring the causes and consequences of this change.

Communicating wisdom: the BBC and the product-oriented era

> It is occasionally indicated to us that we are apparently setting out to give the public what we think they need – and not what they want – but few know what they want and very few what they need. (Reith, founding director general of the BBC, 1922, quoted on www.bbc.co.uk, accessed February 2003)

> [The BBC] was preoccupied with what the audience required, not what it wanted. It was not the BBC's concern to be popular. Instead, it wanted the audience to be a disciplined audience. (Ang 1991: 110)

The BBC was established in 1926. It was granted a monopoly and was sheltered from the profit-making nature of business and the market. Its policy and aim were to provide high-quality education and information as well as entertainment for the nation, following the public service model. Under (Lord) John Reith, the first director general of the BBC, it 'struck a high moral and "socially responsible" note' (Jones 1994: 202). Reith had a missionary almost dogmatic zeal, and created the principles that permeated the BBC from top to bottom (Burns 1977: 37).

Product-oriented approach
Funded by the state, this security ensured 'elitist or paternalist programming which gave people not what they wanted but what the BBC thought they should have' (Budge et al. 1998: 329). Lord Reith 'was an unashamed elitist who believed the BBC should lead public taste by offering high intellectual and moral standards' (Jones 1994: 219). The BBC had 'little anxiety about overriding consumer tastes' (Cave 1993: 20): it was like a traditional, product-oriented, ideological political party, or a doctor or teacher seeking to tell the patient or student what is best.

The BBC thought the audience needed to be 'reformed from above' (Ang 1991: 31). Its product orientation saw viewers not as a market but as a public: 'the audience-as-public consists not of consumers, but of citizens who must be reformed, educated, informed . . . within this context, broadcasting has nothing to do with the consumerist hedonism of commercial television – it is a very dignified, serious business' (Ang 1991: 28). The institution was in the business not of entertainment, but of education (Negrine 1994: 82–83; Wheeler 1997: 94). The BBC at this time therefore followed a simple marketing process; it designed its product to suit what it thought the public needed, communicated it, and delivered it.

Stage 1: Product design

The product was designed according to Reithian principles: what the director thought people should listen to. The focus was on radio programmes, with classical music, plays, poetry, talks and discussions. Pop music was neglected in favour of classic musical; the aim was to 'raise the musical taste of its listeners' and 'it was assumed that once people heard classical music, they would realise its superiority to popular tunes' (Ang 1991: 108). Television did not arrive until 1936, when it was first broadcast from Alexandra Palace. The whole ethos and culture within the institution were also elitist. As Burns (1977: 42) observed, 'BBC culture . . . was not peculiar to itself but an intellectual audience composed out of values, standards and beliefs of the professional middle class, especially that part educated at Oxford and Cambridge.' There was little incentive to step over the BBC line or develop new perspectives.

Stage 2: Communication

The audience were also told how to listen: for example, in the 1930 *BBC Year book* it was stated that 'the listener must recognise that a definite obligation rests on him to choose intelligently from the programmes offered to him' (quoted in Ang 1991: 109). Listeners were not encouraged to have the radio on as background noise.

Stage 3: Delivery

The BBC delivered the product, but did not seek to find out how it was received. As Val Gilgud, then head of the drama department, said, 'we are fundamentally ignorant as to how our various programmes are received, and what is their relative popularity' (quoted in Ang 1991: 110). Even when attempts to conduct market intelligence were made, the willingness to act on them in designing the product was not there. Charles Sipeman, director of talks in 1930, wrote in a memo: 'however complete and effective any survey we launch might be, I should still be convinced that our policy and programme building should be based first and last upon our own conviction as to what should and should not be broadcast' (quoted by Ang 1991: 111).

Consequently, the BBC at this time was very much determined by the producers, not the consumers. As Ang (1991: 117) observed, it had 'an inward-looking, production-oriented attitude which, logically, insists upon the autonomy of the professional in making judgements about the "quality" of the product, without compliance to "outside" demands'. This approach was not without criticism. A Labour MP also complained in the 1930s that the BBC was 'run very largely by people who do not know the working class, do not understand the working class point of view, but are seeking evidently to mould the working class' (quoted in Ang 1991: 108; see also Burns 1977: 43). Only when its market environment was changed did it too have to reconsider its behaviour.

Entertaining to educate? The triumph of sales-oriented media

> The media organisations are substantially part of the business world and embrace profit making as a central objective. (Jones 1994: 211)

> Simply because of its audience reach, broadcasting in general, and television in particular, are inextricably tied up with the cultural sales process. (Frith 1993: 110)

Cause of sales-oriented behaviour

There are many causes of the change in the attitude of the BBC. First, despite the BBC's initial hostility to market intelligence, it couldn't ignore newspaper ratings research or letters from listeners that showed the desire for entertainment (Ang 1991: 111). During World War II the BBC was set the task of programming for the troops and realised it had to respond to demand or they would switch off: one listener complained that 'I'd rather face German guns than hear any more organ music' (BBC website, www.bbc.co.uk/thenandnow/history), so the BBC increased the use of popular music and programmes.

The second factor was competition. The BBC's monopoly was broken in 1955 with the creation of ITV, commercial television, financed by advertising. BBC2 came in 1964, Channel 4 ('better by design') (Negrine 1994: 96) in 1982, and Sky satellite in 1989. In 1971 commercial radio was also allowed. This increased competition for an audience, meaning that even the state-funded BBC had to justify its government funding and charter (Negrine 1994: 84). Commercial TV stations also attracted staff from the BBC: 'television broadcasting staff now had a market to play, instead of competing for rewards within one organisation' (Burns 1977: 51). This increased competition led in the first instance to ratings wars: a desire to design not so much a product that would satisfy all the market as one that would attract the highest audience ratings, so that commercial television could then attract the advertising sponsors. In this respect the move was more towards a sales orientation than to directly responding to consumer needs and wants.

Stage 1: Product design

ITV, the commercially funded channel, designed a popular product with programmes that would attract high audience ratings, such as quiz shows that gave away free goods to participants, and popular US drama series (Ang 1991: 114; Burns 1977: 53). The BBC responded to some extent: different programmes were designed for different audiences, with pressure to deliver more heterogeneous programming (Burns 1977: 48). The BBC conceded it needed to produce new shows 'as ground bait for audiences who might be induced to continue watching programmes of a more informative or intellectually stimulating but less entertaining kind' (Burns 1977: 54), indicating a sales-oriented approach. Product design remained driven by the elite, not the market. A committee under Roy Jenkins which examined the BBC reported that 'we sense some self-indulgence in the production of programmes, with money being spent more to enhance professional esteem and reputation than to increase the pleasure of the viewer . . . sometimes there were even signs almost of contempt for the audience' (Home Office 1977: 93). A BBC worker reported that there was little attention to the audience when creating the news: 'We would say that we've been broadcasting to the people along the corridor not to the people who are listening. You know – one has followed their policy, done the sort of thing that we know will please them, and we haven't really thought about the listener' (quoted in Burns 1977: 200).

There is also a concern today that news reporting has declined in quantity and arguably in quality on the ITV. In 1999 the ITV dropped *News at Ten*; the regulatory body, the Independent Television Commission (ITC) tried to stop this, but then accepted the move to 11 p.m. because ITV 'needed to free its evening schedule for uninterrupted entertainment in order to remain competitive' (Scammell 2000: 173) – although the news was later returned to 10 p.m. The problem is that 'politics is not an audience winner' (Scammell 2000: 173) and a sales-driven or profit-driven ITV or other commercially funded channel has to respond to that.

Stage 2: Market intelligence

The BBC does monitor audience ratings (Ang 1991: 113). Commercially funded television that also needs to attract high numbers, perhaps even more than the BBC, is particularly prone to focusing on ratings figures, but not on audience satisfaction as such. As Cave (1993: 18) observed, there is a problem with media funded by advertising: 'broadcasters get money according to rating figures', favouring 'programmes which are watched with scant enjoyment by larger audiences [rather] than with rapt attention by smaller ones'. However, the Jenkins Committee observed that in the 1970s the BBC's audience research department was swamped by figures and facts, lacking time to analyse and respond to the information (Home Office 1977: 452).

Stage 3: Communication

Commercial television focused on selling programmes effectively, making them seem attractive and ensuring they provided entertainment. As Ang (1991: 27) observed, 'the commercial networks must try to achieve those good ratings results, that is, to maximise their audience, through shrewd and attractive programming'. In terms of overall communication style, whilst director general of the BBC, Hugh Greene worked to reduce old-style deference and adopt less conventional styles. Reports of audience ratings in relation to the competition were also produced. The BBC included new programmes such as chat shows and popular soaps such as *Neighbours*. However, the sales-oriented drive was – and arguably still is – most fully adopted by commercial television.

Stage 4: Delivery

Sales-oriented types of media do not necessarily actually understand their audience, and they certainly do not consider needs as well as expressed wants via purchase. Brittain (1989: 29) argued that 'advertising-financed broadcasting does not accurately reflect consumer requirements' because ratings dominate, minority interests are ignored and ratings figures do not assess quality or satisfaction. Reliance on advertising for an income leads to 'selling audiences to advertisers rather than programmes to audiences' (Brittain 1989: 31; see also Ang 1991: 27; Blumler 1993: 29). It can also lead to a reduction in important, valuable but less popular programmes. For example, Jones argues that the need to make profits led to a reduction in the number of current affairs programmes or their being moved to non-peak viewing times. Alternatively, news programmes became diluted with 'more human interest stories' (1994: 213). In order to gain viewer attention, even news stories focus on what makes a good story or a drama, or has emotional elements. It encourages a focus on politicians' personal lives, or anything that can be seen as controversial. Controversial issues can be easily blown up, so major parties or politicians avoid them where possible, even though it could be argued that non-consensus issues are those that need debate. Sales-oriented types of media may not be in the interest of society or other political organisations, but there can be no doubt that a significant number of media outlets use this approach, encouraging criticisms of political marketing as a whole in the same way as parties that focus on the presentation rather than the substantive product.

Market-oriented media: impossible dream or future reality?

> The BBC no longer stands at the top of society, peering down benignly at its grateful audiences. Instead it is supported by the goodwill of its audiences and its relevance to their wants and needs. It is becoming a supplicant for their time, not a monopolist. It will need them more than they need it. (Mulgan 1993: 98–99)

In recent years, however, the BBC has evolved to utilise a wide range of market intelligence, developing products in response and monitoring the public re-action. It has also sought to provide both majority-popular products and more specific programmes that meet the needs of emerging market segments. It appears to be adopting a market orientation, even if it has yet to follow this approach throughout all of its behaviour.

Cause of market-oriented behaviour

There are many causes of the move towards a market orientation. General changes in society that underlie the overall political marketing revolution clearly affect the media. The more educated people are, the greater their demands are for a wide range of media products. More particularly, the media environment 'has been transformed' since the 1980s (Hodgson 1993: 67). The development of technology enables digital television with the opportunity for direct choice and input into programmes by television viewers. Previously, television was very much a passive experience for the viewer but now there are phone-ins and voting by phone, internet or text. From the 1990s onwards, the introduction of cable, satellite or digital channels has also massively increased the competition for producers and choice for consumers (Beech 2003). Now that there is competition, the market can protect user interests (see Scammell 2000: 170). Even on a terrestrial television level, new channels have been introduced, such as Channel 4. This was designed to be very different, distinctive, with greater freedom to provide more experimental television and to 'provide opportunities . . . for needs to be served which have not yet been fully defined, and for the evolution of ideas which, for whatever reason . . . have yet to be revealed' (Lambert 1982: 100).

Another force is government itself. In 1986 the Peacock report suggested that the broadcasting system could become driven by consumer sovereignty and argued for the introduction of more market forces (Wheeler 1997: 114, 119). Sir Robert Fraser, the first director general of the Independent Television Association (ITA), argued that TV should be about 'popular pleasures and interest' rather than the imposed views of the elite (Wheeler 1997: 119). A 1988 Home Office White Paper, 'Broadcasting in the '90s: Competition, Choice and Quality', viewed audiences as consumers and noted the important of popularity (Ang 1991: 120), as did the 1990 Act (Wheeler 1997: 143; see also Negrine 1994: 87).

The market environment for the BBC in particular is therefore very challenging. As Smith (1993: 4) observed, 'public service broadcasting is having to make its case in a uniquely cold climate, in fact at a time when the very notion of public service has become in many parts of our society an object of general scepticism, amounting to scorn'. The pressure is great for media outlets such as the BBC to become more responsive to viewers. Taking a market-oriented approach involves careful market intelligence (not simply audience ratings), product design and communication, to suit varied markets with developing demands.

Adopting a market orientation

The BBC has made moves towards a market orientation and shown responsiveness to the decline in turnout in the 2001 general election, for example. Committee reports and policy documents suggest growing recognition of the need to monitor public reaction to programmes. In the twenty-first century, the institution has evolved further and developed new products in response to its audience needs.

Stage 1: Market intelligence

Various commissions, government committees and reports discuss ideas about media regulation and the role of the BBC (see Home Office 1977: 3–4). In the 1980s NOP were commissioned to conduct a survey of public opinion on the financing of the BBC (Home Office 1985). The BBC has also conducted market intelligence internally and followed audience research on its own role (Hodgson 1993: 67). It has continued to consult the public and interested bodies, as well as conduct audience research; it held 'The BBC Listens', a series of public events, meeting and opportunities for discussion between product designers and viewers or listeners in 2001, for example. In particular, four public meetings of mostly under-35-year-olds were held in Birmingham, Plymouth, Manchester and Southampton to discuss general election coverage (BBC 2002b). A series of 'customer care' workshops was run to ensure staff respond to viewers and listeners (BBC 2002b). The BBC also has regional advisory councils in England, consisting of viewer and listener panels. On-line there is a 'Connecting with Audiences – The BBC Listens' video (www.bbc.co.uk/england/acc/enfacc.shtml).

Stage 2: Product design

The BBC has developed its product – a range of television and radio programmes – to include popular soaps and series such as *Eastenders* and *Holby City*, but also dramas and creative programmes like *Walking with Dinosaurs*, which broke new ground. It offers popular entertainment but also fulfils its role as a public service broadcaster. For example, Mark Thompson, BBC director of television, said that while 'we don't believe BBC1 is perfect' it was 'investing heavily in high quality UK programmes for the future across all the genres, including those like science, arts and current affairs that rarely find a place in ITV1's peak-time schedule' (quoted in the *Daily Telegraph*, 25 August 2001). It continues to broadcast the Proms, for example, even though classical music does not necessarily attract a majority audience.

In terms of its goal of providing education, this has broadened to include Open University provision, resources for schools and campaigns for adult education. In terms of staff, the BBC recently launched a 'BBC talent' campaign and advertised for anyone with talent in any area of the BBC to come forward, as a means of widening the base of those working in the institution. In technical terms, it has also varied its use of technology and won awards for the creation of interactive radio and television.

The programme policy set for 2002–3 (see BBC 2002d) laid out several goals and principles, delivery of which was to be monitored and discussed in the 2003 annual report. Those statements (cited in BBC 2002d: 2) included 'Strengthening BBC programmes and services' to 'ensure that the overall portfolio has something of value for everyone', and 'Connecting with all audiences' to 'ensure that the BBC is meeting the needs of audiences in all nations and regions of the UK'. The detailed document indicated both maintenance of popular programmes and plans for further development of new products. It included what it termed 'landmark' programmes, such as *The Blue Planet*, delivered the previous year (BBC 2002d: 3). The document also included specified, targeted hours for the year for current affairs and other programmes, such as a minimum 400 hours of children's programmes (BBC 2002d: 7).

The BBC's news reporting, and especially election reporting, continues to be at greater length than ITV's for some programmes. Scammell (2000: 173) noted that in elections the BBC spends more time on substantive policy and issue discussion than does ITV. In the summer of 2003 a row broke out between the BBC and the government over the former's criticism of the government's conduct of the war: this indicates the broadcasters' desire to provide independent judgement of politics. Budge et al. (1998: 339) comment that 'market forces have therefore driven a much wider coverage of political affairs than when reporting could be managed by private contacts among the elite in the 1940s and 1950s'. This is 'a hopeful development which goes against some of the negative trends otherwise associated with commercialisation and the breakdown of the public service model in Britain' (Budge et al. 1998: 339).

Stage 3: Product development
The BBC, while designing aspects of its product to suit the mass market or audience, has also sought to provide quality programming and services for minority groups (Scammell 2000: 174). It therefore includes product development within its market-oriented activities. The argument for including product development within a market-oriented approach is that there are problems with the consumer deciding everything before it is developed. As Cave (1993: 21) argued, 'viewing a television programme is like reading a book or going to a lawyer, in the sense that you only know how much you have enjoyed it after it is too late to do anything about it'. The information is only received after consumption. Smith (1993: 9) also noted with regard to the BBC how 'large numbers of people do indeed want to be given that which they do not yet realise they need. However they may function when consuming physical goods, they may well accept that the imagination benefits from being exposed to unfamiliar cultural experiences.' This is one of the many differences between business and political marketing, although it can also be argued that it is the same with business: new product development theories contend that people do not always know in advance what they may want, let alone need.

Even government committees generally in favour of marketing the media have cautioned against simply following existing public favour. In 1988 the Pilkington Committee argued that 'because in principle the possible range of subject matter is inexhaustible, all of it can never be presented, nor can the public know what the range is. So the broadcaster must explore it, and chose from it first. This might be called "giving a lead" but it is not the lead of the autocrat or arrogant' (quoted in Smith 1993: 9). The BBC made a significant effort at the turn of the century to put out a wide public call for new talent and ideas. As long as new products are carefully developed with some understanding of the market, the public response is monitored, and those products which do not attract support are changed or dropped, this remains part of a market-oriented media approach. There are a number of new product lines developed by the BBC recently.

New market segment: the Asian network   The BBC has developed new products for a market segment, British Asians. In 2002 the Asian network, a digital radio station, was launched. It offers a whole range of information, including sports, entertainment, news and music, but all from an Asian perspective, including global reports. The latest news includes bulletins in Bengali, Gujarati, Hindi, Mirpuri, Punjabi and Urdu; the station has Asian presenters. Programmes include *Devotional Sounds*, *Breakfast* with Gagan Grewal, *Drive* with Sameena Ali-Khan, *Take Two* with Rajni Sharma, *Saturday Sport* with Sanjeet Saund, and *The Mix* with DJ Ritu. This indicates the BBC is trying to provide a service for a particular target market. BBCi (the on-line service of the BBC) also has an information section called 'Asian life'.

Target marketing: launch of new channel BBC3 for youth   The BBC launched a digital TV channel called BBC3 offering new programming in February 2003. The new channel was targeted at young people, with a mix of music, drama, arts and current affairs. The culture secretary, Tessa Jowell, who passed the proposal for the new channel, argued that BBC3 must be 'of a consistently innovative and risk-taking character' and 'a distinctive public service channel that is not competing with what is already out there in a vigorous marketplace' (quoted in the *Guardian*, 18 September 2002), indicating the need for new product development with a market-oriented approach. The channel replaced BBC Choice and in its first night succeeding in attracting four times the audience in some instances. Overall it was watched by an average of 147,000 viewers between 7 p.m. and 12.15 a.m. and drew a 1.32 per cent share of non-terrestrial viewing during its transmission hours, from 7 p.m. until 5.25 a.m., a higher average than BBC Choice (*Guardian*, 10 February 2003). However, ratings dropped soon after and the BBC ran focus groups with students at Bournemouth University to find out what they wanted, testing their reactions to excerpts of BBC3 programmes.

Development of political programming   Additionally, television has recently developed new political programmes in response to concern over the decline in turnout at the 2001 general election. Politicians, the public and the media were concerned that people did not want to vote for their government but were very happy to vote for shows like *Popstars* and *Big Brother*. Television has tried to address this. Politics has been included in soaps such as *Emmerdale* to try to forge a link between popular culture and government politics.

More importantly, television has attempted to adopt a more market-oriented approach to the design of political programmes, trying to respond to weaknesses in previous products which citizens did not find attractive, and also to involve viewers more within the shows. The advance of technology has enabled greater use of the internet, phone-ins and text messages from mobiles to provide more interactive, less passive viewer–programme interaction. The BBC increased coverage and boosted programme funding by £5m for 2003: 'the revamp is intended to increase the number of people watching and engaging actively with the democratic process' (BBC website: http://news.bbc.co.uk/1/hi/programmes/the_daily_politics/2632069.stm). News programmes have been redesigned and two new show formats created. Two examples of this are *The Daily Politics* and *The Politics Show*.

The BBC launched the brand-new politics show *The Daily Politics* on 8 January 2003. It is presented by Andrew Neil and Daisy Sampson on BBC2 every

Tuesday, Wednesday and Thursday. The aim is to analyse and explain why the dominant news stories of the week count and how they affect people's lives. Allowing for greater public input, every day the show calls for members of the public to email or text their opinions to the studio. Additionally, a 'roving reporter' visits a local area to find out what issues are filling up MPs' post bags, and viewers are invited to send in suggestions of local issues for the programme team to investigate. The reporter also aims to canvass the views of local people on the big stories of the day.

The show is clearly keen for viewer input. As the BBC web-site said in February 2003.

Contact The Daily Politics

The Daily Politics wants to hear from you!

Every Tuesday, Wednesday and Thursday Andrew Neil and Daisy Sampson present a new daytime programme of analysis and debate with key politicians and commentators.

Viewers get to comment on the day's burning issues, using e-mail or text messages, which may be read out on air, or posted on *The Daily Politics* website.

If you are a viewer with something to say you can contact us in a variety of ways:

When we are on air, you can text us your comments on 82237 (text messages are at your standard rate, around 10p per message).

You can send us your comments using the form at the bottom of the page, or e-mail direct to Daily.Politics@bbc.co.uk.

Alternatively, you can write to us at:
The Daily Politics
Four Millbank
London SW1P 3JQ.

If you have a query for *The Daily Politics* team, please check our Frequently Asked Questions section before sending a message. It may have an answer for you.

Send us your comments (http://news.bbc.co.uk/1/hi/programmes/the_daily_politics/2634653.stm)

The BBC redesigned and developed its' traditional Sunday lunchtime political programming and launched a new version, *The Politics Show* with Jeremy Vine, to replace *On the Record* in January 2003. The approach was to create a more modern, appealing style as well as engaging the viewers by talking to them directly. The new title, with the word 'show', attempts to be more entertaining. It was described by BBCi as follows: 'From Downing Street to your street, *The Politics Show* reports on policies and government decisions affecting people around the UK.' However, having watched the first episode it could be concluded that changes made are more in line with a sales orientation, focusing on the presentation rather than the product. Indeed, the editor James Stephenson argued that 'we have moved away from Westminster political imagery in terms of the look of the programme, but not the content' (quoted in Lister 2003). For 'look' read presentation, for 'content' read product: there has not really been a change to the actual product. As Lister (2003) observed, 'its very title . . . seems to imply that the governance of Britain is now viewed as show business'. Although the opening is more attractive, with more modern and popular music, and a relaxed studio atmosphere in terms of furniture (sofa rather than formal desk), there was soon a move to the usual traditional news bulletin followed by in-depth talking 'at' the viewer, so audiences may well have left before the more interactive local sections. The show has potential but the BBC needs to monitor it carefully and be prepared to change the actual content if it really wants to reach out to viewers.

Stage 4: Communication

Communication for market-oriented types of media in an era of advanced technology includes not simply the advertising of media products, but interactive communication between viewers and the media organisation, or, in political programmes, between voters and politicians.

Reality shows such as *Big Brother*, *Pop Stars* and *Pop Rivals*, attracting significant audiences and participation in voting by mobile text, phone call or internet, have been discussed with a view to employing their techniques in political programmes. For example, there were at least two public television debates on the future of the monarchy in 2002, jubilee year, which enabled public participation via several means. The public could send comments by email, on-line, and take part in the audience discussion; furthermore their involvement was asked for before, during and after the broadcast of the programme. BBC1's 10 p.m. news launched websites which gave viewers a chance to discuss the news with the presenters in January 2003. The programme can be viewed via the website, and viewers can also take a virtual tour of the newsroom. Other information, on the presenters and the latest stories, is also provided on the website. A BBC spokesperson said the change was deliberately aiming to make BBC's news coverage more interactive, with 'more maps, information, graphics and stills' and 'extra levels of interactivity' planned to be developed in time (quoted in the *Guardian*, 21 January 2003).

One important aspect of BBCi or the general BBC website, which has expanded and performed well (Scammell 2000: 178), is that it keeps the show going on after it has been screened: communication does not end after the programme. *Panaroma*, for example, has archived transcripts of its programmes for viewers to read if they missed the broadcast, as well as viewers' comments on the programme, and reports back and updates from the presenters are posted at a later date. At the end of news programmes or other political programmes or debates, the presenter is now heard saying 'That's all we have time for in the studio, but the BBC website will be taking comments after we go off air', and inviting viewers to enter their opinions that way. In the summer of 2002 the website also had 'Six forum': an opportunity for viewers to set the agenda for the BBC's six o'clock news interactive forum every Wednesday. Comments and transcripts were archived on the website.

The BBC website also has a section called 'Talking Point' on topical issues: the public is invited to send their comments, a selection is posted and archived for others to see, and a vote is held on certain issues. It is a bit similar to our being able to buy videos of movies and watch them over and over again, so the viewing does not end at the cinema. Except that, by providing the opportunity for the viewer to make a comment, the extended communication is made not a passive but an active period. The advantage of greater interaction between viewer and politician is that it holds the potential for creating a more mature dialogue between elite and citizen.

Communication also includes general communication, such as information about the BBC's accounts, viewer figures or issues from the annual report. In 2002 the BBC decided to change the way it issued its annual report. It brought in game show host and former children's TV presenter Gaby Roslin. However, it was criticised for making this 'an increasingly defensive and stage managed event' (Julia Day, *Guardian*, 10 July 2002). The BBC has also engaged in short-term communication, or campaigns, to boost its programming. One example is the campaign to promote digital television, in 'changing faces' advertisements which have celebrities talking to ordinary people about the benefits of digital TV.

Stage 5: Delivery
Obviously the BBC needs to deliver and create viewer satisfaction. Its policy documents indicate an awareness of this. Greg Dyke, its then director general, noted that 'our success has . . . to be judged by the programmes and content we deliver' (BBC 2002d: 3). The BBC issues an annual report on its performance (see, for example, BBC 2002c). The 2001–2 annual report (BBC 2002c) contains measures of audience share relative to other competitors, descriptions of the varied programmes offered, discussion of new staff recruited through the BBC talent scheme, and whether previously set objectives were met. It also includes admission of where goals have not yet been achieved (see, for example, BBC 2002c: 7 and the director general's discussion about not achieving the vision of 'One BBC'). Smith (1993: 5) observed that BBC's management had moved towards marketing models for assessing performance: 'in this new consumerist age they have hurried to wrestle with the specialist language of the mission statement and the performance indicator; they are learning to commercialise, privatise, contract out, create internal markets for services'.

The 2002 annual report event was criticised because the press were banned from attending it and asking the usual questions: instead the report was launched by top BBC executives appearing before the parliament media select committee and meeting MPs in London, followed by a public launch event in Birmingham. This occurred under a new chairman, Gavin Davies: previously the BBC had tried to become more open and accountable, and allowed its governors to face press questions and respond in public at the launch of the institution's annual report under the chairmanship of Sir Christopher Bland. The move away from this naturally raises some questions as to the extent of the BBC's market orientation. In the context of accountability and internal reviews of performance, the British government created a new body, Ofcom, to regulate 'governance' in the telecommunications industries. Gavyn Davies instigated an internal review of BBC governance in response to this, with the report on this acknowledging concern at 'a continuing perception among some members of the public that the BBC is arrogant and inaccessible' (BBC 2002a: 4). The report also promised that the reforms themselves would be evaluated and reported in the 2003 annual report, and that 'the reporting documentation itself and the launch event outside London should provide a more transparent and accessible account of the past year and of the BBC's plans for the future than has previously been produced' (BBC 2002a: 12). Delivery is an on-going activity and the BBC needs to listen to qualitative as well as quantitative measures to feed back into the whole political marketing process when it begins product redesign and development. Marketing the media is a continual activity.

Conclusions

> It is precisely because we are not dealing with baked beans or package holidays but with the communication of ideas, and the dissemination and analysis of news and artistic endeavour, that freedom of entry by producers and freedom of choice by consumers to the maximum feasible extent are so vital. (Brittain 1989: 28)

> Both commercial and public service institutions then cannot, with their specific goals and interests in mind, stop struggling to conquer the audience, no matter whether audience members are identified as consumers or citizens. (Ang 1991: 32)

Applying marketing to the media provides an unusual perspective on an important element of the political system. Sales-oriented types of media would appear to give rise to many issues and questions commonly thrown at political marketing as a whole, suggesting a focus on popularity and entertainment at odds with the more idealistic, traditional goals of the media. As commercially funded media works in conditions which seem to pull more towards such an approach, this provides unexpected support for the public service ethos of the BBC. Although very much product oriented in its initial design, the BBC has over time evolved through the three political marketing approaches as did the Labour party in 1983–97. The BBC has made significant attempts to use political marketing in a market-oriented manner, attempting to identify any weaknesses in its performance and respond to citizen desire for greater participation as well as entertainment and education. However, the extent to which the BBC has adopted a market orientation is clearly limited in some respects. The institution has not fully completed its evolution from a product to a market orientation, and in any case, like all political organisations, it is subject to change and flux. There are doubtless elements of a product orientation remaining. For example, speaking at an academic conference in September 2001, Mark Damazer, deputy head of the BBC news, said that the programme *Challenge the Leader* presented by David

Dimbleby during the 2001 election 'worked in programme terms but it didn't work in terms of the audience'. Overall, however, the development of new products suggests a forward-looking, responsive approach, indicating that the increase in competition, although challenging at first, may be pushing the BBC onto a more positive, stronger footing compared to its commercial competitors.

Criticisms of a move towards market orientation

There are nevertheless many critical arguments against the move towards a market orientation, some of which need to be considered, whilst others perhaps mistaken the true potential meaning of such an approach.

Blumler (1993: 28) argued that there are significant weaknesses in taking the market approach to public television, because 'it misconceives the kind of good that television provides' and 'large-scale communication is not merely a product that may please or displease, but also a mental and spiritual transaction about meanings and relationships'. Another criticism is that it could lead to a focus on majority, not minority, audiences; that moving towards devising programmes according to audience, especially if funded by advertising, will lead to less representation of minority tastes and duplication of popular programme types. This need not be the case with a market-oriented media approach, which includes product development as part of the process. David Liddiment, then ITV's director of channels, said that the 'relentless quest' simply to give viewers what they wanted led to a 'sameness' that reduced television's quality and that he 'worried that [the BBC] is losing sight of its cultural responsibilities in its rush to beat the commercial competition at its own game' (quoted in the *Daily Telegraph*, 25 August 2001: 13). Again, this is not how marketing *has* to be.

One difficulty with the conception of a market-oriented media is that if viewers do not like something, does this mean it should then be dropped? Sometimes new series or programmes take time to develop or simply be watched in order to become popular. In 2000 there was a big debate about the BBC possibly dumbing down, using more simple language to suit the majority audience (Scammell 2000: 173). Even the Jenkins Committee, despite supporting general responsiveness, argued for some limits to marketing: 'audience research is not a substitute for the imagination and the creative decisions of producers. It should not be used slavishly in all forms of broadcasting, particularly not in drama: the last thing we desire is formula-produced series geared to what research purports to say the audience wants' (Home Office 1977: 454).

There are also general critiques of viewing BBC like a business. When Michael Checkland declared that 'the BBC is a billion-pound business' it led to a controversy. Barnett (1993: 1) argued that:

> By any definition, the BBC is not a business. Businesses do not exist as services to the community. No business in the world runs on a guaranteed income, regardless of consumer demand, with obligations laid down by a complicated relationship with Queen and Parliament. Businesses make goods or services for profit. The BBC does not.

Indeed, there is a strong argument that the role of the BBC is to try to solve market failure, representing minorities (Cave 1993: 23) whilst still being responsive to the public as a whole. It is arguably better for the BBC to be popular rather than exclusive or elitist, but there is a dilemma: 'if it shows what people want, it loses its distinctiveness' (Cave 1993: 23). There is also the argument that marketing the media will always be constrained, that true market measures can never be replicated by audience research (Brittain 1989: 30). However, even if there are problems with consumer choice, perhaps it is better for the consumer than the producer to decide what the media should do. As Brittain (1989: 28) observed, 'there is no need to enter into a metaphysical debate whether the consumer is the best judge of artistic quality or the best judge of which programmes will benefit him, or his capacity for citizenship. The point is that no one person or group, or committee, or "establishment" can be trusted to make a superior choice.' Elitism in any sphere of politics is ineffective.

Marketing's support for public broadcasting

> The BBC owes its past, its present – and this future – to the talent and dedication of BBC staff. What Reith started, others continue. But most important of all are the listeners and viewers. They are the real future of broadcasting. (BBC website, www.bccc.co.uk/thenandnow/history/1990sn3.shtml)

The other somewhat ironic conclusion from this chapter is that marketing could help the BBC respond to competition and so to survive in the twenty-first-century marketplace. The BBC could be more likely to be market oriented whilst channels such as ITV are sales oriented. As already discussed, sales-oriented media has extremely problematic potential consequences; as Scammell (2000: 173) observed, 'the more competitive and deregulated the market, the less space for substantive issues, and the more news is focused on softer personality, campaign hoopla and horse-race topics'. Retaining the BBC in its present form can give it a chance to avoid these negative problems, whilst ensuring its responsiveness by adopting a market-oriented approach to the public service institution. Brittain (1989: 47) argued that 'the Government . . . needs to be very sure that it has secured the financing of the informative and minority programmes (public service in the stricter sense) which may not be profitable in the market-place, but which people would still want in their capacity as citizens and voters'. The BBC must use (carefully adapted) marketing – the market-oriented kind – to survive. Mulgan (1993: 93) argued that the BBC will set itself up for attack if 'it continues to seek to justify its existence with rather general philosophical and cultural arguments . . . rather than on simpler relationships to the needs and wants of audiences'.

This also leads to an argument for the BBC being funded differently, because, as Negrine (1994: 99) and others have argued, 'public service broadcasting probably cannot survive in the marketplace and it therefore needs financial, political, and cultural support'. But that does not mean in terms of product performance that it is beyond the market – in fact state funding can enable it to be more market or consumer friendly and more responsive. It also does not mean that other stations should not be commercially funded, because, as has been shown, this introduces elements of competition that encourage the BBC to be more responsive. After all, it was only when competition started that the BBC lost its previously product-oriented attitude.

The marketisation of the media is important for the other institutions and actors in the political system, holding potentially challenging but also positive implications for them. The media provides a more critical environment for party politicians, with greater input by citizens. It can also help stimulate interest in politics that would benefit parties. However, with increased interest comes greater questioning of, for example, delivery in areas like the health service. For the monarchy, the BBC worked supportively to provide popular entertainment for the jubilee, helping to increase public support for the royals.

The media also carries stories of royal scandals directly and quickly to the mass market. Local reporting is important for local government; the media is also of concern to the newly established Scottish parliament in trying to create and maintain a positive place in the eyes of the Scottish public. For charities or interest groups, the media both at a local and regional level is the means by which they can forward their campaigns and gain public attention to otherwise ignored issues. The nature of the media, particularly television, has encouraged charity groups such as Greenpeace to develop sales-oriented techniques that will offer dramatic footage to appear on the evening news. As the next chapter will show, marketing is being used in terms of communication, but also product design, by charities. No longer dependent on good will, they have not only adopted sales techniques such as direct mail but also, more unusually, begun to think about what they offer their 'buyers' or members in return. The political marketing revolution would seem to affect every political organisation regardless of its nature or origins.

Notes

1 Attempts were made to interview the director of marketing at the BBC but were unsuccessful.

Bibliography

Ang, I. (1991), *Desperately Seeking the Audience*, Routledge, London and New York.

Barnett, S. (1993), 'Introduction', in S. Barnett (ed.), *Funding the BBC's Future*, BBC Charter Review Series, British Film Institute, London. pp. 1–2.

BBC (1999), *The BBC beyond 2000*, www.bbc.co.uk/info/news/2000.

BBC (2002a), *BBC Governance in the Ofcam Age*, BBC, London.

BBC (2002b), *BBC English Regions Annual Review 2001–2*, BBC, London.

BBC (2002c), *BBC Annual Report and Accounts 2001–2002*, BBC, London.

BBC (2002d), *BBC Statements of Programme Policy 2002–3*, BBC, London.

Beech, T. (2003), speech presented by Assistant Editor BBC Radio Stoke as visiting speaker at Keele University, 21 March.

Blumler, J. (1993), 'Public Service Broadcasting in Multi-Channel Conditions: Functions and Funding', in S. Barnett (ed.), *Funding the BBC's Future*, BBC Charter Review Series, British Film Institute, London. pp. 26–41.

Brittain, S. (1989), 'The Case for the Consumer Market', in C. Veljanovski (ed.), *Freedom in Broadcasting*, Institute of Economic Affairs, London. pp. 25–50.

Budge, I., I. Crewe, D. McKay and K. Newton (1998), *The New British Politics*, Addison Wesley Longman.

Burns, T. (1977), *The BBC: Public Institution and Private World*, Macmillan, London.

Cave, M. (1993), 'The Role of the BBC: An Economic Evaluation', in Steven Barnett (ed.), *Funding the BBC's Future*, BBC Charter Review Series, British Film Institute, London. pp. 16–25.

Frith, S. (1993), 'The High, the Low and the BBC', in W. Stevenson (ed.) *All Our Futures*, BBC Charter Review Series, British Film Institute, London. pp. 100–111.

Hodgson, P. (1993), 'Quality and Choice: The Future Role of the BBC', in W. Stevenson (ed.), *All Our Futures*, BBC Charter Review Series, British Film Institute, London. pp. 65–76.

Home Office (1977), *Report of the Committee on the Future of Broadcasting*, HMSO, London. Cmnd 6753.

Home Office (1985), *Financing the BBC: A Survey of Public Opinion*, report for the Committee on Financing the BBC, HMSO, London, November.

Jones, B. (1994), 'The Mass Media and Politics', in B. Jones (ed.), *Politics UK*, Harvester Wheatsheaf, London. pp. 198–219.

Lambert, S. (1982), *Channel Four: Television with a Difference?* British Film Institute, London.

Lister, D. (2003), 'The New Politics', *Independent Review* 28 January.

Marsh, D. (1993), 'The Media and politics', in P. Dunleavy, A. Gamble, I. Holliday and G. Peele (eds), *Developments in British Politics 4*, Macmillan, London. pp. 332–349.

Mulgan, G. (1993), 'Why the Constitution of the Airwaves has to Change', in W. Stevenson (ed.), *All Our Futures*, BBC Charter Review Series, British Film Institute, London. pp. 90–99.

Negrine, R. (1994), *Politics and the Mass Media*, 2nd edition, Routledge, London.

Paulu, B. (1961), *British Broadcasting in Transition*, Macmillan, London.

Scammell, M. (2000), 'New Media, New Politics', in P. Dunleavy, A. Gamble, I. Holliday and G. Peele (eds), *Developments in British Politics 6*, Macmillan, London. pp. 169–184.

Smith, A. (1993), 'The Future of Public Service in Broadcasting', in W. Stevenson (ed.), *All Our Futures*, BBC Charter Review Series, British Film Institute, London. pp. 4–13.

Stevenson, W. (1993), 'Introduction', in W. Stevenson (ed.), *All Our Futures*, BBC Charter Review Series, British Film Institute, London. pp. 1–3.

Wheeler, M.(1997), *Politics and the Mass Media*, Blackwell, London.

Yeo, T. (2002), 'Towards a 21st Century Model of Public Service Broadcasting', speech to the Social Market Foundation conference, June.

5

Marketing charities

High ideals, mission statements, and dedicated volunteers may not be enough for non profit organisations in the 1990s. Faced with pursuing lofty goals and paying the rent in a crowded world of service, charitable, and educational charities competing for the same dollars, many non profit organisations – without marketing plans – soon may be taking unwelcome baths in vats of red ink . . . Marketing, a word once never heard . . . is now the No. 1 buzzword. (Schwartz 1991: 20)

Charities were once concerned with benevolent people 'doing good' out of altruism and kindness, for those less well-off in society. Today, charities are in the marketing business. As one charity worker commented, 'the voluntary sector really had to get its act together and become more business-thinking' (Treacy 2000). Marketing is needed to recruit and retain the supporters who then fund and aid the campaigning activity. Not only do charities use direct mail, they use market intelligence to design a 'supporter product' donors will want and also to improve the effectiveness of campaigns, using the media to get their viewpoint across to all of their markets. Political marketing is therefore being used by charities to further their non-business aims to influence government. Political marketing is influencing participation and lobbying: significant areas of political activity in the UK system.

This chapter explores just how they do this and the different approaches they can take, and discusses the issues arising from this. In doing so it utilises analysis of websites and publicly available information about various charities, a number of interviews with charity staff, and other literature on charities and non-profit organisations (in marketing) and interest or pressure-groups (in political science). It also utilises more in-depth primary interview and organisational data gathered whilst studying nine national UK charities. It does not, however, classify a single charity as market-, sales- or product-oriented, and examples used here are for illustrative not assessment purposes.[1]

Marketing charities: the basics

Importance and nature of charities

Charities[2] try to promote a cause or defend a section of society. Distinct from political parties because they do not seek public office in an election, they nevertheless aim to influence politics in the interests of the cause they represent. They offer an alternative form of representation and participation within the political system. Since the 1980s, charities have also grown tremendously in terms of size, activity, range and importance in society and the economy, and continue to do so (see Sargeant 1999: 8). The employment of staff in charities is such as that is sometimes called a 'third sector' because it is economically as well as socially significant. Their political influence upon policy-making within government is potentially substantial (for example, see Grant 1995, 2000; Jordan and Richardson 1987).

Marketing charities: how can we do this?

Charities are technically extra-governmental; nevertheless, they seek to influence politics and society in the interest of the cause they represent. Most charities rely on individual supporters (whether they be members, donors or committed givers) to provide this. As one organisation interviewed said, 'to an extent they drive pretty much everything we do. Without them we wouldn't be able to fund all the [research] we do, we wouldn't even be able to lobby for change through the government because they fund it all.'[3] Supporters who become active within the organisation also help campaigning: high levels of membership suggest the organisation commands public support, and this helps it lobby government. To succeed in campaigning, charities therefore need to find the best means by which to attract and maintain supporters. This is where marketing comes in. For example, Hannagan (1992: 7–8) observed how a charity such as the Royal National Institute for the Blind (RNIB) 'provides a service for the blind while also helping to develop products, and attempting to influence the public in its attitudes and the government in its support for blind people'.

Product

The charity product includes a number of different aspects or activities as well as the supporter package and campaigning activities:

- policies;
- organisation;
- staff – research expertise, lobbying skills, marketing skills, professional skills;
- research;
- website;
- communication;
- information booklets and advice;
- membership or supporters, including recruitment and retention programmes, the support package and participation options;

- local groups;
- events such as support groups, conferences, training days and social events;
- campaigning – methods of lobbying, furthering the cause and pressuring government.

The importance and size of different characteristics will of course vary from one charity to another. In some organisations the focus is at the national level, where supporters are taken care of by large-scale, professionally organised staff and campaigns are run by professional lobbyists. In others, such as the Downs' Syndrome Association (DSA), a significant amount of charity work is carried out by local branches around the country, run by volunteers who have been trained in telephone counselling courses, which offer social events, day trips out for the whole family, coffee mornings, support for new parents of Down syndrome children, and speech therapy (Walsh 2000). The charity product can include support services; for example, the National Society for Prevention of Cruelty to Children (NSPCC) provides counselling for children and parents, young people's centres and supporting witnesses for court cases (www.nspcc.org.uk). Larger charities will be more likely to recruit professional staff; for example, Greenpeace UK employed a consulting company to advise them on recruitment, research, fundraising, media, campaigning and general communications (see www.fundraising.co.uk/news/2001/02/).

The supporter package and campaigning are the most commonly discussed aspects of the charity product. To elaborate further, the supporter package – what charities give to people who give them time or money – can include many different elements, such as a newsletter, information booklets, local groups, training days, rallies, meetings, counselling, information and advice telephone lines, discounted insurance and an organisational credit card. Campaigning itself can be expanded as including:

- trying to influence party policy;
- educating public opinion, using advertising, local events and visits to schools;
- lobbying government, especially over potential or impending legislation, possibly getting onto government committees;
- seeking pledges from candidates at election time;
- seeking media attention through petitions, advertisements, leaflets, demonstrations;
- expanding and mobilising membership to play a role in campaigning;
- sometimes using violence or illegal action.

Market
As with all political organisations, charities do not just market to their supporters (see Sargeant 1999: 17). The market is not just those who pay into a charity, because it is not purely about fundraising but is primarily concerned with advancing a cause. The market for a charity includes:

- the cause it aims to promote (the interest of a section of society, animals, wild-life etc.);
- interested parties (e.g. parents of sick children, carers of the elderly, professionals who deal with sufferers or work in that area);
- the government;
- political parties;
- other charities;
- the media;
- civil servants;
- parliaments;
- supporters;
- staff;
- local groups or branches;
- related state-funded organisations and staff, e.g. health organisations and doctors.

Obviously the nature and relative importance of all these markets varies from one organisation to another. For example, the charity Greenpeace engages in direct action, including illegal action, because their supporters want that kind of campaigning. Other environmental charities such as Friends of the Earth may cover some of the same issues but would not engage in such campaigning. Larger charities may need to segment the supporter market because they are spreading their recruitment strategy so widely, whereas other smaller charities, such as the Alzheimer's Society, have a fairly defined market, thereby being able to limit their efforts to GPs, pharmacies and libraries (Thompson 2000). The DSA identified their market as including parents of Down syndrome children, Down sufferers themselves when they come into adulthood, and the wider family of sufferers and health and education professionals (e.g. midwives, health visitors, paediatricians, teachers, speech and language specialists) (Treacy 2000). Furthermore, each segment needs different products from the charity. The media is important for charities because they use local and national media organisations to communicate with the public. As Grant (1995: 80) observed, 'securing media attention has become a central pressure-group activity'. The NSPCC also targets the media as they need to educate the public to achieve their goals of protecting children.

Supporters: further definition 'Supporters' is a broad term used here to cover the myriad of names given by charities to those (individual, corporate or institutional) who contribute to the organisation in many different ways. Primary research found that they included individual members, donors and committed givers, who may give once a year or every month. They can contribute time and money to the organisation. Although money is the most obvious support an individual can give, time and activity are also important. Supporters can provide ideas and information that fuel organisational strategy and activity: as one charity commented when interviewed, 'members provide ideas, finance but also important is the pool of information they provide'. As the membership officer for the Alzheimer's Society said, 'I don't think we'd be here without members' (Thompson 2000).

Goals

Charities have several goals, including:

- to defend or promote their cause;
- to influence government, politics and society to do this;
- to attract financial and other support to enable this;
- to improve representation and participation in the political system;
- to represent sections of society and causes which may be in the minority and are not covered by mainstream parties or supported by majority public opinion.

Although promoting their cause is the dominant goal, to do this they campaign to influence politics, and to do that they recruit supporters who will finance and help the campaigning. Money is a big factor, but it is the means to another end; as the trust and corporate officer for the DSA said:

> the reason I am here is there are people with Down Syndrome and families who need information and support. And I'm here because I help raise the money that pays for that . . . You have to remind yourself why you're here. Because if you forget or get carried away then I don't think you're doing it properly. Then it becomes like this commercial thing. (Treacy 2000)

Charities also hold more specific goals related to their particular cause, which may alter over time. This can be found in their strategy documents, annual reports or mission statements:

> The NSPCC's mission is to create a society 'that will not tolerate child abuse – whether sexual, physical, emotional or neglect'. (www/nspcc.org.uk, accessed 2003)

> Greenpeace is an independent non-profit global campaigning organisation that uses non-violent, creative confrontation to expose global environmental problems and their causes. We research the solutions and alternatives to help provide for a path for a green and peaceful future. (www.greenpeace.org.uk, accessed 2002)

> Our vision: Imagine a time when every person in the land has equal and ready access to the best information, treatment and care for cancer and when unnecessary levels of fear are set aside. At Macmillan Cancer Relief we dedicate ourselves to working with others to turn this vision into everyone's reality. (www.macmillan.org.uk/aboutmacmillan/disppage.asp?id=40)

> Save the Children is committed to narrowing the gap between reality and our ideal. We start by listening to children – learning about their lives, their hopes and views.

We support practical projects which involve children and their families in improving their day-to-day lives. We also use our global experience and research to lobby for changes that will benefit all children, including future generations. (www.savethechildren.org.uk/functions/indx_abus.html)

The question remains, of course, as to what the best way is to achieve these goals, and like political parties, the monarchy and the media, charities can take all three approaches or orientations to their behaviour. Before we examine this, however, it is worth noting the relationship between the theoretical foundations set out here and existing political science literature.

Existing literature on charities

There is a plentiful literature on how charities recruit supporters, but little on the extent to which they utilise political marketing in its broader sense. The study of interest groups has traditionally been the domain of political science, which focused on analysing the incentives for membership that organisations have, examining how charities play with the costs of membership, or discussing why some people join or do not join. It also discussed the role of interest groups in lobbying government. It is not the point of this chapter – or book – to list, review and critique it all simply to point out how it does not consider marketing.[4] The focus here is empirical. There are, however, a few studies within the existing literature that have acknowledged the use of elements of marketing by interest groups and are worth mentioning (see, for example, Rothenberg 1992; Johnson 1998; Rosenstone and Hansen 1993; O'Shaughnessy and Peele 1985: 115; O'Shaughnessy 1990: 87; Jordan and Maloney 1997). These studies have identified how charities use marketing techniques to communicate with, or sell their product to, potential supporters. Jordan and Maloney (1997) argued that modern large-scale interest groups, using direct mail to solicit financial contributions, targeted the predisposed, thereby only involving a narrow section of society in the cause, behaving like 'Protest Businesses'. This model confines political marketing to the communication of a product, not its actual design, rather as party marketing research used to focus on the use of marketing to sell policies – the sales-oriented approach. The nature of a sales-oriented charity will be discussed, but the new research conducted for this chapter indicated that the dominant trend in charitable behaviour appears to be towards a market orientation, where marketing is used to influence the product, not just its presentation.

Charity political marketing orientations

Like all political organisations, charities can take, have taken and do take any one of three approaches to how they use marketing.

A *product-oriented charity* focuses on arguing for how good it is, on simply doing its job well. Some may see their job as ideological, concerned with battling for their cause, not changing their behaviour to suit membership subscriptions or public or government opinion. They may believe that as long as they all work towards a common goal, people will simply see how good they are and support them automatically, and they will be able to influence government.

A *sales-oriented charity* focuses on using the best communication techniques and methods to persuade government of its cause and supporters of the need to fund the charity. The focus is on advertising, on selling itself to potential members, using all the latest sales gimmicks.

A *market-oriented charity* seeks to advance its cause in the manner desired by the public. It designs its product, including the campaigning and membership package, to suit this: to suit what potential supporters want and what government would be influenced by. In terms of membership, it aims to offer members what they want. If a charity wants to achieve maximum success in recruitment, it needs to adopt a market orientation and to campaign in the most influential way – in a way that reflects government interests also.

The primary research conducted for this chapter indicated that the current trend is more towards a market orientation: however, we will briefly overview the political marketing processes for the first two orientations as well.

The cause and nothing else: product-oriented charities

Charities were successful with this orientation in the past when they held a monopolistic position. Sargeant (1999: 32) observed that 'customers [we]re so reliant on their services' that the organisation could 'adopt a take it or leave it attitude'. Wealth was not so widespread and came from a small number of individual benefactors. Sargeant (1999: 126) explains how 'much early charitable activity was undertaken at the whims of such individuals who were free to indulge their own favourite causes as time and money permitted'. Their attitude to the recipients could be somewhat patronising. Even today, some charities posses a strong ideological belief in the need to promote their cause. This is potentially true of all political organisations in their first stages of existence. As with any new business, it takes entrepreneurial self-belief and conviction to get any organisation over the hurdles of starting up. Another factor encouraging a product orientation is that charities can respond quickly to sudden crises or emerging needs in a way that large, established political parties and government and indeed shareholder-run business cannot. Charities can therefore meet those in need and alleviate suffering more easily – but the speedy response does not facilitate the use of widespread market intelligence before designing the product (see Sargeant 1999: 33).

Product-oriented charities do not use marketing in a complex way; they do what they think is best in a simple process, depicted in Box 5.1.

A few charities remain product oriented today. As one charity interviewed commented, 'we are a particular organisation that believes in a particular set of values, come along and join us if you agree with us. It's not a case of us tapering our message or changing our message to suit our potential supporters. We believe in a particular cause and it's "come join us" on that basis.' However, with

---

Box 5.1 The process for a product-oriented charity

Stage 1: Product design
Design a wide range of behaviour according to what it thinks is right, and assume it will succeed, 'do good' and achieve its goals, as well as receive enough money to do this.

Stage 2: Communication
Information is there if people want to get it, but this is provided with little thought and is not proactive.

Stage 3: Campaign
Inform government as to what they want the government to do.

Stage 4: Delivery
Deliver what they think is best.

---

this approach, the ability to expand the supporter base will be limited, leading many with that kind of thinking to engage at least in sales-oriented forms of political marketing.

Time to get selling: sales-oriented charities

The movement towards a sales orientation occurred alongside substantial growth in competition, partly linked to the decline of political parties as political consumers' first choice for participation. Charities focus on one cause and offer more direct, higher-impact involvement than parties. Fundraising competition is intense, which encouraged the adoption of a sales-oriented approach. This leads to a focus on marketing techniques: direct mail, direct dialogue to raise income from supporters, and media-attention-seeking campaigning techniques such as highly visible demonstrations or illegal action. Another factor is changes in society. Charity literature has noted the importance of social networks in recruitment (Godwin and Mitchell 1984: 830; Knoke 1990b; Rosenstone and Hansen 1993: 23; Verba et al. 1995: 145), but, as with political party membership, these social forces have weakened, leading charities to look for less personal, more technological solutions to persuading people to support their work. Sales-oriented behaviour is the modern response to the decline of social networks. Sales-oriented charities will go through a slightly more complex process, such as that in Box 5.2.

Further elaboration of the most notable aspects of a sales-oriented charity, with relevant empirical examples, follows.

Stage 2: Market intelligence
Sales-oriented charities pay little attention to the nature of their product, which they take as a given, but they do use market intelligence to inform whom they

---

Box 5.2 The process for a sales-oriented charity

Stage 1: Product design
Design a wide range of behaviour according to what it thinks is right.

Stage 2: Market intelligence
Identify the charities most likely to support it, using market segmentation to target them, and discuss how best to influence and persuade government.

Stage 3: Communication
Proactive, entertaining communication designed to attract attention, influence government, raise income from potential supporters; using wide range of marketing techniques such as direct mail, direct dialogue and television adverts.

Stage 4: Campaign
Short-term, one-off appeals; for example, appeal for donations to save a wildlife sanctuary, or to influence forthcoming government legislation

Stage 5: Delivery
Deliver what it thinks is best, promoting it in the most positive way possible

---

target their sales effort at and how they design communication. They try to find out who might be more willing to support them and then target them to sell the product. These charities might also undertake market intelligence with government, identifying its priorities and demands to inform on the way the charities communicate with it.

One way of doing this is by segmentation. A variety of demographic, lifestyle and behavioural characteristics can be used to find the people who are most likely to support the charity. The UK Charities Aid Foundation carried out an extensive survey of charity donors in 1994 and found that donors are, for example, more likely to be female, between 25 and 34, sick and disabled, and less likely to be retired (quoted in Sargeant 1999: 131; see also Sargeant and Bater 1996; Yavas et al. 1980: 43). Lifestyle segmentation means that charities can now buy lists of individuals who have a predisposition to give to particular charitable causes. Charities can profile their existing supporters and utilise the information to understand what their typical supporter might look like. This involves detailed analysis of existing records and databases, or surveying their supporters through, for example, the charity magazine. Pagan (1994) found that the Royal National Institute for the Deaf (RNID) increased the response to its direct mail campaigns by recognising that its donors tend to have a religious and gardening interest and read the *Daily Telegraph*. Charities that have a narrow, more specific market can segment it more easily: as Sargeant (1999: 133) illustrates, 'the Police Dependants Trust has a very narrow recipient base . . . Serving and ex-police officers would clearly be a key target market for this highly specialist organisation.' A charity with a wider market, although having a greater number of potential supporters to target, cannot do so specifically as the nature of supporters is more heterogeneous.

Stage 3: Communication

Charities use the results of market intelligence to aim their communication efforts in a manner that will be most likely to persuade people to support the charity financially. Communication is the 'hard sell' aspect of sales-oriented charity work. It includes offering freebies as inducements to join (e.g. the Royal Society for the Protection of Birds [RSPB] offers a free bird feeder), direct marketing designed according to psychological analysis and market intelligence, pre-tested advertising, and exploitation of current events and stories that stimulate support.

In terms of general communication style, the head of fundraising at the Council for the Protection of Rural England (CPRE) noted how communication from the organisation to supporters had been altered in recent years: from language and presentational forms that were 'grey' and suitable for government officials to a leaflet with effective pictures and clearer points more suitable for the general public (White 2000). Sales-oriented communication can be in the form of symbols. Sargeant (1999: 113) observed how the British Legion uses a poppy that 'has a very powerful and emotive appeal' even though the benefit from giving is still intangible. Charities also make use of organisational Visa cards, with which supporters can raise money through their ordinary shopping (Horne 2000). Amnesty International has its own Amnesty Visa card (Gupta 2000).

Direct mail is a significant tool in the recruitment activities of sales-oriented charities. It is sent directly addressed to named individuals and can reflect each recipient's individual characteristics (see Allen 1997: 15; Roberts and Berger 1989: 224). O'Shaughnessy and Peele (1985: 115) note that as in commercial marketing 'all number of varied messages, exotic gifts, pictures, novelties can be incorporated'. It is designed to get the recipients, attention, explain why they should be interested, instil in them a desire for the product and then encourage them to act (see Stone 1997: 272–273 for a seven-step guide to this). Direct mail can target potential supporters precisely. Charities buy the names and addresses of potential supporters from list brokers. There are three main types of list:

- *compiled (cold) names* brought from list brokers: lists of people who have some identifiable characteristics or set of characteristics, but who've had no contact with the organisation;
- *house (warm) names*: those who have already responded to the organisation, a list kept in the organisation's own database;
- *swapped names*: the house lists swapped with other organisations.

As Charity 1 noted, 'you can go to London and go shopping for names. You can specify the sort of names that you want. These are names that these companies gather from all sorts of sources.' Charities also build up their own lists of warm names, people who have already been touched by the organisation in some way; for example, they may have bought from the catalogue but are not members. Warm names perform better than cold. Most organisations do 'swaps': they swap their own lists of names with non-governmental organisations (NGOs) and charities. Charities 1 and 6 used statistical modelling information to obtain lists of whom to mail. This profiled existing supporters in terms of social grade and interest and then matched them against postal codes. Built in were lifestyle and transaction characteristics (e.g. whether they had bought from the organisation's catalogue). Charities pre-test their direct mail to check the effectiveness of different versions (see Roberts and Berger 1989: 187; Gosden 1985: 179–186; Godwin 1988: 11; Allen 1997: 15; Johnson 1998: 49; O'Shaughnessy and Peele 1985: 115 for further discussion).

Direct dialogue is the newest addition to direct marketing methods. Going into a London tube, or shopping down Oxford Street, as well as through other cities in the UK, you might find yourself approached by a friendly young person wearing the logo-covered T-shirt of a well-known organisation like Greenpeace or Amnesty International, asking you a series of questions and then offering you an invitation to join. The large-scale organisations recently adopted this technique in order to move towards a mass version of individual face-to-face communication. Charities pay agencies to do the work. Charity 8 explained that its telephone agency had people 'who are trained about [the charity] and they learn about [the charity] and they wear T-shirts with [the charity name] on and they stand in various strategic places in the street and talk to people and recruit them for the organisation'. Charity 6 commented that direct dialogue means 'they get the opportunity to ask questions, they get to see a person, to see a face of the organisation . . . they have an interaction'.

Stage 4: Campaign

Sales-oriented charities are likely to engage in campaigning by using the media to gain public attention that then forces politicians to take notice. It is likely to be of a more dramatic and emotive kind, with good visuals, rather than sending in a petition or a well-researched report. Environmental campaigns against the building of a new runway at Manchester airport, for example, gained substantial media attention because campaigners chained themselves to trees and it provided dramatic, exciting news stories for an equally sales-oriented media. Jordan et al. (1994: 551) cite the example of the sinking of the *Braer* oil tanker off the Shetlands Islands in 1993. Following this, several charities launched various appeals, generally accompanied by pictures of wildlife hurt by the incident; wording included the following:

> RSPB is fighting to keep Britain's Birds and marine creatures safe from future disasters. (RSPB)

> The Price of Oil has Just Gone Up. Birds, seals and otters are all facing agonising deaths by drowning or poisoning. (RSPCA/SPCA)

As you read this, Greenpeace is lifting oil stricken birds and animals out of the seas around the wreck of the *Braer* . . . we are using resources we would normally spend on campaigns that aim to stop this kind of thing happening in the first place. (Greenpeace)

Charities such as Greenpeace have used unconventional methods that can be criticised as manipulative. They use highly visual activities involving helicopters, boats, inflatables and direct human-contact protest to fit in with sales-oriented media to obtain more public attention. The NSPCC also recently ran the FULL STOP campaign, which was hard-hitting, using cartoon characters to represent children being hit or abused by adults. It was conveyed through television, posters, billboards and magazines and was supplemented by direct mail to raise awareness of the issue. It had significant affect, achieving recall or recognition by over 90 per cent of adults in the UK (www.nspcc.org.uk).

Success of a sales orientation
In the 1980s and 1990s this approach appeared to be relatively effective, at least in terms of attracting numbers of supporters. The RSPB experienced an almost nine-fold increase in membership from 1971 to 1991, and as Jordan and Maloney (1998: 392) argue, this 'reflects the adoption, and success, of regular high-profile press advertising and increased sophistication in recruitment rather than a change in public attitudes'. Jordan et al. (1994: 549) argued that 'the fact that the RSPB has 852,000 members [in 1991] while Plant Life has 1200 does not necessarily suggest that "birds" are valued so much more by the population than plants, but that the pro-bird organisation has, over time, marketed itself much more successfully'.

Concerns with sales-oriented charities
However, a sales-orientation has limitations and also raises questions and worries about democracy. This approach has given rise to much concern about its affect on participation.

First, direct marketing is based on psychological manipulation in some way, using threats and 'visibility, irreversibility, potential catastrophic consequences, and immorality' (Mitchell 1979: 114; see also Godwin 1992: 311; Jordan and Maloney 1998; Hansen 1985: 81; Godwin 1988: 214). Sales-oriented marketing doesn't respond to demands, it aims to persuade – it is the more manipulative means of political marketing (see also Crenson 1987; Bosso 1995; King and Walker 1992; Mitchell 1979: 120). Another concern is that the use of this type of marketing or recruitment strategy will always be limited by funds. Because direct mail is very costly, poorer charities will be less able to use it (Bosso 1995: 114; see also O'Shaughnessy 1990: 93; Maarek 1995: 144; Johnson 1998: 53), so the richest ones will do better; and richer charities will not necessarily be more democratic or command most public support. Research into smaller charities certainly confirmed their limited ability to engage in direct mail or mass mailings (Walsh 2000; Treacy 2000). Thirdly, because it targets the most likely supporters with a predisposition, it will never broaden but instead narrow overall participation within the political system (see Godwin 1988: 54; Jordan and Maloney 1998: 395–398; Jordan et al. 1994: 550; Kinnell and MacDougall 1997: 149). This prevents charities from achieving their broader goal of increasing participation and democracy within the UK (see Godwin and Mitchell 1994: 829).

Fourthly, sales-oriented charity marketing can lead to a focus on certain issues or aspects at the expense of others, affecting the achievement of campaigning goals and roles in the political system. Greenpeace can also be criticised in campaigning terms: their direct action and media-focused forms of campaigning are sometimes more manipulative and make the appearance of delivery rather than actually changing policy (see Grant 1995: 89). Godwin interviewed the charity leaders of 18 charities and concluded that there was 'a strong association between the degree to which an organisation depends on direct mail and the probability that it will choose highly visible and emotional issues' (1992: 318). Those Godwin interviewed 'made it clear' that the reason they chose issues according to visibility was due to the charity being dependent on direct marketing (1992: 319).

Lastly, direct mail can also be prone to attract disloyal supporters – they come in for the first year with the freebies on offer, then leave. Existing research (such as Jordan and Maloney 1997; Hayes 1986: 134; Mundo 1992: 18) suggests that direct mail-recruited members may be less active within organisations, less attached to organisations, less loyal and therefore subject to significant loss after the first year.

Sales-oriented charities tend not to offer broad, participatory organisational structures for their members to get involved. A member of staff at one organisation said that members had no rights within the organisation; 'we're a limited company . . . we're not a democracy' (see also academic analysis by Grant 1995: 135; and Rucht, 1993: 85). The problem is that supporters are likely to leave (see Rothenberg 1992: 127; Godwin 1988; Godwin and Mitchell 1984: 834; Jordan and Maloney 1998: 406, 1997: 220–226; Johnson 1998: 41; Maarek 1995: 161). A sales orientation may get the 'numbers' but as direct mail is expensive, this may make a loss not only financially in the long-term, but also in terms of lacking an active supporter base to help with campaigning. Indeed, research found that there was a growing realisation amongst charities that face-to-face recruitment can be more effective and attract more loyal supporters than direct mail, especially because the latter is no longer as effective as it once was.

Responsive charity work: market-oriented charities

Like all political organisations, charities have realised that supporters are more critical and that demanding supporters and politicians are more questioning of their recruitment and campaigning activities. Charities have to work harder to achieve their goals; they need to be more responsive to the existing and potential supporter market, and be more effective in campaigning to influence government. As a result, charities are moving to a more responsive, market-oriented model: they do not simply try to sell themselves but attempt to offer supporters what they want. Using political marketing, they try to respond to supporters' demands in order to attract and maintain them. They then use marketing to inform and run their campaigns to influence government. They therefore adopt a market orientation. A market-oriented charity goes through a political marketing process, engaging in various activities and using marketing techniques: see Box 5.3.

```
┌─────────────────────────────────────────────────────────────────────┐
│                                                                     │
│            Box 5.3 The process for a market-oriented charity        │
│                                                                     │
│   Stage 1: Market intelligence                                      │
│                                                                     │
│   Stage 2: Product design                                           │
│                                                                     │
│   Stage 3: Product refinement                                       │
│                                                                     │
│   Stage 4: Communication                                            │
│                                                                     │
│   Stage 5: Campaign                                                 │
│                                                                     │
│   Stage 6: Delivery                                                 │
│                                                                     │
└─────────────────────────────────────────────────────────────────────┘
```

As this process is more complicated, we will explore each stage in turn in greater detail. The theoretical process is summarised stage by stage and then further illustrated with empirical examples from the charities studied.

Stage 1: Market intelligence
Market intelligence is used to:

- discover the demands of the charities' supporters, conducting research into their existing, lapsed and potential supporters;
- identify the needs and wants of the cause they wish to promote and help;
- understand the markets they want to influence in campaigning terms;
- research a particular problem to obtain data to design better solutions or lobby government.

Charities can run focus groups, conduct a survey or ask questions over the phone. They can seek to build up individual relationships with key political figures over time, or pay a research organisation to conduct nationwide surveying and polling. They can carry out informal communication, through meetings for example, with existing supporters and politicians, to ascertain demands and interests and, in the case of supporters, monitor satisfaction and ensure retention.

Research may be conducted, for instance, into the deterioration of an environmental area or dying species. Charities can also segment potential supporters by characteristics such as demographics (e.g. age), geographical location and life-style characteristics.

All of the charities interviewed conducted significant market intelligence. Charity 1 had several members of its staff assigned to this, who tried to work 'amongst potential members to find out what sort of interests and what we need to be saying to them to encourage them to come in'. They ran 'a formal research programme', commissioning questions on omnibus surveys run by market research companies like MORI, and conducting focus groups. Other charities asked their lapsed supporters why they left. Most of the charities interviewed undertook surveys or focus groups of existing supporters: Friends of the Earth conducted a postal survey of supporters involved in their product Campaign Express. Market intelligence identified that whilst some supporters simply want to give money, others want meaningful involvement. As Charity 1 said:

> At one extreme, you've got avid [supporters] who are fanatical . . . and at the other end you've got people who . . . really just want to receive the magazine and are happy in the knowledge that we're carrying out the sort of good work on their behalf . . . they shouldn't be treated the same . . . these people have entirely differ-ent motivations and reasons for belonging and so giving them everything in a pile and saying 'there you are' is not ideal.

Market intelligence can also be conducted informally, to inform everything the charity does. Charity 4's understanding of its potential supporter market was acquired by years of dealing with those they come into contact with. When asked how the organisation knew what members wanted, it said supporters would 'tell you quite often as well actually without you even asking'. Local groups are another means of communication; intelligence can be gathered in the simple form of analysis and discussion at meetings. It can also be conducted to identify those supporters the organisation should have but has not yet attracted. One charity noted how they were aware they were missing potential members: 'we don't seem to get the paediatric units or the people we really want to get to. We're trying to work out what we're not offering them.'

On the campaigning side, market intelligence involves understanding the views of the general public, the media and government or other politicians. It can identify any opposition to the charity's goals. Research is conducted in a more scientific, policy sense, in order to provide evidence for any problems that the charity needs to act on. The results can be used to influence government, the media and the public. The DSA conducted a survey of members' experiences about medical treatment, from which they produced a report about medical dis-crimination that they then used to influence government as well as formulate support services and advice for sufferers (Walsh 2000).

Stage 2: Product design
A market-oriented charity adapts its product to suit the results from market intelligence. The supporter product includes supporter costs (which can vary

with different categories), supporter package (e.g. newsletter, stickers, information booklets, participation rights) and campaigning activities. 'Charities can
create a different supporter product for each group of supporters, identified by
market segmentation, thereby offering supporter-dictated membership products where the individual chooses the package best for him or her. Charities
determine their campaigning or lobbying strategies according to results from
market intelligence about what their cause needs, and what government, the
media and the public is likely to listen to. Charities make significant use of professional staff, who are sometimes recruited not simply on the basis of political
commitment but because of their professional experience in membership or lobbying.

The next stage in the process is designing the product. All the charities interviewed made a cognizant attempt to offer supporters what they might want from
the charities, adapting their product to suit the results from market intelligence.
Charity 1, for example, offered a fairly typical supporter package. It included a
magazine, free entry to particular places, discounted insurance and an organisational credit card. Charity 9 offered a legal advice line, special insurance coverage on cars and houses, and good deals for telephone and internet services. This
was in direct response to 'a demand from new members' and a survey of lapsed
members that said they 'couldn't see a benefit in being a member'.

Charity 4 ran training days for education staff because they would potentially
teach those affected by the issue they deal with. It invited speakers and distributed information packs, and ran conferences around the country for its supporters. Charities may also offer publications and information about the issue they
deal with; they may provide an advice line that enables their supporters to receive
information and support. The DSA has a trained benefits officer qualified to go
to tribunals on the behalf of sufferers (Walsh 2000). Some charities ran local
groups that offer social events and support; for example, in dealing with a particular disease. Support and counselling were a crucial part of their product
offering, because these were what supporters most needed; provision was
through the networking of supporters at the local level. The local groups also
ran fundraising events and outings.

More recently, some charities have begun to create a supporter-dictated
product. They offer different supporter packages for people to choose the one
that best suits them. In terms of money, first they enable supporters to give differing amounts: often several alternatives are given on a mailing form or over the
phone. One option for charities is to offer a fuller package to supporters who
give higher amounts, thereby encouraging greater financial contributions.
Charities offer high-value supporters extra information, invitations to special
events, a video a few times a year, and a possible citation in annual reports and
thanks through the charity's newsletters. Sargeant (1999: 146) noted how the
RSPB launched a mini-campaign around the proposed purchase of particular
land, and donors who had given over £1,000 were also sent 'a pack of correspondence relating to the land purchase, including the relevant council papers',

designed in response to market intelligence which had 'shown that donors in this category were more responsive to reasoned/rational argument'.

Market-oriented charities also differentiate in terms of activity. In terms of involvement, some charities have particular packages for supporters who want to be more active, offering them more information and involvement opportunities. Charity 5 created a new category of activists aside from general supporters. They could register on-line and received four mailings year on a specific campaign with instructions on what to do. This proved 'very successful . . . they just love the fact that they're getting (a) more information, (b) something to do and (c) something to do very quickly and easily'. Charity 7 offered a large number of different products and supporters could choose whatever package they like: there were about 15 different options, created because of 'demand really . . . the services that we provide to people are giving people what they want, when they want it, in the right form'. This shows the market-oriented concept in practice. Charity 6 gave supporters different options 'because we're trying to make more of the organisation available to the right people. **We're trying to ask our supporters to dictate the relationship with us.**'

Greenpeace ran a scheme called Front-Line for supporters who paid at least £20 a month, who received more information, including internal emails when a campaigner from the national organisation returned from an event and wrote a report about it. As Merrett (2000) explained, 'the idea is to give them the opportunity to get closer to the organisation and see a bit of inside information that wouldn't normally be available'. They also ran an Active Supporters Unit at local level for those who wanted to get involved (Merrett 2000). Overall the trend is towards developing membership products and organisational services that respond as much as possible to the demands of supporters. The next stage is then to communicate this to potential supporters.

Charity 5 used its local groups to campaign and speak through local media on local issues. The DSA tried to focus on issues deemed important by their members: 'if you go out to the members' branch meetings and listen to them, listen to the problems they've got in their area, they're telling you what they want: "how do I deal with this?", and then you produce literature [i.e. publications or fact sheets] they need to help them do it' (Walsh 2000). It created new publications with information and advice for supporters on these issues and also used the survey results in reports for government.

In developing campaign strategies to influence government, market intelligence can also be used, and positive relationships can be built up with key players. The aim is to match charity campaign aims with public opinion and party views as much as is possible. However, one of the functions of charities is to offer something different from mainstream political parties and to represent minorities, so following majority public opinion may not be possible: they need to focus on their individual market, not the general UK public. The product can be developed over time; for example, the Samaritans charity tended to be purely for those who were depressed or suicidal, but in recent years they have targeted different segments, such as school children subject to exam stress.

Stage 3: Product refinement
This has four main aspects:

- *Achievability*: ensure the product is achievable in terms of cost, time and other constraints: don't promise to save everything or solve everyone's problems, for example; make focused appeals for support that have a clear aim and delivery potential.
- *Co-operation*: co-operate with other charities when beneficial to achieving one's own goals, or with other organisations or systems.
- *Competition analysis and product differentiation*: consider the main competitors and ensure the charity is distinctive in some way.
- *Support analysis and target marketing*: analyse where support comes from and target new segments of the market – and not just those who have a predisposition; also aim to increase participation.

These are examined in detail below.

Achievability   Like any market-oriented political organisation, charities need to make their proposed product design achievable. They will find greater success if they make focused claims (see Berry 1984: 56; also Jordan and Maloney 1998: 391). If charities do then achieve wider influence, they will be seen as even more successful: better to promise less and achieve more than promise lots and leave supporters unsatisfied. In campaigning terms this includes taking into account government constraints and not asking for everything all at once, but understanding political and financial constraints. It also means being realistic with regard to hoping to change behaviour; for example, not expecting everyone to give up their cars straight away.

Co-operation   Charities can co-operate with related organisations such as local government, hospitals, schools or even other charities when it is in their interest. Co-operative behaviour can add weight to a campaign and be effective in an emergency, such as a war. The charity ChildLine worked with schools to create the programme ChildLine in Partnership with Schools (CHIPS) to make direct contact with children through schools. They also got the charity's on-line help line number put on the back of Kellogg's cereal packets. Seven leading children's charities, including ChildLine, Barnardo's, National Children's Bureau (NCB), National Children's Hospital (NCH), NSPCC, National Council of Voluntary Child Care Organisations (NCVCCO) and the Children's Society, joined forces in December 2000 to establish the Children's Charities Coalition on Internet Safety (CHIS) (see www.childline.org.uk/Campaigns.asp).

Competition analysis and product differentiation   Charities also need to conduct competition analysis to understand whom they are competing with, in terms not just of recruitment but also of campaigning. Charities can then attempt to differentiate themselves from the competition (see Imig 1994: 19).

Friends of the Earth and Greenpeace both deal with the environment, but Greenpeace will take illegal action whereas Friends of the Earth will not – there is a clear difference there, leading them to attract different types of supporters (Merrett 2000). Greenpeace tries to be more confrontational and less compromising. Childline used public figures expert in law to speak at a conference to promote their campaign Child Witnesses in Court, such as Jack Straw (former home secretary, and a lawyer), Hillary Clinton (wife of former US president, and a lawyer) and Cherie Booth (wife of the prime minister, and a top barrister) (see www.childline.org.uk/Campaigns.asp). Another example is Oxfam, which used Gordon Brown, chancellor of the Exchequer, to head their Giving Campaign in Scotland in 2002. Unlike political parties, however, charities tend to avoid negative competition campaigning; as one commented, 'in all our recruitment we talk about what Greenpeace does . . . certainly we would never put down another organisation' (Merrett 2000).

Support analysis and target marketing   Support analysis will enable charities to see not just whom do they attract, but whom they do not, and so target resources and campaigns to attract new groups of supporters, people they may not previously have thought about aiming at. In this way they can use marketing to broaden participation, not hinder it. Childline targeted children to help fundraise, going into schools, offering ideas for activities and producing a teachers' pack. Segmentation can also be conducted to focus efforts on sections of the market not being reached; for example, the elderly if the cause is related to ill-health and lack of exercise. This is not just about attracting donations. Support analysis can also be carried out with regard to those markets whose support the charity needs to obtain in campaigning terms – whether it be certain media organisations, opposition parties or key government ministers.

Stage 4: Communication
Charities communicate their new product to potential supporters and communicate their concerns to government, the public and the media. To do so they use all appropriate forms of advertising, including leaving leaflets and planning posters or advertisements at or in various communication vehicles. Charities choose which method carefully, to ensure it is cost-effective. This is not so much of a selling activity, however, as a way to communicate the benefits and options of supporting. Communication to government is done in a reflective rather than obsessive and overwhelming manner. Market-oriented charities can therefore build a long-term relationship with government, being in a good position to offer expert advice and influence policy development and legislation. Communication also involves long-term projects in raising awareness or educating the public.

As might be expected, charities use advertisements in the press and television. Charity 6 used direct response television, transmitted on satellite TV and Channel 4, which asked people to respond quickly to a number placed 'all over the ad.'. This charity used telemarketing, signing people up over the phone.

Charities that use press advertisement noted that success is more likely if the advert is about a specific, popular issue, but it is somewhat unpredictable. The CPRE had little response from to advertisements in the *Daily Mail* and *Daily Telegraph* about road safety in 1999, yet recruited nearly a thousand members a few years before that from adverts about a housing issue (White 2000).

Continual information is provided cheaply and easily by a website, which the majority of charities now have. This can provide up-to-date information on campaigns, as well as clear and direct means of how to join or support the organisation. Charities now supply a wide range of information on their websites, including policy documents, annual reports, campaign updates and information booklets. Websites are useful in recruitment terms, in helping sufferers and providing information to the media. Charity websites can have important visual impact if well designed; for example, the one for the DSA has very positive, happy pictures of children with Down syndrome.

Communication can include less large-scale means than the direct mail used by large charities. Charity 3 had a stand at conferences on the illness it dealt with, and sent a leaflet dispenser on the organisation to branches; supporters at the branches then placed the leaflets in institutions such as GPs' surgeries, pharmacies and libraries. Local groups also communicate: Charity 8 sent them a membership recruitment pack so that, if existing members met someone who wanted to join, they could sign them up then and there, filling in the form and giving them a receipt, then passing it onto national office. The more involved potential and existing supporters can be the better. ChildLine runs a variety of activities that supporters can take part in, including fun runs, bike rides, social outings at the races and dances, to raise money.

Communication also concerns providing information to those not directly affected by the cause but who come into contact with it. The DSA also worked with another organisation to produce a video for medical students about Down syndrome and ran training days for teaching classroom assistants (Walsh 2000). The NSPCC and ChildLine both undertake research into child abuse so they can provide statistics to help compile reports, campaign and inform government policy. Supporters also receive a wide variety of communication about how they can help: the National Trust (NT) sends out information advertising conservation weekends that volunteers can go on to advance the cause.

Communication involves long-term communication with key groups, users, experts – any market which the charity needs to advance the cause. The DSA produced a report over medical discrimination and held meetings with the Department of Health following its publication, as well as achieving an early day motion in Westminster (Walsh 2000). It also includes providing useful advice to those who may suffer because of the issue the charity addresses, such as booklets for how to gain government benefits. The Samaritans used the slogan 'Whatever you're going through, we'll go through it with you', not to gain money, but to attract people to use their organisation – to help people. Marketing *can* be combined with good old-fashioned charity principles.

Stage 5: Campaign

Charities run a short-term burst of campaigning to recruit supporters, involve supporters in a particular activity, or lobby government intensely. This need not be manipulative, simply informative, strong and well-planned.

Market-oriented campaigns vary in nature. Amnesty International run 'urgent action' letter-writing campaigns for certain prisoners (Gupta 2000). The British Heart Foundation (BHF), concerned with reducing ill-health through heart disease, involves itself in educational communication to promote better fitness and so reduce the problem. They run several campaigns and events including marathons and jogs, and have even communicated in the form of children's books, such as *Artie Beat's Picnic*, which promote healthy eating to children and parents (www.bhf.org.uk). Save the Children ran a campaign called 'Beat Poverty', which urged people to take action by writing to their MP (www.beat-poverty.org/content.asp, accessed 2003). ChildLine undertook a number of campaigns to advance their goals including, 'Commercial Sexual Exploitation of Children', 'Internet Safety' and 'Child Witnesess in Court' (www.child-line.org.uk). In 2003, Oxfam engaged in various campaigns, including 'Cut the Cost', which tried to reduce the cost of medicines for poor countries; 'Education Now', to try to educate every child in the world; and 'Conflict', to try to reduce the problems brought about by war (see www.oxfam.org.uk/campaigns.html).

Greenpeace trains its active supporters to help advance campaigns; they 'are specifically trained up to be speakers on a specific issue' and then speak at local meetings and radio (Merrett 2000). Members of the Active Supporter Unit were also asked to write letters several times a year; for example, on the issue of Norwegian whaling; in 1999 members were asked to write to ordinary Norwegian people to tell them their point of view (Merrett 2000). Developing a more market-oriented approach, Greenpeace has increasingly used researchers to inform its campaigns. Campaigns can also be used as one-off attempts to raise the supporter numbers; local branches in the Alzheimer's Society run campaigns to get members, for example (Thompson 2000). Greenpeace also ran a lapsed reactivation phone campaign, to contact people who had lapsed ten years ago (Merrett 2000). Market-oriented charities are therefore more likely to make provision for members who wish to be more active than are charities that adopt a sales-oriented approach. Not *all* supporters will be active, because some still want to only pay money or engage with the organisation on limited terms; it is simply that if a charity is market-oriented it will provide different options for involvement and supporters can choose that which suits them best.

Stage 6: Delivery

Delivery has four main aspects:

- *Deliver the supporter package* and monitor satisfaction.
- *Deliver campaign goals*: progress to influence public affairs needs to be communicated to supporters.

- *Supporter retention*: charities also invest in ensuring retention, making sure that new members renew and stay as supporters.
- *Upgrading supporter contribution and involvement*: over time supporters can be contacted and moved up the contribution scale.

The first aspect is self-explanatory; the others are detailed below.

Deliver campaign goals   Market-oriented charities make sure that they communicate progress on campaigning – that they deliver the broad, cause-related goals, as these are one of the main motivations for joining. Without this there are problems: Charity 9's survey on lapsed members cited a 'lack of communication' as a major reason for leaving. Charity 1 noted that 'there's an awful lot of stuff that we do that we need to talk to members about to get it across to them'. It reported its action in the supporter magazine and in mailings for donations. Charity 2 let its supporters know of any campaign successes, taking particular care to inform supporters if their own activity made a difference and had an impact on public affairs. Charity 6 informed its supporters about campaign progress through its magazines, and even phoned its high-value supporters to inform them individually about a result on a current campaign.

Amnesty International tells its members where direct action through letter writing has had an impact on releasing prisoners (Gupta 2000). The CPRE sent a *Planning Update* to known activists that gave them more information about other campaigns and what to do (White 2000). Greenpeace also gives details of its global campaign expenditure in its annual report (www.greenpeace.org/Annualreport-2001/voice.htm). Save the Children has a section called 'campaign news' on its website (www.savethechildren.org.uk/campaigns/index.html). Charities also convey progress to the media, though the issuing of press releases to all media organisations and on their websites (see www.childline.org.uk/Newsandmedia.asp for example).

Furthermore, there is a strong belief amongst charities that if at least a part of the supporter base is active this helps campaigning or influencing government. Charity 1 noted that high membership 'is a great lobbying and persuasive tool to dangle in front of the government from time to time'. Charity 5 argued that 'if you don't get citizen action and you're trying to get a bill through parliament you might as well piss against the wind':

> We can go to government and business and ask them to do something . . . but where's the actual political will for them to do it? The political will is only really going to come from aware and active citizens, people who know the facts. An MP sitting in parliament is only really going to act if their constituents kick up a fuss. So again that's why we're coming down to actual individuals who for us in an organisation are critical.

Supporter retention   There is little point putting substantial effort into attracting supporters in the first instance only to lose them after a year. As Charity 1 noted, 'there are some tricks that are pretty common knowledge: that you try and get them onto direct debit [sometimes called committed giving] as quickly as you can. The fallout from people on direct debit is much lower.' But they need more than this. New members are often put on a particular programme designed to make them feel valued and introduce them into the organisation so that they sustain their relationship with it over the subsequent years. Greenpeace has a detailed programme for new members to ensure they are satisfied with their membership. In the first three months after joining they are placed in a welcome cycle; they receive a welcome pack (cards on the organisation and what it does, or a fuzzy globe for those recruited by direct dialogue); six weeks later they receive a follow-up, such as a photo-card or a picture of the earth, with details of how they could get involved and options to choose from, while direct-dialogue recruited supporters receive fuzzy felt things to put on their globe; only then do they go onto the standard cycle for existing members (Merrett 2000).

People who leave are called lapsed supporters and they can be sent several reminders as part of a renewal cycle. Charities can try ringing people up or contacting them by post, which is one to one and personal (see Jordan et al. 1994: 552; Rothenberg 1988: 1147). However, some charity issues make it difficult to do this; for example, the Alzheimer's Society notes how if someone's membership lapses it is a very sensitive matter, because it could be the person who suffered from dementia died (Thompson 2000). Charity 1 sent three reminders if people stopped supporting: if there was still no response, their names went off the supporter list but were retained and kept on the database. Those supporters can be contacted and invited to rejoin several years later, a strategy which proves quite effective. Another aspect to understanding retention is that supporters' demands may change over time and the charity must respond to this (Mundo 1992: 23).

Charities with high-value supporters will ensure they contact them a certain number of times each year and maintain a personal, friendly relationship with them. They may even keep a record of the supporters' circumstances and nature so they can continue a conversation with them from one contact to the next without having to remember all the detail (see Sargeant 1999: 141 and interview data). Relationship marketing may offer a valuable perspective in retention of supporters generally (see Sargeant 1999: 146; Jordan et al. 1994: 552). As Kinnell and MacDougall (1997: 147–148) noted, 'maintaining a strong relationship with donors over a long period of time is a central requirement of charity marketing. The difficulties and expense of recruiting new donors have led to increased emphasis on the importance of building stronger relationships with existing donors and supporters.' Charities have even advertised for jobs such as 'relationship fundraiser'. Kinnell and MacDougall (1997: 148) argue that relationship marketing in the voluntary sector is about involving donors. Organisations should try to ensure their contributors 'feel a sense of ownership of the organisation's objectives and aims'. This is a new area with regard to marketing generally, let alone political marketing, however, so this will require literature written about businesses to be adapted to suit politics (see Worthington and Horne 1996: 192–193, for example).

Upgrading supporter contribution and involvement   Charities can also try to make supporters more active and contribute increased amounts over time. In terms of money, charities can, with care, increase the amount given and its frequency (Sargeant 1999: 136). In terms of activity, this can also increase their attachment to the organisation, and therefore their support loyalty. Charities are trying to move individuals from the outside of the participatory circle to further in, nearer the most active supporters. Charities may initially recruit people because of tangible, material incentives, but if they increase contact between themselves and the members, they may gain more in terms of higher financial contributions and activity in the long term. Charity 1 knowingly recruited people 'at a fairly low level in terms of their knowledge about [the cause] . . . and once they're in, the plan is then to sort of raise their awareness and their knowledge throughout the course of their membership'. This would suggest a more positive assessment of the participation offered by organisations than existing literature currently offers.

Conclusions: marketing charities and democracy

Although there are charities that still engage in sales-oriented-type activity, market-oriented charities use the political marketing activities of market intelligence, careful product design, communication and delivery. They attempt to understand what their supporters want from the organisation and design their supporter package to reflect this. By analysing their supporter base they can also offer a supporter-dictated membership package so that individual supporters can choose the option that best suits them, ranging from a one-off financial donation, through regular giving, to active involvement in local groups, meetings and lobbying. Charities use various techniques to contact potential supporters, such as direct mail and direct dialogue. They make sure they tell their supporters of campaign progress and continually evaluate and discuss the response to all aspects of organisational behaviour, not just the recruitment packages sent out by direct mail. Overall they adopt the market-oriented concept and become market oriented: they design their behaviour to meet potential and existing supporters' demands in order to obtain and maintain their support.

Charities are beginning to realise that they can use political marketing not simply to sell their organisation, but also to ensure that they offer something people will want to support. Further research is needed to assess the extent to which this approach has permeated the charity sector, but it is clear that comprehensive political marketing has the potential to help the non-profit goals of these non-business enterprises, to 'do some good': a public, political use of marketing. All charities need to be financially aware: using marketing to stay in touch with their donors and offer the best possible service to the cause or section of society they are trying to support does not reduce it all to being about money or return on investment.

The marketing of charities raises questions about the effects on participation and charities' broader goals. Although, as already explored, it seems sensible to accept research that suggests that sales-oriented charities do not have the socio-psychological, more stable support built up through solidary activities upon which to call and sustain long-term support and activity (Godwin and Mitchell 1984: 837), the market-oriented approach may offer a solution to this. Charities that try to become market oriented, to market the product not just the presentation, are realising the importance of increasing the attachment and involvement of supporters, to provide stable financial income but also to help with campaigning. As a member of staff at Greenpeace commented, 'our supporters are completely the reason that we exist' and 'the life-blood of the organisation' (Merrett 2000). While more detailed research may be needed to assess the overall impact of market-oriented charity behaviour, the latest approach has more potential for charities and a more positive outlook for the political system as a whole. Charities aim to influence policy, often in areas like health and education, and in doing so work closely with the public sector. The behaviour of hospitals and GPs is therefore a significant concern for health-related charities. The next chapter will discuss the marketing of health.

Notes

This chapter builds upon and develops ideas first made public in an article submitted and accepted by the *Journal of Public Affairs* in 2001, originally due to be published in spring 2003, actually published in autumn 2003 (vol. 3, no. 4).

1 Interviews were conducted with recruitment, marketing or member staff between August and November 2000, mainly face to face, bar two conducted over the phone, and semi-structured with some open-ended questions. Information gathered by interview was supplemented by analysis of the charities' documents and websites. Participants agreed to be interviewed as long as it was confidential, so any material with direct reference to these interviews is coded as Charity 1, Charity 3 etc. All were national, relatively large-scale organisations based in London; they covered a wide range of areas including environment, animal rights, human rights, health, professional and consumer. The interviews were conducted as part of a mini-research project within the politics department of the University of Aberdeen, devised by the author whilst working with William Maloney and Grant Jordan. A survey to a larger number of organisations, with the questions informed by interview data, was also drafted, but before it was finalised and sent out the author obtained a lectureship in the management department.

2 Otherwise referred to as pressure groups, interest groups, non-governmental organisations, non-profit organisations or voluntary organisations. There are, of course, differences between the terms used, but the word 'charity' is retained here because it is utilised most widely within the actual charity world, and definitional argument is not the purpose of this chapter: for discussion on this see, amongst others, Grant (1995).

3 Comment by staff member within a national charity interviewed for this research; the organisation wished to remain anonymous.
4 Further analysis of the literature can be found in Lees-Marshment (2003).

Bibliography

Allen, M. (1997), *Direct Marketing*, Kogan Page, London.

Berry, J.M. (1984), *The Interest Group Society*, Glenview, IL, Scott, Forseman/Little, Brown.

Blois, K.J. (1996), 'Relationship Marketing in Organisational Markets: When Is It Appropriate?', *Journal of Marketing Management* 12: 161–173.

Bosso, C.J. (1995), 'The Colour of Monday: Environmental Charities and the Pathologies of Fund Raising', in A. Cigler and B. Loomis (eds), *Interest Group Politics*, CQ Press, 4th edition, Washington, DC. pp. 101–130.

Burnett, K. (1993), 'The Challenge of Relationships', *Fund Raising Management* July: 44–54.

Burns, B. (2000), Interview by J. Lees-Marshment with Brendan Burns, former policy chairman of the FSB (Federation of Small Businesses), 6 November.

Christy, R., G. Oliver and J. Penn (1996), 'Relationship Marketing in Consumer Markets', *Journal of Marketing Management* 12: 175–187.

Cigler, J.A. and B.A. Loomis, eds (1998), *Interest-group Politics*, 5th edition, University of Kansas, Congressional Quarterly, Washington, DC.

Commonwealth Federation (1996), 'NGOs: What They Are and What They Do', Commonwealth Foundation, http://carryon.oneworld.org/com.

Conway, T. (1996), 'Relationship Marketing within the Not-for-profit Sector', in F. Buttle (ed.), *Relationship Marketing: Theory and Practice*, Paul Chapman, London.

Crenson, M.A. (1987), 'The Private Stake in Public Goods: Overcoming the Illogic of Collective Action', *Policy Sciences* 20: 259–276.

Dunleavy, P. (1991), *Democracy, Bureaucracy and Public Choice*, Harvester Wheatsheaf, London.

Ewing-Cook, C. (1984), 'Participation in Public Interest Groups', *American Politics Quarterly* 12(4): 409–430.

Godwin, R.K. (1988), *One Billion Dollars of Influence*, Chatham House, Chatham, NJ.

Godwin, R.K. (1992), 'Money, Technology, and Political Interests: The Direct Marketing of Politics', in Mark P. Petracca (ed.), *The Politics of Interests: Interest Groups Transformed*, Westview Press, Boulder, CO.

Godwin, R.K. and R.C. Mitchell (1984), 'The Implications of Direct Mail for Political Organisations', *Social Science Quarterly* 65: 829–839.

Goodwin, R.E. and K.W.S. Roberts (1975), 'The Ethical Voter', *American Political Science Review* 69: 926–928.

Gosden, F.F. Jr (1985), *Direct Marketing Success: What Works and Why*, John Wiley, New York.

Grant, W. (1995), *Pressure Groups, Politics and Democracy in Britain*, 2nd edition, Harvester Wheatsheaf, London.

Grant, W. (2000), *Pressure Groups and British Politics*, Macmillan, Houndmills, Basingstoke, and London.

Gray, R. (2000), 'How the NSPCC is a Boom for Brands', *Journal of Marketing* May.

Gray, V. and D. Lowery (1996), 'A Niche Theory of Interest Representation', *Journal of Politics* 58: 91–111.

Grover, R. (1991), 'Fighting Back: The Resurgence of Social Activism', in E.J. McCarthy and W.D. Perreault (eds), *Applications in Basic Marketing: Clippings from the Popular Business Press*, Irwin.

Gummesson, E. (1987), 'The New Marketing: Developing Long-term Interactive Relationships', *Long Range Planning* 20(4): 10–20.

Gupta, S. (2000), Interview by J. Lees-Marshment with Sanjeev Gupta, supporter acquisition manager at Amnesty International, by phone, 5 September.

Hannagan, T. (1992), *Marketing for the Non-profit Sector*, Macmillan, London.

Hansen, J.M. (1985). 'The Political Economy of Group Membership', *American Political Science Review* 79: 79–96.

Hayes, M.T. (1986), 'The New Group Universe', in A. Cigler and B. Loomis (eds), *Interest Group Politics*, CQ Press, Washington, DC. pp. 135–145.

Hirschman, A.O. (1970), *Exit, Voice and Loyalty: Responses to Decline in Firms, Organisations and States*, Harvard University Press, Cambridge, MA.

Horne, S. (2000), Presentation on charity marketing, Aberdeen University.

Imig, D. (1994), 'Advocacy by Proxy: The Children's Lobby in American Politics', paper prepared for the annual meeting of the APSA, New York.

Johnson, P.E. (1995), 'How Environmental Charities Recruit Members: Does the Logic still Hold Up?', paper delivered to the American Political Science Association, Chicago.

Johnson, P.E. (1998), 'Interest Group Recruiting: Finding Members and Keeping Them', in A.J. Cigler and B.A. Loomis (eds), *Interest Group Politics*, 5th edition, CQ Press, Washington, DC. pp. 35–62.

Jones, B. and D. Kavanagh (1994), 'Pressure Groups', in B. Jones (ed.), *Politics UK*, Harvester Wheatsheaf, London: pp. 220–237.

Jordan, A.G. and J. Richardson (1987), *Government and Pressure Groups in Britain*, Clarendon Press, Oxford.

Jordan, G. (1994), 'Why Bumble Bees Fly: Accounting for Public Interest Participation', paper presented at ECPR Joint Sessions, Madrid.

Jordan, G. (1998), 'Politics Without Parties: A Growing Trend?', *Parliamentary Affairs* 51(3): 314–328.

Jordan, G. and W. Maloney (1997), *The Protest Business: Mobilizing Campaigning Charities*, Manchester, Manchester University Press.

Jordan, G. and W. Maloney (1998), 'Manipulating Membership: Supply-side Influences on Group Size', *British Journal of Political Science* 28: 389–409.

Jordan, G., W. Maloney and A.M. McLaughlin (1994), 'Interest Groups: A Marketing Perspective on Membership', P. Dunleavy and J. Stanyer (eds), *Contemporary Political Studies: Proceedings of the Annual Conference of the Political Studies Association*, Political Studies Association.

Keith, R. (1960) 'The Marketing Revolution', *Journal of Marketing* January: 35–38.

King, D. and J.L. Walker (1992), 'The Provision of Benefits by Interest Groups in the United States', *Journal of Politics* 54: 394–426.

Kinnell, M. and J. MacDougall (1997), *Marketing in the Not-for-profit sector*, Butterworth Heinemann, Oxford.

Knoke, D. (1981), 'Commitment and Detachment in Voluntary Associations', *American Sociological Review* 46: 141–158.

Knoke, D. (1986), 'Associations and Interest Groups', *Annual Review of Sociology* 12: 1–21.

Knoke, D. (1988), 'Organisational Incentives', *American Sociological Review* 53: 311–329.

Knoke, D. (1990a). *Organising for Collective Action: The Political Economies of Associations*, Aldine de Gruyter, New York.

Knoke, D. (1990b), 'Networks of Political Action: Toward Theory Construction', *Social Forces* 68(4): 1041–1063.

Kotler, P. (1991), *Marketing Management: Analysis, Planning, Implementation and Control*, 7th edition, Prentice-Hall, Englewood Cliffs, NJ.

Kotler, P. and A. Andreasen (1991), *Strategic Marketing for NonProfit Organisations*, 4th edition, Prentice-Hall, Englewood Cliffs, NJ.

Lancaster, G. and L. Massingham (1999), *Essentials of Marketing: Text and Cases* 3rd edition, McGraw-Hill.

Laundy, L. and C.B. Weinberg (1990), 'A Marketing Audit of the British Columbia Society for Human/Animal Interaction', in C.H. Lovelock and C.B. Weinberg (eds), *Public and Nonprofit Marketing: Readings and Cases*, Scientific Press San Francisco. pp. 61–70.

Lees-Marshment, J. (1999), 'Broadening the Concept of Marketing: How to Market a Political Party', Working Paper XI, Department of Government, University College Cork (National University of Ireland, Cork, July.

Lees-Marshment, J. (2001), *Political Marketing and British Political Parties: The Party's Just Begun*, Manchester University Press, Manchester.

Lees-Marshment, J. (2003), 'Marketing Good Works: New Trends in How Interest Groups Recruit Supporters', *Journal of Public Affairs* 3(3).

Maarek, P.J. (1995), 'Direct Marketing Methods', in P. Maarek, *Political Marketing and Communication*, John Libbey, London. pp. 137–162.

Maloney, W.A., G. Jordan and A.M. McLaughlin (1994), 'Interest Groups and Public Policy: The Insider/Outsider Model Revisited', *Journal of Public Policy* 14(1): 17–38.

McCarthy, J.D. and N.Z. Mayer (1977), 'Resource Mobilisation and Social Movements: A Partial Theory', *American Journal of Sociology* 82: 1212–1241.

McFarland, A.S. (1976), *Public Interest Lobbies: Decision Making on Energy*, American Enterprise Institute, Washington, D.C.

Medley, G.J. (1990), 'Strategic Planing for the World Wildlife Fund', in C.H. Lovelock and C.B. Weinberg (eds), *Public and Nonprofit Marketing: Readings and Cases*, Scientific Press San Francisco. pp. 47–52.

Merrett, G. (2000), Interview by J. Lees-Marshment with Gillian Merrett, high value supporter fund-raiser with Greenpeace, 12 September.

Milbrath, L.W. and M.L. Goel (1977), *Political Participation: How and Why Do People Get Involved in Politics?*, 2nd edition, University Press of America, Lanham.

Mitchell, R.C. (1979), 'National Environmental Lobbies and the Apparent Illogic of Collective Action', in C. Russell (ed.), *Collective Decision-making.* Johns Hopkins University Press, Baltimore, MD. pp. 87–121.

Mundo, P.A. (1992), 'Organisational Analysis of Interest groups', in P.A. Mundo, *Interest groups: Cases and Characteristics*, Nelson Hall, Chicago. pp. 18–38.

Nichols, J.E. (1995), 'Developing Relationships with Donors', *Fundraising Management* August: 18, 19, 47.

Olson, M. (1965) *The Logic of Collective Action*, Oxford University Press, London.

O'Shaughnessy, N.J. (1990), 'The Peevish Penmen: Direct Mail and US Elections', in N.J. O'Shaughnessy, *The Phenomenon of Political Marketing*, Macmillan, Basingstoke. pp. 87–97.

O'Shaughnessy, N.J. and G. Peele (1985), 'Money, Mail and Markets: Reflections on Direct Mail in American Politics', *Electoral Studies* 4(2): 115–124.

Pagan, L. (1994), 'Testing out Support', *Marketing* 12 May: 43.

Putnam, R.D. (2000), *Bowling Alone: The Collapse and Revival of American Community*, Simon and Schuster, New York.

Richardson, J. (1995), 'Market for Political Activism: Interest Groups as a Challenge to Political Parties', *West European Parties* 18(1): 116–139.

Roberts, M.L. and P.D. Berger. (1989), *Direct Marketing Management*, Prentice-Hall, Englewood Cliffs, NJ.

Roelf Bult, J. (1996), *Target Selection for Direct Marketing*, Rijksuniversiteit, Groningen.

Rosenstone, S.J. and J.M. Hansen (1993), *Mobilization, Participation and Democracy in America*, Macmillan, New York.

Rothenberg, L.S. (1988), 'Organizational Maintenance and the Retention Decision in Groups', *American Political Science Review* 82(4): 1129–1152.

Rothenberg, L.S. (1992), *Linking Citizens to Government: Interest Group Politics at Common Cause*, Cambridge University Press, New York.

Rucht, D. (1993), '"Think Globally, Act Locally?" Needs, Forms and Problems of Cross-national Co-operation among Environmental Groups', in D. Rucht, *European Integration and Environmental Policy*, Belhaven, London.

Sargeant, A. (1999), *Marketing Management for Non-profit Organisations*, Oxford University Press, New York.

Sargeant, A. and K. Bater (1996), 'Market Segmentation in the Charity Sector: Just What is the Potential?', Working Paper 96/05, University of Exeter.

Schlegelmilch, B.B. and A.C. Tynan (1989), 'The Scope for Market Segmentation Within the Charity Sector: An Empirical Analysis', *Managerial and Decision Economics* 10: 127–134.

Schwartz, K. (1991), 'Nonprofits' Bottom-line: They Mix Lofty Goals and Gutsy Survival Strategies', in E.J. McCarthy and W.D. Perreault (eds), *Applications in Basic Marketing: Clippings from the Popular Business Press*, Irwin. pp. 20–21.

Sherman, E. (1999), 'Direct Marketing: How Does it Work for Political Campaigns?', in Bruce I. Newman (ed.), *Handbook of Political Marketing*, Sage, Thousand Oaks, CA., pp. 365–388.

Sinclair, B.W. (1982), 'Political Consultants: The New King-Makers Work their Magic', *Washington Post* 5 June: A-6.

Smith, P.R. (1993), 'Direct Marketing', in P.R. Smith, *Marketing Communications: An Integrated Approach*, Kogan Page, London.

Stone, B. (1997), *Successful Direct Marketing Methods*, NTC/Contemporary Publishing, Chicago.

Thompson, D. (2000), Interview by J. Lees-Marshment with Dorothy Thompson, membership officer of the Alzheimer's Society, by phone, 5 September.

Topolsky, M. (1974), 'Common Cause?' *Worldview* 17: 35–39.

Treacy, T. (2000), Interview by J. Lees-Marshment with Tara Treacy, trust and corporate officer of the Downs' Syndrome Association, 11 September.

Truman, D. (1951), *The Governmental Process: Political Interests and Public Opinion*, Knopf, New York.

Uhlaner, C.J. (1986), 'Political Participation, Rational Actors, and Rationality: A New Approach', *Political Psychology* 7(3): 551–573.

Uhlaner, C.J. (1989), 'Relational Goods and Participation: Incorporating Sociability into a Theory of Rational Action', *Public Choice* 62: 253–285.

Verba, S., K.L. Schlozman and H.E. Brady (1995), *Voice and Equality: Civic Voluntarism in American Politics*, Harvard University Press, London.

Viguerie, R. (1981), *The New Right: We're Ready to Lead*, Viguerie, Falls Church, VA.

Walsh, E. (2000), Interview by J. Lees-Marshment with Ellie Walsh, administrator of the Downs' Syndrome Association, 11 September.

Watts, D. (1997), *Political Communication Today*, Manchester University Press, Manchester.

White, S. (2000), Interview by J. Lees-Marshment with Stephen White, head of fundraising at the CPRE, 13 September.

Worthington, S. and S. Horne (1996). 'Relationship Marketing: The Case for the University Alumni Affinity Credit Card', *Journal of Marketing Management* 12: 189–199.

Yankelovich, S. and White Inc. (1985), *The Charitable Behaviour of Americans, Management Survey*, Independent Sector, Washington, DC.

Yavas, U., G. Riecken and R. Parameswaren (1980), 'Using Psychographics to Profile Potential Donors', *Business Atlanta* 30(5): 41–45.

6

Marketing health

Few NHS organisations yet practise marketing consciously but many of its ingredients are already familiar to them. (Sheaff 1991: 1)

Under the old regime consultants could afford to develop specific areas of medicine governed by their own interests. Under the new regime, hospital portfolios must carefully match the needs of their specific market, thus ensuring that adequate levels of demand can be maintained. (Sargeant 1999: 240)

We must also accelerate the pace of change in our public services. And all with one aim in mind: to redesign our public services around the individuals they serve. (Blair 2001)

The National Health Service (NHS), and how it can meet the needs of its market, are a major topic of political debate. The NHS has become one of the top issues in voters' minds, and the market-oriented Labour party was elected in 1997 with the pledge of improving the system. Marketing techniques and principles have been introduced into the NHS since the 1980s, but existing empirical studies and informal conversations with health practitioners suggest that the actual practice of marketing in health falls short of full-scale development to, and implementation of, a market orientation. Public satisfaction with the NHS is generally poor. It is therefore an important issue for political marketing scholarship.

Marketing and health were first connected in academic literature by the first journal article by Zaltman and Vertinsky (1971). The majority of academics observing this and working in this area tend to come from management science, applying theory once intended for business. Literature in that discipline falls into two areas; services marketing (which includes financial and travel services as well as the public sector; see Laing et al. 2001) and non-profit marketing. Yet within the mainstream marketing academic environment, not all of this literature has been adapted to suit the different conditions that all political organisations present. There is also a literature called public sector management, but Graham (1994: 365) suggested that 'despite the attention marketing would like to have in the public sector it is still seen as irrelevant or inappropriate by academic contributors in the field of public administration'.

Health was only recently included within the discussion of political marketing.[1] As health is a major political issue for parties, it seems sensible to include it within political marketing. It is also an area studied from a policy perspective within political science. It is subject to government influence and always will be, no matter how involved business or private finance becomes. It is an area where elites (health care professionals) and masses (patients) relate to each other and interact. It contains professional, expert ideals and is not yet accepted by society as an area that can be purely left to the business market. As one academic observer noted, 'the private sector measurements are efficiency and profitability', while the 'dominating ideas' in the public sector are 'justice and democratic control' (Walsh 1994: 67). It is politics, it is not a business, it is subject to marketing, and so it is part of political marketing.

Indeed, in a speech shortly after being elected to his second term, 'Reform of the Public Services', Tony Blair (2001) made clear the political and government focus on public services, and the need to adopt marketing approaches, specifically a market-oriented approach:

> Public services need reform if they are to deliver the uniformly high standards and consumer focus that people expect in the twenty-first century . . . Unlike 1945, people don't put up with the basics. In a consumer age, they expect quality, choice and standards and too often don't experience them . . . there are some things that the public sector can learn from the private sector. Private companies can in many cases be more responsive to the immediate needs of demanding consumers. If they don't they go out of business. They know that poor service, lack of courtesy, massive delays, destroys their image and their success. It would be surprising if the public sector could not learn something from that responsiveness to consumers. The best parts already do.

The basic frameworks used here are designed to facilitate discussion of the issues surrounding health care marketing. They do not replicate, or try to compete with, the detailed marketing-focused theories offered by current services marketing literature within management studies. This chapter simply aims to explain why health care is being subject to marketing and how marketing might be applied, and to raise some of the issues in applying marketing to a public sector area, rather than to offer a full academic analysis of marketing models of health care.

Like other chapters, it does not claim to provide an empirical, positivist test of the degree of health care marketing. There is, though, a difference between this and previous chapters: whilst there is only one monarchy, only two major parties, only one BBC and only one Scottish parliament, the number of health organisations is in the hundreds. This is also true of education and local government, dealt with in later chapters. In these areas, it is not possible within the constraints of this book to provide the same kind of focused, empirical discussion that can be conducted with a smaller number of political entities. Furthermore, this chapter on health in particular relies substantially on existing studies rather than conducting primary research, because whilst it does not make sense to try to replicate these, it would reduce the value of the book if the chapter were omitted solely because this area has already been researched. The main value in discussing marketing and health care is that it demonstrates the overall argument of the book: that marketing is being used in a wide range of organisations. There are major forces pushing for the marketing of health care, including the NHS being the point of delivery for New Labour's party election promises. Nevertheless, as will be explored, there are many issues with this as with any area of political marketing.

Theory: the components of health care marketing

Health is conventionally thought of as a public service (for discussion about public service marketing in general see Hannagan 1992; Collins and Butler 1998; Sheaff 1991; Chapman and Cowdell 1998; Walsh 1994; Graham 1994; Laing and McKee 1998; Citizen's Charter Unit 1992; Holloway et al. 1999; Bottery 1998; Christy and Brown 1999). As Sheaff (1991: 39) commented, 'marketing can and should be applied to NHS services but simply imitating commercial marketing is unlikely to be successful or desirable'.[2]

Nature of the organisation
Health care includes health care organisations, such as hospitals and GPs' (general practitioners') surgeries, and also more general health support, including psychological and social factors. The main focus here will be GPs' surgeries and hospitals. The NHS has historically presented many problems (see Sheaff 1991). There is a huge variation in practice, wide geographical distribution of resources, a 'highly individualistic approach by medical practitioners to their work' (Laing and Galbraith 1997: 115), and demand has increased (Bottery 1998: 43).

Product
The basic product is health care, but it is extremely intangible, both physically and mentally, and includes many factors, such as:

- treatment of an illness – e.g. detection, administration of medicine, operation, rehabilitation and convalescence;
- support for ill-health – e.g. terminal care;
- health professionals and administrative staff, their training and working conditions;
- hospital and surgery waiting rooms;
- doctors' bedside manner;
- appointment system and receptionists' manner;
- reputation or league table position;
- consultation, diagnosis, treatment and after care;
- promotion of good health, factors encouraging good health, and action against ill-health e.g. poor housing or diet.

Although the main aspect of the product might be the treatment, with the end goal being a return to full health, other factors are also important (see Strachan 2002; Kinnell and MacDougall 1997: 78; Sheaff 1991: 29; Hannagan 1992: 35 for further discussion). Tappin (2003), for example, cited a new health centre as a new product that was communicated to staff as an investment within their workplace. Consumer behaviour analysis suggests that patients often assess delivery success on factors other than treatment, whilst many health care organisations apply marketing to the other factors such as a doctor's bedside manner, more than the actual main treatment, (Chapman and Cowdell 1998: 104).

Goal

The most dominant goal is to provide the best possible health given set resources. The NHS in the UK traditionally tried to provide good quality health care free of charge to anyone who needed it, but today there is concern about the extent to which the NHS is really able to achieve this. Dr Giri Rajaratnum, director of public health for North Stoke and South Stoke Primary Care Trusts (PCTs), argued that the purpose of the NHS was:

> to secure through the resources available the greatest possible improvement in the physical and mental health of the nation by:
> - Promoting health.
> - Preventing ill-health.
> - Diagnosing and treating disease and injury.
> - Caring for those with long term illness and disability who require the services of the NHS. (Rajaratnum 2003)

Market

The most obvious market for the health service is patients. However, this view is oversimplistic and highly debatable. It could include various groups (Sheaff 1991: 51), which are overlapping but potentially conflicting, including:

- medical professionals (doctors, nurses, consultants, health visitors, community and district nurses);
- support staff (receptionists, cleaners, building maintenance, security);
- politicians and civil servants;
- the health authority, central government and local government;
- patients, patients' relatives and carers;
- related organisations, e.g. nursing homes, local council and charities;
- media;
- suppliers of technology, medicine (e.g. the pharmaceutical industry), laundry services, food.

It could be argued that although overall the entire population is the market for the NHS, and perhaps within this voters are dominant because they determine who is in government, which in turn decides health policy. As Pauline Strachan (2002), medical advisor to NHS Grampian noted, there is significant 'potential for tension between needs of individual, community and population'. Furthermore, as Rajaratnum (2003) observed, politicians are one of the key audiences for the NHS, but they need to ensure 'it maintains their power'. Central government also takes advice from medical professionals or pharmaceutical companies (see Duckenfield 2003), which can have more influence on policy, especially if the governing party is more product oriented: government may be more inclined to take the view of the health practitioners rather than the users of the health service.

Delivery and assessing performance
The complex nature of the product makes it difficult for assessment of delivery to be made. The standard measure of profit used in the business world cannot be used in the political arena (see Kinnell and MacDougall 1997: 75). Rajaratnum (2003) explained how Stoke PCT used statistics on progress with reducing heart disease or life expectancy, but of course, such results can be affected by a whole variety of factors, including education, average income in the area, housing, the provision of leisure facilities by the local council and the behaviour of the people themselves – casual factors not controllable by a primary care trust (see also Strachan 2003).

As already noted, a market orientation has not permeated all areas of the health system. The chapter will therefore outline and illustrate the nature of all three approaches, beginning with a product orientation.

Product-oriented health care: doctor knows best

Definition of a product-oriented health care organisation
A product-oriented health care organisation will think it knows what is best for the patient and design its product or service according to what the health professionals think is best. Little or no room is given to the concerns and ideas of the patient themselves; no market intelligence is undertaken; the patient is expected to be deferent to the doctor's judgement. See Box 6.1.

A product orientation was once very prevalent in health care. It has been undermined by changes in government policy and increasing questioning and criticism by patients, but it is none the less still prevalent throughout the system. Sargeant (1999: 236) contends that many organisations 'still have no conception of the term "customer", and remain steadfastly focused on management issues related to the product/service being provided'. The approach therefore 'regards the patient as being in passive receipt of their treatment and affords little scope for a genuine interaction to take place between the healthcare provider and its patients' (Sargeant 1999: 238). Previously, people had much less choice and acted out of habit. Furthermore there were no general standards of health care to be met, and standards varied significantly between regions. In terms of communication, 'management may hold the view that patients will find their way to it

---

Box 6.1 The process for a product-oriented health care organisation

Stage 1: Product design
A product-oriented health organisation will focus on the product, not the consumer, and design its product according to what decision-makers – doctors or politicians – think is best. They do not listen to patients or the general population, because they have the medical training and expertise necessary to judge, and judge more successfully.

Stage 2: Communication
A product-oriented health organisation may neglect communication, assuming patients will find the service on offer if they need to. Doctors and other medical staff assume they will get patients whatever they do, and will receive local standing and respect because of their medical expertise and trust in their ability. Support for their work is assumed.

Stage 3: Delivery
Product-oriented health care organisations treat their patients in the way medical staff think is best and measure success in the way they judge is possible. They do not seek to question whether they are meeting all their patients' needs; they follow their own priorities because the medical practitioner knows better than anyone else. They will not attempt to solicit feedback on whether they are seen to perform satisfactorily overall. They aim to deliver what they think is best. Overall, product-oriented health care suggests a more traditional, 'doctor-knows-best' approach, far removed from the idea of the consumer or patient being king.

---

without help' (Hannagan 1992: 154). One GP surgery held various clinics, on smoking and asthma for example, but only communicated these via the practice notice board, demanding that the patient go to them to find out, not the other way round.

Perhaps surprisingly, empirical research suggests that much of the UK's health care is product oriented. Teasdale (1992: 62) observed that the NHS 'is a very large organisation which decides for itself what is best for patients, and then develops its services accordingly. Patients are expected to be grateful for what they are offered, and to put up with delays or other inadequacies because we tell them we are short of resources.' Laing and Galbraith (1997)'s work on acute NHS hospital trusts in Scotland suggested that there is a significant lack of focus on the needs of the patient, with the views of the professionals remaining paramount: 'the prevailing structures reflect the established professional aggregations of staff as opposed to the aggregations of services demanded by the market' (see also Kinnell and MacDougall 1997: 75; Sargeant 1999: 239). Patients of health care did not have the knowledge to act like consumers (Sargeant 1999: 247; see Wilson 1994; Laing et al. 2002: 112). There was also no competition (Sargeant 1999: 239–240).

Painted hospitals but wait to get in there? Sales-oriented health care

Definition of a sales-oriented health care organisation
A sales-oriented health care organisation will design its service according to what the decision-makers or elites think is best, but aim to present it in a way that attracts and pleases patients. The focus is not on the product, but on the presentation of the product or service, to provide patient satisfaction. The designers are those in charge – be it politicians, civil servants, managers or doctors – rather than those who actually receive the product. See Box 6.2.

Causes of a move to sales orientation
Government legislation and increasingly critical patients have encouraged hospitals and GP surgeries to move to a sales orientation: not really changing the product but focusing on better communication (Sargeant 1999: 250; Meidan and Moutinho 1993: 205). However, the understanding of marketing is generally very narrow in scope (Laing and Galbraith 1995: 7). Sheaff (1991: 34–35) commented that 'governments are likelier to use marketing of NHS services as a cosmetic for existing health policy rather than to assist the NHS in meeting consumer demands and needs'. Laing and Galbraith (1995: 9), in their study of Scottish hospital acute trusts, argued that 'internal considerations remain pre-eminent in dictating the service products offered by the unit, but supporting sales and promotional activities are developed in order to secure custom'. A sales orientation is at least partly possible because of the complexity of health: consumers of health care cannot judge their treatment so easily (see also Gilligan and Lowe 1995: 47; Sargeant 1999: 242). It is also easier to change, easier to demonstrate, and may have more influence than the actual treatment quality – at least in the short term.

The only major changes that sales-oriented organisations undergo are in presentation and staff. In the 1980s there was a big transformation in the 'presentation' of health – the development of leaflets, the refurbishment of waiting rooms, new signs and new desks for the reception. One example of this is that the South Thames Regional Authority (1994: 6) argued that good practice in a GP surgery was to provide a well-signposted, well-lit building, with a good waiting area, that would welcome patients and have a positive affect on their health care experience. Also, GPs now choose whether to use hospitals or not, and the response of the latter has been to create 'selling' departments or staff 'whose primary function is to solicit business from health authorities and GP fund holders' (Sargeant 1999: 240). Yet such factors do not actually consist of anything to do with the health care or treatment being offered.

In terms of market intelligence, research has been conducted into service satisfaction – that is, what determines a patient's assessment of the product delivery – but these results are used in communication efforts rather than product design. As Laing and Galbraith (1995: 7) noted, much marketing within the NHS 'has been technique driven and centred on the activities of the designated

---

Box 6.2 The process for a sales-oriented health care organisation

Stage 1: Product design
A sales-oriented health care organisation designs its product to suit what it thinks is best. There is no regard for public opinion or demands, or the need to change behaviour to suit other bodies.

Stage 2: Market intelligence
A sales-oriented health care organisation will conduct market intelligence (debate, discussion, commissions, focus groups, polls, reports) on the reaction of its market to its behaviour and performance, to find out where it has strengths and weaknesses; what patients like about the treatment and service; what they think could be improved; and what the health care organisation may have a good or bad reputation for, especially locally.

Stage 3: Communication
A sales-oriented health care organisation will create and run an effective communications system to publicise its best work to its market, including prospective patients, other health care providers and prospective staff. Responding to the results of market intelligence, it may attempt to downplay its weaknesses and focus on its strengths. For example, it may seek to attract more patients from a target market such as the locality. It may showcase one aspect of its treatment that is known for being excellent. Communication is designed to improve the reputation of the health care organisation, and its form and style will be designed to suit its market. Communication includes material on websites, surgery guides or leaflets. It can also include the downplaying of any potential negative publicity from any problems that arise or complaints that are made.

Stage 4: Campaign
A sales-oriented health care organisation may also undertake mini-campaigns to boost its reputation and attract new patients, or advertise particular treatments, clinics or new service of any kind. It may also engage in social marketing campaigns to persuade people to behave in a particular manner.

Stage 5: Delivery
Sales-oriented health care organisations will treat their patients and intend to deliver the intended outcome, but in a way which aims to deliver what the organisations think is best.

Stage 6: Communication of delivery
The health care organisation will also attempt to communicate the work it has done.

"marketing" professionals within the organisation'. A sales-oriented approach can also lead to social marketing – campaigning to try to change society's behaviour, according to what the elite think. Social marketing is the application of marketing concepts and techniques to the marketing of various socially beneficial ideas, and it can be done in response to public needs, but in a sales-oriented environment is more likely to be driven by health practitioners or politicians. This aspect of sales-oriented health care may be considered less unethical than party campaigning, for example, because there is an argument that campaign and communication can be used 'for the good' of society: social marketing, on a particular disease or issue, is trying to change behaviour in the interest of society as a whole.

However, if it really is trying to change behaviour (see Kinnell and MacDougall 1997: 79) then it is difficult to see it as market oriented, especially if the content and design are to 'preach' correct behaviour. Other campaigns may also involve short-term communication to promote a new service or attract new patients to counteract falling numbers at a GP's surgery. They may be carried out to provide positive publicity for a health organisations. Sales-oriented health organisations will try to communicate anything positive whilst reducing information and media awareness of any problems. This is a more persuasive form of delivery; placing greater emphasis on presenting rather than actual delivery. It may focus on more visible achievements, such as a new building or refurbished waiting room, rather than an actual improvement in health that is harder to measure.

The rising costs of the NHS and concerns about inefficiency have stimulated at least a partial move towards market-oriented political marketing. Gilligan and Lowe (1995: 14) observed that health care organisations currently face 'some of their biggest changes and challenges of the post-war period', which has led to 'a substantial rethink of how they are run'. Like all other political organisations, health care organisations have faced increased pressure to become market oriented because of the changing nature of users.

Market-oriented health care

Definition
A market-oriented health organisation would seek to design its product to meet the needs and wants of the patients it seeks to treat. It would conduct market intelligence to determine the demands of its patients and respond to these in designing the product. Whilst naturally using professional judgement on how to meet patients' needs, the users' demands would be placed above those of the provider of the service. See Box 6.3.

Causes of a move towards market orientation
One major change is the information available to patients (Strachan 2003). Berkowitz and Flexner (1980) argued that increasingly people are becoming 'activist health care consumers'. The internet provides a plethora of world-wide information; there are also health magazines, medical textbooks, libraries, media, trusts and foundations (Laing et al. 2002: 121). There is home diagnostic equipment available in the shops. Political consumers are more critical and desire

---

Box 6.3 The process for a market-oriented health care organisation

Stage 1: Market intelligence

A market-oriented health care organisation will conduct a wide range of market intelligence (debate, discussion, commissions, focus groups, polls, reports, from the public, related bodies and health staff) about what the organisation is good at and not good at, and think about how it might be improved. It is concerned with what the public need and want from it, not just what they think of it as it is. It will therefore include debates about the nature and role of health staff, service delivery, health priorities and best treatment, and involve related outside bodies and parliamentarians as well as the views of the public.

Stage 2: Product design

A market-oriented health care organisation designs its product, including treatment, manner of staff, waiting times and nature of the buildings, to suit the results from market intelligence. It aims to respond in the most effective manner to the demands of patients and allocate resources accordingly.

Stage 3: Product adjustment

- *Achievability:* Staff in market-oriented health care organisations will not promise what they can't deliver: they will aim to be as accurate as possible in predicting the timing of treatment and its outcome, and to ensure that general expectations, standards and promises can be fulfilled and achieved.
- *Internal reaction analysis:* For the product design to be effective, it needs to be supported by the staff within the organisation, so any proposed changes to the product may need to be adjusted to take account of the views of staff.
- *Competition analysis:* It will take into account the needs and views of any competing organisations, such as other health care providers or hospitals, and adjust its behaviour to suit them, maybe cutting back on some services or developing new services to meet a need not met by other organisations.
- *Support analysis:* A health care organisation may target some product changes in particular areas where it is especially weak or does not meet demand or attract patients. For example, it may develop a clinic to deal with drug abuse if this becomes a particular problem in the locality, or change its hours to suit working parents.

Stage 4: Implementation

For political marketing to work it has to be implemented effectively, using all the guidelines from marketing management literature. The findings from Stages 1–3 of the process must be implemented and a majority within the organisation need to accept the new behaviour broadly and comply with it. The organisation must therefore proceed carefully, especially if major change is required. Any change also needs to be carefully communicated and explained, and extra training offered if needed to help staff comply with the expected new behaviour.

continued on next page

Box 6.3 continued

Stage 5: Communication
The health care organisation will then communicate its work effectively and efficiently, using all the techniques, tools and staff of a sales-oriented organisation. Communication is designed to ensure that the public is aware of the work of the health care organisation, how they may participate and what the service offers them. The style of communication is also geared to suit the audience: for example, if the organisation seeks to reach particular patients it must communicate somewhere they will see the information, and in a manner they can easily access and understand.

Stage 6: Campaign
A market-oriented health care organisation may undertake mini-campaigns to boost its profile, attract new patients, or highlight a new service available.

Stage 7: Delivery
The health care organisation will treat the patient in the manner proposed, and aim to achieve the best possible outcome which meets the patient's needs to the best possible extent.

Stage 8: Communication of delivery
It will also attempt to communicate the work it has done; for example, making it clear to individual patients what the outcome is, and to the local community. It will also solicit feedback and user opinion on, for example, the effect of particular treatment in case any improvement might be made in future. This stage will be continual.

a greater say in their health treatment (Sargeant 1999: 247; Laing and Galbraith 1997: 116). Supporting the idea of the political marketing revolution as a whole, the national media is also cited as a factor in causing patients to be more critical health care consumers (see Laing et al. 2002: 115), because the media always picks out negative stories: 'one 90-year old lady left on a trolley is a story, one hundred treated well is not'. In recent years a number of stories have hit the headlines, such as the Alderhay Scandal and the Harold Shipman case in 2002, where there were reports of atypical numbers of babies dying at Alderhay hospital and of elderly patients dying under the care of GP Dr Shipman, and these have remained in people's minds. The consequence of this has been an increased focus on the empowerment of health users (Laing et al. 2002: 95; Meidan and Moutinho 1993: 205; Griffiths 1988; Gilligan and Lowe 1995: 3).

Furthermore, the public has become increasingly vociferous about its concern for the quality of health care being offered in the UK, which puts greater pressure on market-oriented parties seeking electoral support to deal with the issue (see Lees-Marshment and Laing 2002; and Laing et al. 2002: 115). Combined with the ideology of the Conservative governments of the 1980s in favour of markets and cutting public spending, this has provided the political will power to introduce marketing (see Griffiths 1983: 9; DHSS 1984: 9). Kinnell and MacDougall (1997: 84) contend that marketing:

> has a major role to play in the new competitive NHS specifically in relation to con-
> sumer orientation and the identification and targeting of patients' needs. Ensuring
> a responsive health service and providing a balance between cost containment and
> quality improvement will be the main objectives for marketing in the NHS into the
> twenty-first century.

Stage 1: Market intelligence

Market intelligence informs behaviour in many respects, including users' needs, priorities, staff concerns and future societal changes (Sheaff 1991: 85; Kinnell and MacDougall 1997: 82). There is a rich variety of methods open to the NHS, as with any organisation (for further detail see Kinnell and MacDougall 1997: 82; Sheaff 1991).

The market intelligence method chosen will depend on the aspect of user opinion or needs and wants being researched, plus factors such as cost and time to conduct these methods. Individual GP surgeries conduct market intelligence research, for example, through patient suggestions forms in the practice, by ana-lysing complaints, by conducting satisfaction surveys or by analysing local needs (Kinnell and MacDougall 1997: 83; Sargeant 1999: 248). Large practices may even employ a member of staff specifically to carry this out. GPs need to think about both the current and future health care needs of current and potential patients, and to use researchers to gather statistical data on the catchment area, in order to identify different needs and plan what services to provide. A commu-nity may have particularly high numbers of children, the elderly or asthma suf-ferers. New patients are normally asked to undergo a free health check which also provides useful information on patient needs. If GPs simply consult their patients and offer them choice in treatment, this is a form of market intelligence or market-oriented product design. Patient choice is an increasing theme in policy and academic discussions (see, for example, Gage and Rickman 2000; Coulter et al. 1999; Murley 1995; MORI 1997; Curtis et al. 1998; Dixon et al. 1997; Ovretveit 1996; IPPR 2002).

Market intelligence is not just concerned with patients. As Duckenfield (2003: 124–125) noted, the National Institute for Clinical Excellence (NICE) conducts research with the government, the pharmaceutical industry and patient groups. Duckenfield (2003: 127) found that NICE consulted industry more than patient groups – but perhaps this is indicative of an incomplete market orientation.

Indeed, public consultation exercises – a traditional means of political activ-ity – are, as Duckenfield (2003: 131) suggests, 'actually mechanisms of political marketing'. One notable example of this is that on 31 May 2000 the Labour government launched a nationwide consultation exercise on the NHS. The sec-retary of state for health, Alan Milburn, said 'I want to be able to say that for the first time in the twenty first century, we have an NHS that is there not just for some patients, but for everybody.' The government distributed 12 million leaflets in surgeries and hospitals around the country that invited people to list the three things they most wanted to see improved in the NHS. Leaflets were also made available in supermarkets such as Safeway, shops such as Boots, opticians and public libraries. The government ran a series of focus groups to explore the public's priorities for improving the NHS; six modernisation action teams were created to bring together professionals, patient representatives, front-line staff and other key players to give their views on what should be in the national plan, in the areas of partnership, professionals, performance, patient empowerment, patient access and prevention. However, the process was subject to extreme criticism and problems, because the leaflets gave a misleading date, which gave the impression that it was too late to reply: it seemed the deadline was only 24 hours away and therefore the reply could not arrive by post in time.

The New Labour government also initiated a people's panel to talk about health. They also planned to conduct 'patients' fora' for 2004, with five being conducted in Stoke-on-Trent, for example, the idea being to 'listen to what local councils are saying in terms of their needs for health' (Tappin 2003).[3] The trust also draws on 'expert patients'; 'people we can learn from', who have been ill and can also share their experience and support future patients (Tappin 2003). Similarly, NHS Grampian engages in consultation exercises, focus groups and the use of public representatives to involve the public in making decisions (Strachan 2002). In Scotland, there are also health councils: 15 independent bodies that represent the opinions of patients and the public.

Health-care organisations can also take account of how patients and GPs choose, that is, consumer behaviour. Within health there are various models of consumer behaviour (see Laing et al. 2002: 104–105, 107, for further details). The consensus from research is that patients assess the quality of the health care on three main intangible factors, seen by Bopp (1990) to be expressive caring, expressive professionalism and expressive competence. As these are intangible, patients use other indicators to make such assessments. The SERVQUAL model can be utilised here (see Lytle and Mokwa 1992 for further details). Further research examines how to enhance service quality and the gaps between expectation and delivery conceptualised by Parasuraman et al. (1988). There has also been significant research over the last 35 years into what aspects of medical care most affect patients' perceptions of service quality, which health organisations can draw upon.

Stage 2: Product design
The move to designing health with the market in mind has come from government changes in regulation. Government policy has increasingly placed greater emphasis on consumer satisfaction: designing the product to suit the patient (see for example DHSS 1989, 1984; Kinnell and MacDougall 1997: 72; Sargeant 1999: 239–240). In 1991 the Patient's Charter was published, with a second edition issued in 1995, and this arguably marked a significant shift towards a market-oriented approach by recognising patients' rights and basic standards to expect from the health services.

There are subtle signs of a more responsive system. GPs have moved focus from cure to preventative health care. Some GPs engage in a monitoring system, seeing their patients regularly for a check-up whether they are ill or not (see Sargeant 1999: 240). GPs may run health or wellness clinics and seek to facilitate healthier lifestyles. Indeed, health promotion is an important part of the product. According to Pauline Strachan (2002), it includes immunisation pro-grammes; lifestyle – diet, physical activity and harm avoidance, including nutri-tion and physical activity prescription programmes; and screening programmes – genetic screening, antenatal screening for conditions such as Down syndrome, cystic fibrosis, and colorectal and breast cancer.

Opening hours are also a significant characteristic; one surgery holds evening clinics to maximise the number of women likely to attend for cervical smear tests; evening hours are generally important for those who work in the day. Also important is the nature of the facilities within the surgery building, such as a play area for children, as well as its location with regard to access by its catchment area. The system for making an appointment to see a GP is also an important issue. After conducting market intelligence into what patients thought of the service, health staff found that one major area of concern was waiting times. They therefore introduced a staggered appointment system so that there were always a number of appointments for relatively urgent cases within three days, whilst most would be available within a week, but a fair number of spaces were kept clear for the most urgent to see a doctor within one day.

Hospitals also have greater incentives to offer a wanted product since GPs will now choose between different hospitals when deciding where to send their patients. Hospitals no longer receive patients automatically but compete against each other for custom. As Sargeant (1999: 240) noted, in the new market 'hospi-tal portfolios must carefully match the needs of their specific market, thus ensur-ing that adequate levels of demand can be maintained'. However, Laing and Galbraith (1997: 116) argued that 'there is little evidence that acute trusts are responding to these mounting market-led pressures'. They conducted research by means of an in-depth study of acute NHS trust hospitals in Scotland. The organisations do not offer an integrated and market-focused service, so the effect on 'the delivery of services and achieving a shift from a product to a market-led approach' has been extremely limited (Laing and Galbraith 1997: 118). Therefore there has not been a 'refocusing of services on the needs of patients rather than those of service professionals' (Laing and Galbraith 1997: 118).

Over the past few years I have easily been able to get visiting speakers from the NHS to talk to students about marketing health, and there is clear awareness amongst practitioners of the need to respond to and listen to patients and the public. However, not all staff are familiar enough with marketing to be able to understand completely what it could be about, what they could do to be more responsive (Kinnell and MacDougall 1997: 73). Laing and McKee (1998: 582) found that 'the appointment of dedicated marketing managers, or the establish-ment of dedicated marketing departments, has been the exception rather than the norm'. Marketing managers in the NHS often work in isolation, so they do not have anyone with the same tasks or approaches to support them. This is made worse by the natural hostility towards marketing and the introduction of commercial methods into the public sector (see Laing and Galbraith 1996).

Stage 3: Product adjustment

Achievability   Like political parties, health care organisations need to ensure they can achieve their promises and meet the demands they say they will. Particularly as demands in health will always exceed the possible supply, it is very important to adjust the product on offer to make it achievable, or delivery will always fall short of expectation. This may lead to demand management to ensure that the public do not have unrealistic expectations: see below under 'Stage 5: Communication' (see Chapman and Cowdell 1998: 123).

Internal reaction analysis   It is important to involve staff in any proposed changes, consulting them where appropriate, in order to aid implementation. This was noted by Tappin (2003) to be of high priority in the PCT in Stoke, for example. Other organisations conduct internal market intelligence to ensure their staff are happy. For example, one GP's surgery talks to staff at a weekly meeting and also disseminates external market intelligence to them there.

Competition analysis   As Sargeant (1999: 240) noted, hospitals need to give 'careful consideration to the relative skills of other providers in their area'. Health-care organisations need to identify the competition and try to differentiate themselves from others. There may also be sense in co-operating with some other organisations where service gaps exist: 'collaborative agreements could be developed to ensure that adequate coverage of all medical specialisms is provided within one geographical region' (Sargeant 1999: 251). Co-operation can also be beneficial for health promotion; for example, with organisations such as councils on issue like housing.

Support analysis   This involves segmenting the market and focusing or targeting resources on certain groups. Demands are rising faster than the resources to meet them (Strachan 2003; see also Kinnell and MacDougall 1997: 83). For example, Stoke PCT has a programme called 'Sure Start' and other measures which focus resources on the more deprived areas (Tappin 2003). Other initiatives have been non-smoking clinics, with targets to achieve for those affected by smoking (Tappin 2003). Targeting resources on deprived areas is particularly important given that they will tend to demand, expect and use less from the NHS but possibly need more, as noted by Pauline Strachan (2002) (see also IPPR 2002). GPs can offer clinics for smoking, asthma, diabetic and heart trouble. Segmentation is also important, because different groups have different needs and ways of access to health care that need to be taken account of when designing the product.

Strachan (2003) noted how the homeless are not registered; those who are working may need to take time off work or to obtain child care to get treatment; the elderly need public transport; and those living in remote and rural areas also need transport and branch surgeries to gain access to health.

Stage 4: Implementation

Marketing health care is not easy, especially as internal organisation and culture are very important in the overall success of marketing. There is a natural opposition to marketing: Laing and Galbraith (1995: 6) noted that 'the health service tends to view itself as being unique and as fundamentally different from other sectors of the economy, resulting in a reluctance to adopt and absorb new ideas and approaches from other spheres'. Sheaff (1991: 155–156) argued that leaders need to give support and reward marketing behaviour (see Sargeant 1999: 251). It is generally difficult for any product design to be implemented throughout the NHS. As Laing and Galbraith (1997: 119) noted, although in business there are specified standards of care, which can be implemented throughout branches nationwide, 'within the NHS, specifically in acute trusts, there is a lack of such standardisation or harmonisation of service delivery in terms of speed, specification and standards across service professionals working for the same organisations'. In health care, there are a number of different providers of the product. As Sargeant (1999: 242) observed, a patient going to hospital for just a routine operation 'will have to deal with administrative staff, nurses, anaesthetists, catering staff, hospital porters, a variety of physicians, and their own surgeon'. Implementation is crucial but not easy to achieve.

Stage 5: Communication

Health-care organisations can use communication both internally and externally. Communication within the health service can be about informing and reminding the public, rather than persuading as with sales-oriented organisations. For example, as GPs develop new preventative measures such as wellness clinics, they need to let their patients know about this new product aspect. GPs need to give out information about the need for child injections and flu and to advertise in places where their target audience – patients – will see the adverts. Posters about clinics, say, may be displayed in the waiting room or in local libraries and community centres. GPs could be more advanced and send out letters or direct mail to those most likely to respond, using a database of patients' records. New patients are also given a practice leaflet outlining the services available and introducing the key staff. The same type of communication can be used more widely; Stoke PCT has a leaflet for the public entitled 'Your Guide to Local Services' (Tappin 2003) and also appreciates the importance of internal communication with staff. Tappin (2003) noted how the Stoke PCT had initiated a PCT newsletter to ensure staff were informed of any developments. Newcastle-under-Lyme Primary Care Group (2000) also produces a newsletter. Health organisations need to put out positive stories to counteract the natural negativity of the media, and to try to improve public perception of health provision (see Tappin 2003; also noted by staff connected with other health organisations, informally consulted for this study). One problem with communication is the cost of producing leaflets, designing and maintaining websites and employing public relations staff: this can prove a barrier to providing market-oriented communication.

Demand management or demarketing – whereby instead of trying to increase demand for a product the organisation tries actively to reduce it – is also an important aspect of market-oriented health care. Research into health care marketing has found that one of the major difficulties in achieving satisfaction is that there is often a mismatch between customer expectations, as identified by market intelligence, and actual delivery (Sargeant 1999: 242). The health care organisation therefore needs to try to manage demands through its communication – or even go as far as to demarket to reduce demands (see Mark and Brennan 1995, for example). Communication can also be used to reduce or respond more effectively to demand. Increasingly, health care organisations are using communication to encourage patients to engage in self-diagnosis and treatment of minor ailments, to cut down demand on the system. As Sargeant (1999: 249) observed, most GPS have 'spent at least one sleepless night attending to a range of relatively minor call-outs which could easily have waited until the following day for a routine appointment at the surgery. Marketing can help educate patients to recognise how best to use the services that the GP can provide.' Upon joining a new GP surgery after moving, I was given a rather hefty booklet on how to deal with minor ailments. In addition, NHS Direct was created as a means to reduce demand on GP and hospitals. This is a telephone service on which people can speak to trained nurses who can give them advice on minor conditions or refer them to a GP or hospital for more serious conditions. Demarketing is therefore another means of trying to manage demand. As Mark and Brennan (1995: 17) note, it has not been studied. In health care, as resources provided by the state (or privately paying consumer) decline, the population ages and patients become more critical and demanding, there is sometimes the need to reduce the demand for the health product. Prioritising funds for neglected sections of society, such as single mothers or the elderly, can seek to meet market demand, thereby retaining a market orientation.

Stage 6: Campaign
Health organisations may undertake public information campaigns or engage in social marketing: campaigns to influence people's behaviour or actively to encourage them to use certain products. There is increasing concern about and emphasis on health promotion, to prevent problems occurring in the first place. In Aberdeen, for example, Health Promotion (promoting better health through activities such as walking, a good diet and avoiding smoking) ran a shop on the high street and engaged in producing leaflets on local walks to improve fitness. The Scottish Health Executive ran a number of television adverts in 2002 to try to encourage the public to stop smoking, use public transport etc. (see Douglas

2002). Health promotion organisations run throughout the UK: Stoke-on-Trent also has a directorate of health promotion. Like other agencies, Stoke Health Promotion deals with sexual health, oral health, immunisation, alcohol, children and families, teenage pregnancies and drugs. The unit has a wide range of staff, including posts in media and marketing, and engages in overall marketing activities, such as intelligence, design and product, creating business plans, and completing reports to analyse delivery and effectiveness. But the unit's specific goal throughout all this is to promote better health – to reduce illness before it gets to the local doctor or hospital.

In terms of techniques, all the usual marketing tools are used by health promotion: advertisements, leaflets, posters, gimmicks, radio, television and print media. North Stoke PCT Health Promotion recently ran a campaign on sexual health, in conjunction with an international and national promotion and World AIDS Day. It used adverts in newspapers and on television, a poster placed in local council and gay venues, flyers and leaflets (see www.shepstoke.com/shep/default.htm for further details). In this way health care organisations actually try to reduce demand, rather than stimulate it as businesses do. However, health education campaigns can be prone to failure if 'they do not take into account why people act as they do' (Hogg 1999: 52; see also Douglas 2003). To be more effective, campaigns need to be market oriented in themselves and driven by the market they're trying to influence, not the ideals of the professionals. The nature of communication and the mass media also needs to be taken into account (see Budd and McCrone 1981; for further details on social marketing see, for example, Fox and Kotler 1980, and Kotler and Roberto 1989). Campaigns may also involve short-term communication to launch a new service of some kind.

Stage 7: Delivery

Delivery is very important, obviously, but there are various difficulties associated with delivery of health care. As Laing et al. (2002: 51) noted, the 'delivery of health care within modern health systems is concerned to a significant degree with the management of a complex set of inter-organisational and inter-professional relationships'. Central government faces many obstacles when trying to control always the delivery (see Laing and Lees-Marshment 2002). One of the difficulties with delivery in politics is that users are not looking for the product or policy as such, but for the benefits it is expected to bring (see Hannagan 1992: 13). A further complication is that the users themselves at last partly determine delivery: illness can be a consequence of poor diet, lack of exercise, and bad habits such as heavy drinking and smoking.

Another aspect of the importance of delivery is the procedures for dealing with anything that goes wrong or if a patient wants to complain. Tappin (2003) noted that in the Stoke PCT, 'we have to make sure that patients' complaints are listened to in a robust, open and transparent way', and Stoke has a patient advisory liaison service (PALS) to deal with complaints. It is in the interest of any trust to handle any complaints carefully, especially if the media is alerted to any problems.

Stage 8: Communication of delivery
Communication of delivery will also be carried out. The organisation will continually seek to communicate any progress it makes or responses it gives to concerns. This can be done in a variety of ways, through meetings, reports, media
events or information on a website.

Overall analysis of the degree of market orientation in the health service

Despite the pressures to change, empirical studies indicate that the market-
oriented concept (as opposed to communication and market intelligence techniques), has been slow to develop within the NHS (see Laing and Galbraith 1995:
6). Clearly, some changes have occurred: there are more responsive doctors,
improved waiting times, prettier waiting rooms and an increase in choice. There
is also greater emphasis in GP surgeries on preventative health care: GPs 'play a
greater role in enhancing the overall health of the nation and for the first time
many have had to consider researching the ongoing needs of those individuals
comprising their local community' (Sargeant 1999: 240). There are health practitioners who do believe that the public and patient should be involved in the
NHS (Rajaratnum 2003; Strachan 2002). Rajaratnum (2003) argued that 'it's not
sufficient to leave it up to the political leaders of the time'. Any member of the
public should be involved:

- 'as a taxpayer, with views about how the money should be spent and value for
  money';
- 'as a patient, with preferences about diagnostic and therapeutic interventions
  and how they should be delivered';
- 'as a local citizen, with views about what services should be provided in the
  locality'.

But more detailed research still suggests major characteristics that indicate a
lack of a market orientation. For example, Laing et al. (2002: 95–96) conclude
that existing data suggests that 'in the majority of cases patients are typically not
involved' or given any choice of hospital or consultant. Laing et al. argue that in
primary care 'patient views would to date appear ultimately to take second place
to professional judgement' (2002: 95). Other research indicated that GPs do not
even ask their patients when choosing secondary care (e.g. hospitals) for them
(Gage and Rickman 2000).

Obstacles to developing a market orientation
Despite pressures from government to focus on customer demands, evidence suggests this has not happened, perhaps because the impetus has come from government policy rather than being developed internally (see Laing and Galbraith
1995: 6; Kinnell and MacDougall 1997: 71).

Internal organisational obstacles and culture

Implementation is not easy (see Meidan and Moutinho 1993: 205–206). Health professionals and the culture around them can provide opposition to the marketing of health. Laing et al. (2002: 96) note that 'limited patient participation' is due to 'the long-established paternalistic ethos of the NHS'. Internal culture is definitely a barrier (see also Graham 1994: 370; Christy and Brown 1999: 102; Hannagan 1992: 41).

Market intelligence results and costs

It is not a straightforward process to identify patients' needs and wants. The concept of needs is very complex and open to debate. Furthermore, demand is often unpredictable (Sargeant 1999: 242). Meidan and Moutinho (1993: 207) argue that the health care market is usually hard to analyse, that health care marketers have less good-quality secondary data about their consumers, and that target market selection is difficult, because there is often public pressure to attempt to reach the whole market rather than to zero in on specific target groups.

Another issue is that market intelligence can simply uncover that the public and NHS staff want different things. The 2002 Labour government's national consultation merely produced contrasting 'wish-lists'. The results showed the public and NHS staff had different views: the public wanted more staff, shorter waiting times and fewer managers, while staff preferred better pay, training and managers. The market intelligence exercise was also criticised by other parties as a waste of money: Liam Fox, Conservative health spokesman, said 'Ministers could have discovered the same thing by buying anyone a drink in any pub in any part of the country. This scandalous waste of NHS resources is typical of Tony Blair's obsession with spin and presentation' (quoted in the *Daily Telegraph*, 16 June 2000).

Ethical and professional objections from health practitioners

Those within the public services often misunderstand the nature of marketing and reject its potential applicability to their work (see Chapman and Cowdell 1998: 39). Laing and McKee (1998: 582) interviewed staff within NHS trusts in Scotland and found that most thought 'an overtly commercial approach to marketing would not be appropriate for, or even transferable to, the NHS'. One of the difficulties with the use of marketing is that it is often confined to communication.

Nature of the product: naturally constrained choice

It is not always possible to offer the citizen choice. As Walsh (1994: 67) argued, 'the public sector is not a "real" market where consumers can choose which product to buy and refuse to buy, or exit, if they are not happy'. Chapman and Cowdell (1998: 64) provide the example of an individual suffering pain in her or his big toe. Although the person is the primary market, they note how her or his need 'is for relief from pain and cure' but:

the degree of choice open to [her or] him is limited. S/he may have chosen [her or] his particular doctor for a number of reasons: the distance of the surgery or medical centre from [her or] his home, the friendliness of the receptionist and staff, the reputation of the practice, etc. It is likely, however, that there are relatively few practices within a reasonable distance.

Choice may also be limited by geography and transport factors (see Laing et al. 2002: 106). Meidan and Moutinho (1993: 205) also note how consumers are constrained by a lack of choice and information. Gage and Rickman (2000: 4) argue that the 'institutional arrangements' in the NHS prevent patients from 'doctor shopping'.

Patient unwillingness to act as consumers

The other side of arguing that health professionals need to give patients choice is that, for this new political marketing relationship to work, patients need to take their rights and responsibilities seriously. Laing et al. (2002: 101) note that the effectiveness of increased choice 'is ultimately dependent on the willingness of consumers to change their established patterns of behaviour'. They need to exercise their rights but also 'accept the responsibilities given to them' (Laing et al. 2002: 101). This may include complaining, voicing their opinion. Research by Laing and Hogg (2002) indicated that patients were not exercising their right to choose a hospital. It may also mean participating in health programmes such as exercise or reducing alcohol intake in order for medical treatment to be effective. If health consumers do need to act in a certain way for the market-oriented political marketing relationship to work in health, there will need to be general education and a change in attitudes.

Lack of resources to meet insatiable demand

Laing and McKee (1998: 583) noted how often there is little time for marketing: 'given the frequently urgent need to focus on ensuring the Trust's survival in the face of financial crises, demands for managerial efficiency savings and the reconfiguration of clinical services, marketing was viewed as a discretionary long term strategic activity'. Staff in the health-service are increasingly under pressure to perform under difficult circumstances, as well as to adopt new ways of working and undertake training, and they suffer from low morale. Rajaratnum (2003) argued that in the NHS as a whole, 'we never have sufficient resources to do what we need to do'. Not all demands in health care can be met: they are insatiable.

Conclusions

There is very clearly a demand and need for marketing in health care, and awareness of its potential by staff. There is increasing emphasis on patient choice and consultation and a concern about patient needs, but there are also many obstacles to using marketing really effectively. The current situation in the UK is that while patients are less deferential, more questioning, and professionals are increasingly responsive to their needs and trying to provide improved services, there is still a long way to go before a market orientation is achieved throughout the entire organisation.

The existing lack of market orientation within the NHS could, arguably, explain much of the voter dissatisfaction with it. This is a problem for the governing parties, whose support depends on delivery of a promise to make the NHS better. The pressure is on them to find a way to make the NHS more responsive, but it is a vast and diverse organisation, and its organisational and cultural characteristics do not make easy the introduction of a market orientation, so the task ahead is huge. This highlights the difficulty of parties becoming market oriented and asking for support on the basis of outputs, and the difficulty with political marketing in general. It is not an easy business. Marketing health also raises a number of debatable, ethical questions. The biggest concern is that patients cannot and should not be treated as consumers. Health professionals question the value of patient input and choice. Health practitioners, with greater knowledge and training than patients, question the ability of patients to make informed choices (see Laing et al. 2000: 11; Klein 1977: 90). As Hogg (1999: 48) noted, pure consumerism 'does not take account of the complexity or intimacy of the professional–patient relationship and the importance of trust in that relationship'.

It could be argued that it is in the interest of the market – that is the patient – for professionals to use their expertise and judgement to make a decision and design the product. We have already seen that it can be argued that there is a need for politicians to lead in some circumstances and a need for creativity in media provision; now we see an argument for the need for the judgement of health professionals to prevail when determining treatment, and the equivalent is true of education. Thus, whilst there are many pressures for health care to become market oriented, there are many practical obstacles and ethical arguments against its doing so. This is true of all public services. The next chapter will explore this further by analysing the increased marketisation of university education.

Notes

1 See, for example, the 2003 special issue of the *International Journal of Non-profit and Voluntary Sector Marketing* entitled 'Broadening the Concept of Political Marketing', which contains papers on health, education and government communication, and Lees-Marshment (2001a, 2001b, 2003a, 2003b, 2003c).
2 It should be noted that marketing the NHS is not the same as internal markets within the NHS, or as the market provision of health care. Sheaff (1991: 30), for example, commented that if research recommended marketing to the NHS, that would not be 'to recommend market provision of health care; it may do the opposite'.
3 Different terms, such as 'forum', or 'panel' are used to represent different forms of market intelligence, but no standard or methodological definition of each one exists as yet.

Bibliography

Berkowitz, E.N. and W. Flexner (1980), 'The Market for Health Services: Is there a Non-traditional Consumer?', Health Marketing and Consumer Behaviour 3(1): 57–68.

Blair, T. (2001), 'Reform of the Public Services', speech, 16 July, www.p,.gov.uk/news.asp?Newsld=2305, accessed April 2002.

Bopp, K.D. (1990), 'How Patients Evaluate the Quality of Ambulatory Medical Encounters: A Marketing Perspective', *Journal of Healthcare Marketing*, 10(2): 6–15.

Bottery, M. (1998), *Professionals and Policy: Management Strategy in a Competitive World*, Cassell, London.

Brown, P. (1992), 'Alternative Delivery Systems in the Provision of Social Services', *International Review of Administrative Sciences* 58: 201–214.

Budd, J. and R. McCrone (1981), 'Health Education and the Mass Media: Past, Present, and Potential', in D.S. Leather, G.B. Hastings and J.K. Davies (eds), *Health Education and the Media*, Pergamon Press, Oxford.

Chapman, D. and T. Cowdell (1998), *New Public Sector Marketing*, Financial Times, Pitman Publishing, London.

Christy, R. and J. Brown (1999), 'Marketing in the Public Services', in S. Horton and D. Farnham (eds), *Public Management in Britain*, Macmillan, Basingstoke. pp. 94–106.

Citizen's Charter Unit (1992), 'Raising the Standard: Britain's Citizen's Charter and Public Service Reform', Foreign and Commonwealth Office, London.

Collins, N. and P. Butler (1998), 'Public Services in Ireland: A Marketing Perspective', Working Paper VII, Department of Public Administration, National University of Ireland, Cork, August.

Coulter, A., V. Entwistle and D. Gilbert (1999), 'Sharing Decisions with Patients: Is the Information Good Enough?', *British Medical Journal* 318: 318–323.

Crowther, C. (1995), 'NHS Trust Marketing: A Survival Guide', *Journal of Marketing Practice: Applied Marketing Science* 1(2): 57–68.

Curtis, R., T. Kurtz, R. Curtis and L.S. Stepnick, eds (1998), *Creating Consumer Choice in Health Care: Measuring and Communicating Health Plan Information*, Health Administration Press.

Department of Health (2000), 'The NHS Plan: A Plan for Investment, a Plan for Reform', www.nhs.uk/nhsplan.

DHSS (Department of Health and Social Security) (1984), *Inquiry into the Management of the NHS (Griffiths Inquiry)*, HMSO, London.

DHSS (Department of Health and Social Security) (1989), *Working for Patients*, HMSO, London.

Dixon, P. and R. Carr-Hill (1989), 'The NHS and its Customer. III: Customer Feedback Surveys: A Review of Current Practice', Centre of Health Economics, York.

Dixon, P. et al. (1997), *Patient Movements and Patient Choice*, report for NHS Executive, York Health Economics Consortium, University of York.

Douglas, F. (2002), 'Social Marketing and Health Promotion', presentation at Aberdeen University, 12 March.

Duckenfield, M. (2003), 'Nasty or NICE? The National Institute for Clinical Excellence and Technology Assessment', *International Journal of Nonprofit and Voluntary Sector Marketing*, special issue on *Broadening the Concept of Political Marketing*, ed. J. Lees-Marshment 8(2): 122–133.

Fox, K. and P. Kotler (1980), 'Marketing of Social Causes: The First 10 Years', *Journal of Marketing* 44: 24–33.

Gage, H. and N. Rickman (2000), 'Patient Choice and Primary Care', Working Paper, Department of Economics, University of Surrey, 15 June.

Gilligan, C. and R. Lowe (1995), *Marketing and Health Care Organisations*, Radcliffe Medical Press, Oxford.

Graham, P. (1994), 'Marketing in the Public Sector: Inappropriate or Merely Difficult?', *Journal of Marketing Management* 10: 361–375.

Gray, A. and B. Jenkins (1994a), 'Ministers, Departments and Civil Servants', in B. Jones (ed.), *Politics UK*, Harvester Wheatsheaf, London. pp. 402–425.

Griffiths, R. (1983), Letter to Norman Fowler, 6 October, in *The Griffiths Report*, NHS Management Inquiry Report, DHSS, London.

Griffiths, R. (1988), 'Does the Public Service Serve? The Consumer Decision', *Public Administration* 66: 195–204.

Hannagan, T. (1992), *Marketing for the Non-profit Sector*, Macmillan, London.

Hogg, C. (1999), *Patients, Power and Politics: From Patients to Citizens*, Sage, London.

Holloway, D., S. Horton and D. Farnham (1999), 'Education', in S. Horton and D. Farnham (eds), *Public Management in Britain*, Macmillan, Basingstoke.

IPPR (2002), 'Not for Profits and Patient Choice: The Route to Better Health care?', www.ippr.org.uk/research/files/team24/project84/NFPs%20and%20Choice%seminar%20summary%20.doc, accessed July 2001.

Kinnell, M. and J. MacDougall (1997), *Marketing in the Not-for-profit sector*, Butterworth Heinemann, Oxford.

Klein, R. (1977), 'The Conflict Between Professionals, Consumers and Bureaucrats', *Journal of the Irish College of Physicians and Surgeons* 6(3): 88–91.

Klein, R. (1995), *The New Politics of the NHS*, 3rd edition, Longman, London.

Kotler, P. and R.N. Clarke (1987), *Marketing for Health Care Organisations*, Prentice-Hall, Englewood Cliffs, NJ.

Kotler, P. and F.L. Roberto (1989), *Social Marketing: Strategies for Changing Public Behaviour*, Free Press, New York.

Laing, A. and A. Galbraith (1995), 'Strategic Marketing in the NHS: Kwik-health NHS Trust', *Journal of Management in Medicine* 9(2): 6–13.

Laing, A. and A. Galbraith (1997), 'Matching Structure and Strategy: Towards a Market Orientation in Health Care', *Journal of Nonprofit and Voluntary Sector Marketing* 2(2): 114–124.

Laing, A.W. and G. Hogg (2002), 'Political Exhortation, Patient Expectation and Professional Execution: Perspectives on the Consumerisation of Health care', *British Journal of Management* 3(2): 173–188.

Laing, A. and J. Lees-Marshment (2002) 'Time to Deliver: Why Political Marketing Needs to Move Beyond the Campaign', paper presented at the PSA conference, Aberdeen, April.

Laing, A.W. and L. McKee (1998), 'Structuring the Marketing Function in Complex Professional Service Organisations', *European Journal of Marketing* 34(5–6): 576–597.

Laing, A., B. Lewis, G. Foxall and G. Hogg (2001), 'Predicting a Diverse Future: Directions and Issues in the Marketing of Services', *European Journal of Marketing* 36(4): 479–494.

Laing, A., M. Fischbacher, G. Hogg and A. Smith (2002), *Managing and Marketing Health Services*, Thomson, London.

Lees-Marshment, J. (2001a), 'Comprehensive Political Marketing: What, How and Why', *Proceedings of the Academy of Marketing Conference*, held at Cardiff University, 2–4 July.

Lees-Marshment, J. (2001b), 'Let's go Comprehensive: Reaching the Full Potential of Political Marketing', *Proceedings of the Political Marketing Conference*, held in Dublin, September.

Lees-Marshment, J. (2003a), 'Editorial', special issue on *Broadening the Concept of Political Marketing*, ed. J. Lees-Marshment, *International Journal of Nonprofit and Voluntary Sector Marketing* 8(2): 104–105.

Lees-Marshment, J. (2003b), 'Marketing Political Institutions: Good in Theory but Problematic in Practice?, *Academy of Marketing Conference Proceedings*, University of Aston, 8–10 July.

Lees-Marshment, J. (2003c), 'Political Marketing: How to Reach that Pot of Gold', *Journal of Political Marketing* 2(1): 1–32.

Lees-Marshment, J. and W. Wymer, eds (forthcoming), special Issue on *Political Marketing, Journal of Nonprofit and Public Sector Marketing*.

Loveday, P. (1991), 'Public Sector Marketing: A Critical Appraisal', in C. O'Faircheallaigh, P. Graham and J. Warburton (eds), *Service Delivery and Public Sector Marketing*, Macmillan, Sydney. pp. 17–35.

Lytle, R.S. and M.P. Mokwa (1992), 'Evaluating Health Care Quality: The Moderating Role of Outcomes', *Journal of Health Care Marketing*, 12(1): 4–14.

MacStravic, R. (1975), *Marketing Health Care*, Aspen, Gaithersburg.

Mark, A. and R. Brennan (1995), 'Demarketing: Managing Demand in the UK National Health Service', *Public Money and Management* July–September: 17–22.

Meidan, A. and L. Moutinho (1993), *Cases in Marketing of Services: An International Collection*, Addison-Wesley, Wokingham.

MORI (1997), *The Extent and Determinants of Patient Choice of GP Practice*, report for NHS Executive.

Murley, R., ed. (1995), *Patients or Customers: Are the NHS Reforms Working?*, Institute of Economic Affairs, London.

Newcastle-under-Lyme Primary Care Group (2000), *Newsletter* 1(11), www.newcastlepcg.co.uk.

O'Fairchellaigh, P. and P. Graham (1991), 'Introduction', in C. O'Faircheallaigh, P. Graham and J. Warburton (eds), *Service Delivery and Public Sector Marketing*, Macmillan, Sydney. pp. ix–xiii.

Ovretveit, J. (1996), 'Informed Choice? Health Service Quality and Outcome Information for Patients', *Health Policy* 36: 75–93.

Pagan, L. (1994) , 'Testing out Support', *Marketing* 12 May: 43.

Parsuraman, A., V.A. Zeithaml and L.L. Berry (1988), 'SERVQUAL: A Multiple Item Scale for Measuring Consumer Perceptions of Service Quality', *Journal of Retailing*, 64(1): 12–40.

Petrochuk, M.A. and R.G. Javalgi (1996), 'Reforming the Health Care System: Implications for Health Care Marketers', *Health Marketing Quarterly* 13(3): 71–86.

Pirie, M. and R. Worcester (2001), *The Wrong Package*, report on a MORI poll by the Adam Smith Institute, London. Also at www.mori.com/polls/2001/asi.shtml or www.adamsmith.org.uk.

Posneet, J et al. (1996), *Primary Care Consortia and Patient Choice*, final report for NHS Executive, York Health Economics Consortium, University of York.

Rajaratnum, G. (2003), 'Health Marketing: Views from a Practitioner', presentation by the Director of Health, North Stoke and South Stoke Primary Care Trusts, Keele University.

Royal Pharmaceutical Society of Great Britain (2002), 'Pharmacists Working for a Healthier Scotland', advertisement within Scottish Conservative Party conference programme.

Sargeant, A. (1999), *Marketing Management for Nonprofit Organisations*. Oxford University Press, Oxford.

Sheaff, R. (1991), *Marketing for Health Services*, Open University Press, Milton Keynes.

South Thames Regional Authority (1994), *Primary Health Care in a General Practice Setting: A Model of Good Practice*, Directorate of Nursing, Quality and Programmes.

Strachan, P. (2002), 'Healthcare Marketing', presentation by Medical Adviser, NHS Grampian, at Aberdeen University, 4 March.

Tappin, M. (2003), 'Marketing Health', presentation at Keele University on Marketing Health.

Teasdale, K. (1992), *Managing the Changes in Health Care*, Wolfe, London.

Walsh, K. (1994), 'Marketing and Public Sector Management', *European Journal of Marketing* 28(3): 63–71.

Wilson, A. (1994), *Emancipating the Professions*, John Wiley, Chichester.

Zaltman, G. and I. Vertinsky (1971), 'Health Services Marketing: A Proposed Model', *Journal of Marketing*, 35: 19–27.

7

Marketing university education

> The marriage of the ideas of 'consumerism' and 'education' seems strange for many of us, for we have been led to believe that ideas are priceless and that they are 'free' . . . thus, to make ideas 'buyable' is a new concept and, for most academics, theoretically uncomfortable. (Academic, quoted by Brookes 2003: 139)

> It is now 'a buyers market'; 'people exercise a right to choose' and 'fashions in courses and institutions have a big effect. As consumers of education, students have a right to expect good quality education. (Educational Marketer I 2003)

> The shift of power from producer to consumer is now hitting universities . . . Scholarship is now a global business. (Wakeford 2000)

> The idea that academics are somehow 'intellectual monks', to whom people will turn for an education because of the perceived quality of an institution . . . [is] now hopelessly out dated. Students have a much wider choice of courses than they had even ten years ago and because of this can 'pick and choose' the institutions at which they want to study. (Sargeant 1999: 21)

This chapter applies political marketing to education. Education is one of Tony Blair's number one issues, apparent from his famous 'education, education, education' sound-bite when he was opposition leader.[1] It is not free to use marketing as it wishes, because it is subject to government regulations, and so it presents all the usual challenges of marketing a non-business, political organisation. Universities are very elite institutions, concerned with the development and dissemination of specialised knowledge and expertise. Nevertheless, students are more questioning of intellectuals – even of professors – and as one marketer commented (Thorley 2003), students no longer automatically trust universities or accept 'that university knows best'. It is 'a buyers' market at the moment:' consumerism has permeated the student ethos. Marketing staff – even whole departments – are being created in universities as they struggle and compete to recruit more students or better students. This raises many questions: should education – degree courses – be designed to suit market demand? Can you expect professors to change what they research and teach to suit the tastes of school children? Will the development of marketing interfere with or aid university goals? Is a marketised system good for the country?

Limitations of space have necessitated a focus on universities, although research was conducted on schools and many of the trends described here reflect practice there as well as within further-education (FE) colleges. In terms of literature, analysis of educational marketing can of course draw on the general public service marketing research, as was done with health in the previous chapter, but there is little specific research on marketing universities. Services literature includes organisations such as banking, but areas such as education are political and different to finance or legal services, so the value of the literature is limited for this topic. Additionally, as in Chapter 6, empirical discussion here is, by necessity, not as focused as that in chapters that are studying one or two entities. An assessment of the degree of market orientation of just one university would require greater in-depth research to ensure a fair judgement, and if ever carried out would necessitate a number of controversial and ethical issues being overcome, as institutions would be naturally protective of the results.

The chapter will simply outline theory and illustrate it using a variety of examples, drawn from existing secondary sources and observation, together with material obtained from presentations, interviews and informal conversations with marketing staff at a number of educational institutions. It is fully acknowledged that the issues, themes and questions raised by this chapter are worthy of an in-depth empirical study across a large number of institutions: hopefully this chapter will help to stimulate such work.

Marketing universities: the basics

Product
The university product is broad and varies, but includes:

- 'education';
- degrees – the final grade;
- knowledge and understanding;
- in some degrees, directly vocational training for a specific job, e.g. medicine;
- transferable skills – presentation skills, team work, reading and writing, which can be used after university;
- skills that will help students' job prospects;
- accommodation;
- social activities;
- computer, library, technological and communication facilities;
- finances – financial support and bursaries, and on the other hand tuition fees and top-up fees;
- support services, e.g. counselling and learning support;
- an overseas or international student office;
- internal organisation and structure;
- institutional reputation.

Table 7.1 Market sections for universities

	Details
Students	Prospective and existing; returning; undergraduate, postgraduate; overseas, part-time, mature
Parents	Provide financial and other support; influence student choice
Careers advisors, school and FE teachers	All have potential to influence student choice
Staff	Academic, administrative, support and auxiliary staff; their training and unions; have a vested interest in the organisation; run the organisation
Research funders	Governmental organisations, e.g. ESRC, AHRB; non-governmental grant-making trusts that support particular research; RAE and reputation a factor here
Alumni	Provide extra funds for universities; provide word-of-mouth reputation and publicity
Assessment organisations	RAE assesses research; QAA assesses teaching; other bodies assess, for example, disabled access to university
Government	Source of funding, legislation, regulations, assessment procedures, targets, admissions etc.
Accredited organisations	Colleges accredited to teach certain aspects of the universities' product or whose course and award qualification universities recognise; occurs especially with overseas institutions; provides money and links which encourage recruitment of overseas students
Local and national media	Publicity can contribute to reputation for teaching and research excellence, innovation; universities or departments publicises work of academic staff; this helps to get best students, best staff and funding
Society	Education is a benefit to society as a whole

Source: building on Sargeant (1999: 218–219)
Notes: AHRB = Arts and Humanities Research Board; ESRC = Economic and Social Research Council; QAA = Quality Assurance Agency; RAE = Research Assessment Exercise.

The product is broad; as Thorley (2003) argued, it's not a product as such; 'it's an opportunity for education, experience, a lifestyle that may lead to a degree'.

Market
The university market is diverse and is therefore highly complex (Hunt and MacKay 2001, for example): see Table 7.1.

The power or dominance of one group over another changes over time. Parents are more influential now as more are paying towards or for their children's university education directly. Universities are recognising this; e.g. the University of Stirling has a section on its website directly written for prospective parents: 'When your child goes to university you naturally want to know that they will be well looked after. Below you'll find links to information on what the University does to make your offspring's time with us happy and safe' (www.external.stir.ac.uk/undergrad/parents/index.php).

Goals

Universities have several goals, which are debatable and subject to government influence, such as:

- training, spread of skills, spread of knowledge;
- education for its own sake – the pursuit of knowledge;
- research to provide an objective analysis of the real world – more independent than e.g. the media;
- consultancy advice on what might work best, e.g. best treatment for certain illnesses.

Universities often have their own mission statements or visions. Leicester's mission statement says that the university aims at 'the advancement of knowledge, the diffusion and extension of arts, sciences and learning and the provision of liberal, professional and technological education and will strive to enhance its position as a leading research and teaching institution, cultivating the synergy between research and teaching' (www.leicester.ac.uk/cwis/university.html# mission). Cambridge University holds its mission as being to 'contribute to society through the pursuit of education, learning, and research at the highest international levels of excellence' (www.admin.cam.ac.uk/univ/mission.html). Universities can adopt any one of our three approaches.

Product-oriented universities: professors know it all

Definition of product-oriented universities

A product-oriented university will think it knows what is best for students and design its product, including degree course, assessment, organisation and facilities, according to what the academics think is best. Little or no room is given to the choice and demands of students themselves; no market intelligence is undertaken; students are also expected to defer to and never question the judgement of academics. See Box 7.1.

Universities are traditionally product oriented; they do design their 'product' to suit what academics think and want; it fits with the whole history of university education. It was education for the elite, beginning with Oxford and Cambridge. In 1950 there were only 24 universities. University was and is also concerned with selection by academic ability, so was inherently elitist. The entire university product was very much delivered in a way that best suits the needs of the institution or academic rather than those of the student (Hannagan 1992: 32). As Boxall (1991: 12) observed:

> the activities and priorities of universities have traditionally been determined primarily by the preferences and aspirations of their academic staff . . . Indeed, the

---

Box 7.1 The process for a product-oriented university

Stage 1: Product design
The highest academics within a university design its product to suit what they think is best. There is no regard for prospective or current student demands, or the need to change behaviour to suit parents or politicians. The word of the professors is supreme: they are the ones who have the most expertise, knowledge and experience and should judge how the product should be designed.

Stage 2: Communication
Academics assume their work, particularly research, will be communicated without any effort on their part. Furthermore, they are not concerned with communicating all their work: it has a value in its own regard and does not need justifying – knowledge for knowledge's sake. The institution assumes it will attract students because of its reputation, which has been earned over a number of years, through research and former students' word of mouth.

Stage 3: Delivery
Product-oriented universities educate their pupils by ensuring they pass through their degree for the required number of years, achieving what academics think they should.

   These universities do not seek to question whether they are meeting all their students' needs, or whether the student is equipped for the wider world, because academics know better than anyone else and seek to serve their own interests. They will not attempt to solicit feedback on whether they are seen to perform satisfactorily overall. They aim to deliver what they think is best.

---

very essence of a university has been the self-determining community of academic professionals, whose rights to set their own agenda were enshrined in the unwritten charter of academic freedom.

   University communication used to be extremely long-winded and not geared to the student or any form of advertising. Sargeant (1999: 22) outlines how some universities felt advertising their courses would lower their perceived quality and how 'until recently the advertising of undergraduate courses was taboo in the UK'. There was 'a gentlemen's agreement between universities to avoid unseemly competition', which 'precluded the use of advertising except during the clearing process'. The prospectus was not used to communicate with students: as Hannagan (1992: 32) observed, universities would 'produce lists of long established courses in prospectuses which tend to be handbooks for the staff of the institution rather than a marketing vehicle directed at potential students', and courses 'are delivered in a way that best suits the needs of the institution rather than those of the client and customer'.

   Today, this idea is out of date. 'All but the Oxbridge universities are now finding themselves having to compete hard to attract the brightest students'

(Sargeant 1999: 21) and, furthermore, to attract wider funding just to survive, let alone develop as they would wish.

The era of glossy prospectuses: sales-oriented universities

Causes of change towards a sales orientation
The director of marketing for Aberdeen University (Manders 2002) cited greater competition as a key stimulant to the use of marketing communications. There are now many more institutions offering degree and higher-education level qual- ifications, for a wider and more diverse range of students. In 1992 the govern- ment removed the distinction between university and polytechnics, so that they all compete with each other. Universities have had to compete for funds, resources and students. There was a massive expansion in student numbers as well as diversification in their nature. Total student numbers rose from 50,000 in 1939, to 324,000 in 1963, to over 1.6 million in 1997 (Holloway et al. 1999: 206; Sargeant 1999: 200). University education is no longer for a privileged elite. There are therefore more students and places available, and universities compete for the best and for the numbers to get the funding to keep themselves going.

Definition of a sales-oriented university
A sales-oriented university will design its product, including degree course, assessment, organisation and facilities, according to what the academics think is best, but present it in a way which appeals to students. The focus is not on the product, but on the presentation of the product, to attract students to the univer- sity and make them think that the academics are doing a good job. See Box 7.2.

A sales-oriented university retains broadly the same product as product- oriented institutions, except for recruiting more managers, accountants and marketing, advertising or PR professional staff. It does, however, conduct market intelligence to understand student choice, which then informs communication. There are a large number of influencing factors, such as athletic facilities, avail- ability of financial aid, conversations with former students and social activities, not just the academic reputation of the institution (Grabowski 1981). Manders (2002) conducted research to understand the University of Aberdeen's consu- mers, noting that students decide earlier on a university or course, using a range of information sources. The course is the prime factor, followed by reputation, and location is an issue.

Universities need to identify which factors might be most important, maybe for their specific institution as opposed to all, or for particular groups of students (e.g. mature students may be more interested in child care facilities than the number of student pubs!). Overseas students also think differently, considering academic reputation first, then content and international reputation of the insti- tution, with non-academic factors such as the guarantee of accommodation and cost of living or fees being perhaps more important than for home students (see Sargeant 1999: 229; HEIST 1995). St Andrew's University, for example, offers

---

Box 7.2 The process for a sales-oriented university

Stage 1: Product design
A sales-oriented university designs its product to suit what it thinks is best. There is
no regard for public opinion or demands, or the need to change behaviour to suit
other bodies.

Stage 2: Market intelligence
A sales-oriented university will conduct market intelligence (debate, discussion,
commissions, focus groups, polls, reports) on the reaction of its market to its
behaviour and performance, and to find out where it has strengths and weaknesses,
what students like about the courses and what they think could be improved, and
what the university has a good or bad reputation for.

Stage 3: Communication
A sales-oriented university will create and run an effective communications system
to publicise its best work to its market, including prospective students, funders,
bodies such as the ESRC and those measuring its performance, and politicians.
Responding to the results of market intelligence, it may attempt to downplay its
weaknesses and focus on its strengths. For example, on open days it may seek to
attract more students from a target market such as the locality. It may showcase one
aspect of its teaching which is known for being excellent. Communication is designed
to improve the reputation of the university, and its form and style will be designed to
suit its market: e.g. for prospective students, it might be fun, easy, attractive adverts
as much about the night life as about the education on offer. Communication
includes material on websites, prospectuses, leaflets, materials available at recruitment fairs, press releases and documentation presented to any assessment of the university's work, e.g. in the RAE or QAA. It can also include the downplaying of any
potential negative publicity.

Stage 4: Campaign
A sales-oriented university may undertake mini-campaigns to boost its reputation
and attract new students; for example, via open days.

Stage 5: Delivery
A sales-oriented university will educate its students and produce research, but in a
way which aims to deliver what the university thinks is best.

Stage 6: Communication of delivery
The university will also attempt to communicate the work it has done; for example,
publicising good research results.

---

different links on its website for prospective undergraduate students coming
straight from school and for overseas and mature students. Keele found that students were influenced positively if they visited the campus, thereby leading the
university to focus communication on getting students to open days.

Universities increasingly put much more effort into promotion and recruitment. A university recruiter I interviewed said that the amount universities spend on marketing had increased substantially alongside the professionalisation of communication (Educational Marketer I 2003). The trend as seen from awards by HEIST (a marketing organisation for higher education which grants awards) is towards the most modern, snappy, designer-based slogans: 'selling education . . . in line with selling any commercial product' (Educational Marketer I 2003). Whilst some universities remain more traditional, others are producing communication designed in a similar way to that of record shops and magazines for young people, to ensure universities are relevant institutions (Educational Marketer I 2003).

Universities may establish a logo or brand in order to ease communication to students. Aberdeen decided its brand personality was 'proactive, accessible, helpful, friendly, forward thinking, confident, relevant credible, reputable, exciting, fun' (Manders 2003). The University of Essex decided its brand was all about standing out from the crowd; the idea that if a student went there she or he would be unique and have valuable attributes others did not (Educational Marketer I 2003). The university then used this theme in its communication. For example, on the front cover of the prospectuses for various years were rubber ducks, or elephants, or fairy cakes, all of them yellow except for one red one standing out as special. The cover of the prospectus for 2004 shows gingerbreadmen, one with the university scarf on it (University of Essex 2003).

Communication is used in two stages, before and after the application. The overall process can take up to 18 months (Thorley 2003). Pre-application marketing (adapted from Manders 2002) includes development of theme, slogan and images; advertising using radio, press, cinema and billboards, e.g. at train stations; direct mail – postcards, newsletters, posters and bookmarks; prospectuses, both hard copy and on-line; open days, both general and specific; links with schools and higher education colleges; conventions; application support by phone line and website information; and university education fairs.

After students have been through the admissions process and been offered a place, and while they are still deciding on the offers made, communication is extremely important in influencing that final 'buying' decision (see Sargeant 1999: 221). All marketing staff interviewed noted the importance of communicating with students after the offer of a place, with differentiated communication for each time in the year (Manders 2002; Educational Marketer I 2003; Educational Marketer II 2003). Aberdeen sent a postcard headed 'Do you remember your first' to students after they had attended an open day event (University of Aberdeen 2002b). Similarly Keele sent out various material to students after they had been accepted, including a CD-Rom. Aberdeen also targeted late applicants through clearing, even advertising on billboards at Edinburgh railway station after results were out, telling students the university was still open for clearing. Aberdeen put considerable effort into improving the application process and offering support to prospective students (Manders 2002). The university revamped the system dealing with enquiries so that it could keep in touch with students more effectively, offering free phone lines and free post options, dealing with as many as 400 emails a day Manders (2002).

There is currently emphasis on widening participation in the UK, reaching out to students from a wider range of social and economic backgrounds. Sales-oriented universities are trying to do this through carefully designed communication. They are doing research to try to figure out what young people want, how to reach them, how to encourage them to find out about universities (Educational Marketer I 2003). Universities also produce and use CD-Roms to make it attractive to students to find out about them through new media: the University of Stirling (2003) sends its prospectus on CD-Rom. Overseas students also require a more comprehensive communication strategy (Sargeant 1999: 229). Websites of universities often have a special section for prospective international students, with advice on issues such as language training and support and travel. Product packages can also be created to suit the overseas market: for example, some institutions offer an accommodation and fees package to overseas students to study for an MBA, understanding that accommodation is a big issue for overseas applicants. Universities such as Abertay and DeMontford have also produced adverts for cinemas.

For 2002/3 Keele created a new slogan: 'love–learn–live'. The aim was to make people want and ask for the prospectus (Thorley 2003): an attention-seeking strategy. A student wearing a hat with a heart on it was pictured below the slogan, a partly serendipitous design as a student happened to be walking past when pictures for the prospectus were being taken, but it made students at fairs want the prospectus. Keele also dropped the traditional message from the vice-chancellor (Thorley 2003). The overall design was much more suited to the student reading it. The Open University (OU) have used direct mail to reach their audience, which is traditionally wider, composed of part-time students studying at a distance. In 2002, the OU's leaflets, with butterflies and slogans such as 'stand out from the crowd', were commonly inserted in publications such as the woman's magazine *She*.

Universities can also engage in short-term communication, in the form of a campaign. Aberdeen University hase run two campaigns: first 'Right Time Right Place' (2000/1) and then 'Straight A Campaign – Putting You First' (2001/2; see Manders 2002). This theme ran throughout all their promotional material. On open days students were given a red bag with themed material inside. The bag itself was bright red, with information on it as shown in Figure 7.1.

Within the bag was the usual information – prospectus, campus map, the day's events – but there was also a continuation of the day's theme. There was a bright red postcard listing the key advantageous facts about the university: see Figure 7.2. The red theme was continued throughout the open-day guide, travel guide and campus map, placed in a professional clear folder. There was also an attractive postcard from the university sports council.

Keele also tried to 'sell the sale', running a campaign to increase attendance

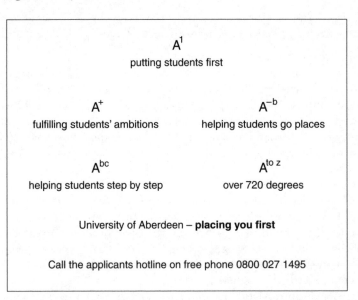

Figure 7.1 University of Aberdeen's Straight A Campaign 2002, bag cover

The University at a glance

- The University of Aberdeen was founded in 1495
- Internationally distinguished
- Campus based university
- Over 720 flexible degree programmes
- Library containing over 1,050,000 volumes
- Over 1000 computers are available for student use
- All new students are guaranteed accommodation

- There are over 150 sports clubs and societies
- 92% of academic staff are research-active
- 97% of our graduates enter directly into work or further study training
- We have over 10,600 students
- 115 nationalities are represented
- Student population is 48% men and 52% women

Figure 7.2 University of Aberdeen postcard, 2002

at open days, with pink or green postcards and invitations, very different in style to the traditional formal letter. If prospective students did not respond and book a day, they were sent reminders as well as a final reminder for the last open day of the year (Thorley 2003).

Of course, as with political parties, a sales-oriented approach can only have limited impact. The real key to success is to offer a superior product – but in university marketing this is not a simple idea to put into practice.

Market-oriented university: improving quality of service

Causes of move to a market orientation

At the start of the twenty-first century, universities are increasingly attempting to look at the product they offer, and gear it to suit the results of market intelligence, in order to attract the best students and survive. The whole marketplace for universities is changing as I write: the vice-chancellor of my current institution recently wrote, 'the whole system is becoming more exposed to market forces and we cannot avoid reflecting this in the way we manage the University' (April 2003).

Whilst student numbers have increased, government or state funding to pay for their education has been reduced or restricted. This makes it harder for universities to maintain unpopular courses or unproductive staff: reorganisation, managed rebalancing, voluntary redundancies and even sacking of some staff is being introduced into the UK higher education system as institutions struggle to find a way to survive in changed conditions. To do so, they are attempting to analyse market demands and examine their actual product, not just the presentation, in order to attract students.

Similarly, the introduction of tuition fees and the decline of the maintenance grant system have led students to act more like consumers. As one marketer commented, now 'people exercise a right to choose' and 'fashions in courses and institutions have a big effect' (Educational Marketer I 2003). Students – or their parents – now directly finance their individual course of study. Their expectations are higher. Students will complain if they do not get what they want. The focus is on the delivered product; it is no longer a case of just producing glossy brochures to attract their attention and then forget all about marketing once you've got them there.

Attention has therefore moved to the nature of the product or service on offer. As the University of Aberdeen's strategy document said, 'we must define our programmes and process to meet market changes' (University of Aberdeen 2001). Forward-looking institutions are now adopting a market orientation to get ahead of the game now they are in the twenty-first century, and this approach may offer a way of doing this. However, it is not as easy in practice as the theory might suggest. The difficulty is doing all this in an era of cutbacks, increased competition and fights for scarce resources: as Baines and Lynch (2003) suggested, 'Britain's Higher Education Institutions face fundamental and unprecedented pressures.'

Definition of a market-oriented university

A market-oriented university would seek to design its product, including degree course, assessment, organisation and facilities, to meet the needs and wants of the students it is intending to educate. It would conduct market intelligence to determine the demands of its students and respond to these in designing the product. Whilst naturally professional judgement would be used on how to meet those needs, student demands would be placed above those of the professional. See Box 7.3.

Box 7.3 The process for a market-oriented university

Stage 1: Market intelligence

A market-oriented university will conduct a wide range of market intelligence (debate, discussion, commissions, focus groups, polls, reports, from the public, students, related bodies, staff) about what the organisation is good at and not good at, and think about how it might be improved. It is concerned with what students need and want from it, not just what they think of it as it is. It will therefore include debates about the nature and role of academics, degrees, the timing and content of the course, and which transferable skills are desirable, and will involve related outside bodies as well as the views of the general public.

Stage 2: Product design

A market-oriented university designs its product, including courses, assessment, teaching format, staff expertise, administrative support, computer and library facilities and accommodation, to suit the results from market intelligence. It aims to respond in the most effective manner to the demands of students and allocate resources accordingly.

Stage 3: Product adjustment

- *Achievability:* Staff in a market-oriented university will not promise what they can't deliver: they will aim to be as accurate as possible in predicting the quality of education, the options available and its outcome, in order to ensure that general expectations, standards and promises can be fulfilled and achieved.
- *Competition analysis:* The university will take into account the needs and views of any competing organisations, such as another local university, or the other main lead in a particular field, and adjust its behaviour accordingly. This may mean developing a new course not offered by the other local university, improving an existing course, creating superior computer facilities, or emphasising particular centres of research excellence or innovation to mark it out as different from other institutions.
- *Internal reaction analysis:* For the product design to be effective, it needs to be supported by the staff within the organisation, so any proposed changes to the product may need to be adjusted to take account of the views of academics. If they strongly oppose a particular change it may be impossible to implement it anyway. It may be necessary to adjust the product design to suit the personal views of academics, given their particular expertise and training – rather as parties need to take account of their ideology and history. Universities and parties are both concerned with values and ideas, not just making a profit, so those who work within these organisations can be cautious about changing what they do purely to suit the market. If not carefully managed, the culture and attitude of staff can prove a barrier to ensure the successful implementation of marketing.
- *Support analysis:* A university may target some product changes in particular areas where it is especially weak or does not meet demand or attract students. For example, it may develop a course to deal with a new emerging topic to attract its potential market, or change its hours to suit mature or part-time students in full-time employment.

continued on next page

Box 7.3 *continued*

Stage 4: Implementation
For political marketing to work it has to be implemented effectively, using all the guidelines from marketing management literature. The findings from Stages 1–3 of the process must be implemented and a majority within the university need to accept the new behaviour broadly and comply with it. The organisation must therefore proceed carefully, especially if major change is required. Any change also needs to be carefully, communicated and explained, and extra training offered if needed to help staff comply with the expected new behaviour; for example, clear guidance on the nature of the Research Assessment Exercise (RAE), or expected demands of the Quality Assurance Agency (QAA), or time to prepare a new topic for a new degree course.

Stage 5: Communication
The university will then communicate its work effectively and efficiently. Communication is designed to attract potential students but may also be aimed at existing students to maintain satisfaction. It may, for example, communicate the range of welfare services available to students, the range of course options or the social activities on offer, so the students may participate fully in all the university has to offer. The style of communication is also geared to suit the audience: for example, if the organisation seeks to reach particular students it must communicate somewhere they will see the information, and in a manner they can easily access and understand.

Stage 6: Campaign
A market-oriented university may undertake mini-campaigns to boost its profile, attract new students (e.g. mature or local students), or highlight a new degree course available, or graduate school, or centre of research. Campaigns may also be carried out during the clearing process after school exam results.

Stage 7: Delivery
The university will aim to deliver the proposed product once the students are in place. It aims to achieve the best possible outcome which meets their needs to the greatest possible extent.

Stage 8: Communication of delivery
It will also attempt to communicate the work it has done; for example, highlighting good research results, performance in assessment measures, or the job destinations of its graduates.

Stage 1: Market intelligence
Universities need to identify what student demands and expectations are. For example, the University of Aberdeen conducts focus groups, internal meetings and marketing audits and obtains feedback from applicants to inform its recruitment process (Manders 2002). In 2002 Keele University appointed a new market

intelligence officer to conduct research into market demands, in order to inform their decisions about the development of new courses. Elaine McFarlane (2003) noted that the reason to conduct such intelligence was:

- to ensure the university's product, i.e. degrees, are what the market wants;
- to ensure courses equip students with the skills employers want;
- to identify potential areas of growth to increase recruitment;
- to understand its market better;
- to identify the best areas to commit resources to.

Universities can utilise all the market intelligence techniques that any organisation has open to it, and would seek to analyse and understand potential and existing students. This therefore includes consumer behaviour analysis (Brookes 2003: 141). This information would be used to improve the product design, not just inform communication, and universities would seek to identify what students want those characteristics to be like, not just which are important. A key difference between a sales- and a market-oriented university is that whilst the former would concentrate market intelligence efforts on prospective students, the latter would also consider students once they are at the institution, and endeavour to adapt courses and facilities to suit their demands once in place. Staff–student liaison committees and feedback forms are important sources of market intelligence on the product as it is delivered, and can be used to help develop future products. Keele undertook market intelligence amongst its existing students when it was considering changing the nature of its core first year courses. Stirling University conducted research into student learning when undergoing a redesign of their teaching methods within their degree courses (McAuley 2003). Staff can also be a valuable source of market intelligence, especially young staff with new ideas, or those who have worked at several institutions and therefore bring greater objectivity to discussion.

Stage 2: Product design

There has been a move towards realising that universities need to market the whole product, not just the degree. One marketing professional I interviewed said that the trend was towards realising that the student lifestyle was important, not just the academic aspects of the university (Educational Marketer I 2003). Another issue is that the undergraduate, postgraduate, research and conference aspects of a university are all different products or brands, and need to be designed and communicated in different ways (Educational Marketer I 2003).

Staff Professional or administrative staff are extremely important to the success of marketing, and universities have tended to increase their use of marketing professionals (see Sargeant 1999: 205; Educational Marketer I 2003): as Brookes (2003: 137) said, 'marketers are presently, and will continue to be, much sought after commodities in universities'. Warwick University has a marketer, or someone looking at marketing, in each department. The University of Aberdeen appointed a new marketing professional to help with its recruitment when it started seeing a fall in student numbers (Manders 2002). At first staff dealt with recruitment, but this was developed to create a new Directorate of Marketing, the first to be introduced in a traditional Scottish University (University of Aberdeen 2001). The aim of the unit was to 'develop a corporate marketing strategy', to 'have responsibility for the position of the University in its various market places' and to 'provide an integrated, systematic and co-ordinated approach to marketing'. Not all staff have marketing backgrounds but the trend is in that direction (Educational Marketer I 2003; Brookes 2003). Academic and support staff are vital, as is their training (Holloway et al. 1999: 211). There has been an effort to try to redress the imbalance in terms of gender and ethnic minorities amongst academics. However, it remains the case that universities are overstocked with white males, especially at the top.

Courses   In terms of courses, product design in a market-oriented university can involve dropping some courses – 'sometimes we've shut down degrees that are just not recruiting' (Educational Marketer I 2003) – alongside the development of new courses in response to demand. The use of market intelligence at Keele has led to changes in titles, prevented some courses going ahead because there was not enough market, and supported the launch of other degrees (McFarlane 2003). Keele dropped ancient history, for example, but developed a new degree in media, culture and communications, whilst Essex developed a new undergraduate degree in management, economics and mathematics for 2004. Manchester University developed a new degree in 2002 called a BSc (Hons) Degree in Audiology; the university's website section on new courses states that such development is 'in response to recent proposed restructuring within the audiological profession' and that 'the programme has been designed to incorporate education and training tailored to the needs of the profession, as well as meeting the aims of a higher education qualification (www.man.ac.uk/study/ugrad/new.html, accessed July 2003).

Admissions process   A prompt, efficient and friendly admissions service is an important part of university activity. Even the most reputable institutions can lose out because of not seeming responsive at this stage and therefore suggesting an inferior product once the student arrived (Sargeant 1999: 220–221). Recruitment should be seen as a service, not just an attempt to get students into the university. For example, the student recruitment and admissions service at Aberdeen University (2002) listed various services it provided, including presentations to parents; student presentations on student life; information on bursaries and scholarships; and information on many aspects of student life, e.g. accommodation, facilities for study and leisure, costs of living, financial advice and much more. The Robert Gordon University has a customer services department that provides information and support to students on aspects such as finances.

One aspect of the product that will change in the forthcoming years is fees: as the government is allowing the introduction of top-up fees price will become another element in marketing university education. A fair amount of analysis and some guesswork will have to be carried out as institutions estimate what they can charge students without losing numbers and while maintaining income, all the time asking 'what will the student think?' (Educational Marketer I 2003).

Stage 3: Product adjustment

Achievability   Staff have to be careful not to promise what they cannot deliver. When I was teaching this subject, my students recalled vividly being promised facilities such as computer rooms within their halls of residences when they applied, only to arrive and find they were not there: even three years on they still remembered the broken promise. Often universities cannot simply follow demand, and there needs to be some adjustment to offer a realistically achievable product.

Competition analysis   Universities need to analyse whom they compete against. They can then discuss the strengths and weaknesses of competitors and try to differentiate themselves from the main competitors, or to turn weaknesses (e.g. not being an established or ancient university) into a strength (e.g. being new and friendly, with innovative, young staff). Universities need to do this for students but also in terms of attracting staff and considering all aspects of the product. A less-established university may offer more support for non-traditional students, for example, resulting in a lower dropout rate than a redbrick or Oxbridge. These last have obvious strengths of name and wealth, but newer universities may be able to boast that they have a more socially diverse student population than the elite universities could ever have. Competition analysis requires universities to step back slightly and make tangible what it is they do well and what they do not do so well, to inform product adjustment and communication. For example, Aberdeen's prime weakness is location – far from anywhere, located in the north-east of Scotland. Keele's weakness is that it lacks a major city and lacks name recognition: about 60–65 per cent of students have never head of Keele (Thorley 2003). The problem is that it is named after a village, and although this is completely unrelated to the quality of education, prospective students fear that it cannot be that good if they have never head of it. The university's marketing plan therefore has to counteract these negative images, highlighting open days, as visits to campus work effectively to turn those negative perceptions around. It needs, for example, to communicate the benefits of Keele's unusual dual honours degree (Thorley 2003).

Competition analysis can, however, lead to co-operation as well as competition. Manchester University and UMIST are due to merge in October 2004, for example. Keele worked alongside Staffordshire University to raise awareness of higher education amongst the local school students because it was of mutual benefit. Interestingly, staff suggested that in the sector 'there is a certain amount of co-operation' and sharing of best practice via the professional association for university recruiters (Educational Marketer II 2003).

Internal reaction analysis   This is difficult for a university. To keep staff on board, ideally they will be consulted on required changes. The move to a market orientation, however, is complete anathema to most academics, used to a more elite, state-funded environment. Discussions with marketing staff suggest that whenever they suggest a change in communication, let alone the actual product, they are almost always met with hostility from some departments or disciplines within the university. 'You have to bring people with you', for change to be effective (Educational Marketer I 2003), but if a suggested new design involves reducing staff within a particular subject area because it is not popular with students, it is impossible to satisfy all internal demands. Too much internal reaction analysis can slow progress. One marketer said of prospectuses that 'you can tell the ones that have been done by committee', as they tend to lack understanding or a brand, and send confused images such as a montage of pictures; an 'old fashioned approach to marketing' (Educational Marketer I 2003). Another staff noted how they had moved away from traditional shots of old university building and academics had objected, but 'your main market is 17–18-year-olds, not 50-year-old professors' (Educational Marketer II 2003).

Support analysis   Universities often aim for particular target markets, such as local students or mature students. There has recently been an increasing focus on widening access to universities, so that they aim to attract a particular target market, such as students from the local comprehensive school which has not previously sent many pupils to university (see Mitchell et al. 2003, for example). They can also target sections of the market, such as parents. Aberdeen University held parents' information evenings not just in Aberdeen but around Scotland, attracting over 1,000 parents in 2001 (University of Aberdeen 2002c), clearly targeting that influential market. Schools are another target: 'some people in the sector believe that if you're in the schools constantly that is the way to do it' (Educational Marketer II 2003).

Stage 4: Implementation
Like political parties, senior academics and marketers in universities will often face obstacles to implementing a market orientation and any change to the product design it brings with it. One member of staff recalled conducting a meeting early on in her appointment and receiving objections when she used the words 'product' and 'market', and there was opposition even to the idea of introducing a open day. Another staff member said that 'most do not like marketing or view it as inappropriate because they believe that education should not be viewed as a product to be sold and that their disciplines do not need a "sales pitch" to make them popular'.[2] Another educational marketer noted that in all

universities 'there are academics who feel that is not what their job is about' (Educational Marketer II 2003). Even involving staff in open days can prove problematic; one head of department admitted letting an ineffective and off-putting academic do the open days because the department didn't want more students anyway, as they wanted a lighter workload! Another issue is that any proposed changes to the core product – to the degree programme – require effort by academic staff. It is not easy for staff to change what they research and teach; the knowledge and skills take several years to acquire and cannot be altered to suit the results of focus groups without considerable effort on the part of the academic. As Thorley (2003) noted, 'you may be challenging dearly held beliefs'. Another issue is basic administrative links to enable marketing strategies to be effective. Internal organisation can play a part: in some institutions, admissions are separated from recruitment, recruitment from widening participation, and so forth, so that units all involved in marketing do not work together (Educational Marketer I 2003).

Stage 5: Communication

Communication involves all the methods and techniques outlined for a sales-oriented university, but it goes beyond mere recruitment and is designed with an understanding of, and market intelligence on, its market demands in mind. Market-oriented universities will build up a relationship and track students right from application through to taking up their place: this links back to the admissions process described in the section on product design. Communication with students through the admissions process and whilst they are choosing which offer to take up is also important, right through until the final decision to come. This is true of postgraduates as well as undergraduates. Thorley (2003) spoke of the use of relationship marketing – trying to keep contact with prospective students throughout the time from first enquiry to taking up a place. Prospective students can often obtain a copy of a prospectus by filling in forms on-line: the most advanced universities also ask for data such as subject interested in, email address and age, so they not only monitor interest but keep contact with that enquirer through a relationship-managed system. Building up a personal relationship can be more effective than spending lots of money on advertising.

As Sargeant (1999: 220) observed, 'favourable publicity about the activities of students and/or staff, links with feeder institutions, open days, special events etc. can all help create and reinforce positive attitudes towards an organisation'. Word of mouth is often important as well, and good links with the community help make for a positive reputation on the grapevine. Liaison with local schools and colleges is important too. In 2001, Keele introduced UNIWORLD on the web to inspire young people whose parents had not been to university or were from poorer backgrounds to consider universities. Activities were designed to suit children from age 12–13, to explain to them the advantages of university and dispel negative myths (www.keele.ac.uk/depts/aa/widening/uniworld). Obviously websites are a key part of communication. New technology can play an important role in making prospective staff and students feel welcome to a university: increasingly, universities are using panoramas and providing live web-casts of part of their campus in an attempt to introduce the user to the institution.

Marketing could and should also be applied to recruiting staff. Universities need to determine the benefits of their staff training, resources, culture etc. and communicate them to prospective applicants. Some forward-thinking universities have sections dedicated to prospective staff who may be considering applying for a position; these sections outline the advantages of working for that particular university, thereby increasing its chances of obtaining the best possible application pool.

Stage 6: Campaign

Campaigning includes the activities discussed for sales-oriented universities, but focuses these. Keele recently introduced open days at weekends when it is easier for students and their parents to visit a university, and it tries to ensure that not all academics are in suits – they need to be welcoming rather than formidable, whilst retaining professionalism. Keele also thanked people for coming and applying (Thorley 2003). Aberdeen University tried to encourage students to attend open days despite the geographical distance, by putting an 'advert' in for them into the last page of the prospectus (University of Aberdeen 2002a): see Figure 7.3.

The style is very much suited to the prospective student, and deals with Aberdeen's potential weakness of geography by suggesting that there are cheap and easy travel options to the university. Open days need to be designed with the audience in mind. Students are not likely to be impressed by having to sit through long lectures by dithering and meandering academics. Market-oriented universities need to put on show the academics who are most likely to be attractive to

---

Here's something to think about.

YOUR FUTURE

At our Open Day we'll give you the answers.

- **Tour** our departments
- Talk to our staff and students
- Find out how a degree from the **University of Aberdeen** will give you **a better job**
- Stay overnight on 26th in student accommodation and **party the night away** at our Students' Union (don't worry, we'll entertain your relatives and teachers)
- For those of you staying overnight **cheap return coach travel** from Edinburgh, Glasgow and Dundee is available

Figure 7.3 University of Aberdeen's advert for an open day, 2002

prospective students, such as those who are younger, or the most effective at communicating, or knowledgeable yet also approachable, or involved in exciting and topical research. They also need to cater for all of their audiences and other aspects of the university product, including sessions for parents, now acknowledged as one of the key markets and decision-makers.

Stage 7: Delivery; Stage 8: Communication of delivery
Delivery in education is increasingly important, not the least because it is a key voting issue on which the market-oriented political party in government needs to be seen to deliver success in order to be re-elected and maintain public support. Measuring delivery in universities is, however, problematic. Like other public services, universities are increasingly subject to assessment, the results of which are widely publicised. They can produce annual reports (see, for example, Keele University 2001, 2002) and monitor statistics such as open day attendances and acceptances from applicants, but the general trend is not to see massive increases in student intake numbers unless you make a major change such as introducing an open day for the first time (Educational Marketer I 2003). Lucky universities with sudden jumps in undergraduate applications are those such as St Andrew's when Prince William went there in 2001 (Educational Marketer I 2003). Universities are subject to assessments of their research output through the RAE and of teaching quality by the QAA. Prospective students and funders can use this information to make a choice. One issue is dropout; for example, larger, well-known city universities may attract students easily but have a high dropout rate; the actual quality of student experience may be questionable.

Conclusions: marketing education and public services generally

> The mission of non profit organisations often requires them to take a long-term view rather than pander to current popular tastes . . . A university seeks to transmit skills, knowledge, and ways of thinking and reasoning that will have extended value to students – not simply to amuse and inspire them for the duration of the course in question. (Lovelock and Weinberg 1990: 7)

Marketing can make academics more responsive, more willing to change to suit student demand where possible. In theory, it can mean that money goes where it is most wanted, where the greatest demand is. Students are closer to the labour market and so may be better able to judge it and therefore which degree should be provided. Marketing, if used effectively, properly and carefully, can provide a useful debate and dialogue between staff and students, universities and society, as to what is most needed and how it should be provided (see Harvey and Busher 1996: 31; Pardy 1991; Christy and Brown 1999: 101).

Competition can also bring universities into the twenty-first century, stimulating a response to emerging, new and topical subjects that may never have stood a chance in the old elitist system. It may threaten some institutions, but, ironically, the less traditional schools and universities, although in a weaker position initially, may in the long term prove to be more responsive and market oriented, and therefore do better, than established places, because they have to use marketing and not just be sales oriented. One member of staff involved in marketing whom I interviewed said that marketing strategies were used more in new universities; the more established institutions had 'not had the imperative to move with the times' (Educational Marketer I 2003) because they were not as affected by the changes in market forces. Lori Manders, the director of marketing at Aberdeen, recalled how before she went to the institution there was a degree of complacency; it expected students just to turn up, but over the years this had lost the university its market share (Manders 2002). Of course the correlation between use of marketing and the type of institution requires further testing, but marketing could make education more responsive and up to date.

Nevertheless, there are many issues in trying to market education. The market-driven, product-design aspect threatens traditional academic values. The pro-vice-chancellor of Warwick University, in response to government plans to introduce top-up fees or change the state funding of universities in general, stated in 2002 that 'the Government's view is anti-intellectual . . . It has an unhealthy focus on education being for the economy, rather than for knowledge's sake' (quoted in Brookes 2003: 135). University is not a business; it is intended to offer a range of subjects, to foster collegiality; it is against the philosophy of education to do otherwise (see Moore 1989: 120; Gibbs et al. 2003; Jarratt 1985: 33; Harvey and Busher 1996: 29).

Furthermore, basing educational choice on the market poses potential problems. As Sargeant (1999: 201) noted, because universities now need to adapt to meet the demands of students, since they are the paying consumers, 'demand for subjects deemed to be of crucial importance to the future health of the economy – such as the sciences or engineering – [is] often sadly lacking'. If universities were completely led by the market, educational provision would significantly change and be subject to fashion; television, for example, can influence the choices made not just by students but by parents (Educational Marketer I 2003). 'If you were totally market-led' the institution would offer just three degrees in, for example, law, psychology and criminology (Educational Marketer I 2003). Universities are much more subject to market forces. Not all subjects are sexy; yet 'if you were a business and that was a paint colour that wasn't selling you'd just close it down' (Educational Marketer I 2003).

Another major difficulty with universities is that the product cannot be changed as demand alters. As one marketer said, 'you can't bring courses on-line fast enough': it takes at least 18 months to create a new course in terms of policies, documents, committees and recruitment (Educational Marketer I 2003). Subjects and staff expertise in an unpopular subject may be needed to inform the development of another new area – such as political marketing, which requires elements from both traditional political science and marketing management studies. Furthermore, demand can fluctuate and may rise again, so staff need to be retained in case this happens. Indeed, 'these things go up and down'

(Educational Marketer I 2003): numbers fall but then can rise again, and if you remove staff on the dip they can be costly if not impossible to get back. Academics are highly skilled and take years to train. This issue is facing all universities, even traditional ones. In July 2003, for instance, an article in the *Daily Telegraph* stated that Durham University was seeking to close Middle and Far Eastern studies because of budget constraints, and that there had been objections from academics, international foundations and even the foreign office (*Daily Telegraph*, 5 July 2003: 6).

As in health, choice is limited by various factors. Increasingly, for example, consumers of universities may also face this dilemma as students and parents pay directly for education, encouraging students to try to live at the parental home to save money.

Again as with health, there is a strong argument that the professionals – those who have trained for school teaching or academic research and teaching – should be the ones to decide what is taught and how it is taught, because they have the objectivity and expertise. Marketing appears to threaten that, although it does not have to. There can be a blend of listening to market demand and using professional judgement to respond to it. But certainly there has been increased power given to parents within schools and students have greater choice and power within universities, threatening the traditional professional autonomy that educationalists once had.

Universities are now subject to market forces, but they are nevertheless not as free as businesses to develop. Institutions cannot simply expand their numbers; government restricts the growth and sets them targets (Thorley 2003), and they are fined if they attract too few or too many students. Keele, for example, applied in 2002 to be able to take more students for the degree in media, culture and communications, but this was not accepted and they were limited to taking up to 40 students despite receiving 450 applications. The demand was there, but they were not allowed to respond to it. Universities are not as free to take risks or expand as businesses are: 'it isn't like marketing in a free market'; 'you're not free in terms of what the government does' (Educational Marketer I 2003).

Central government or market faces obstacles in always trying to control the delivery (see Laing and Lees-Marshment 2002), especially, for example, who delivers it, such as a teacher in a school (Christy and Brown 1999: 98). Harvey and Busher (1996: 27) noted how in schools:

> Teaching as a craft is dependent on teachers' interpersonal skills and the social interactions of groups of students. Even if a curriculum is prescribed, as it has been in state schools in England and Wales since 1988, how staff teach and how students respond to their pedagogy will vary. Schools . . . provide something which . . . in its creation, is largely inseparable from the interactions of teacher/providers and student/clients.

As with health, the end output of education is at least partly determined by the political consumer. We can offer all the good teaching in the world, but in part the success of the students depends on their abilities and effort. As Hannagan (1992: 51) observed, 'pupils and students can play a large part in the delivery of education and training – they are participants in the process', and learning also depends on the interaction between students (Harvey and Busher 1996: 26). Another problem is that market intelligence costs: there is not enough money to conduct intelligence about all proposed new courses, leaving product development decisions to be taken in a vacuum without accurate knowledge of the market. Devoting significant resources to market intelligence takes limited funds away from product design and delivery. Numerous academics have questioned the application of marketing to the public services generally (see, for example, Graham 1994: 361; Brown 1992: 204; Walsh 1994: 67). It is a debate that will continue.

Clearly marketing has entered the educational sphere, but in reality the practice of marketing is relatively underdeveloped. A survey commissioned by the Adam Smith Institute on the public services indicated that they are not delivering what people want. The report indicated that the public services in Britain follow their own agenda, not what people want them to do: 'only a very few undertook market research to discover what their public thought they ought to be doing, and which services they should be providing. Most looked at what they were already doing, and sought to do it in more efficient and user-friendly ways' (Pirie and Worcester 2001: 7). This is a problem because the public services affect people's daily lives. As such these services are becoming an increasingly important issue in party and electoral politics, and hence the political system generally, as many people debate the best way to produce the services needed given the resources available (Collins and Butler 1998: 1).

The legislature that changes the policy implemented in these services is also of great concern: changes in tuition fees and state funding are debated within parliaments, the institutions set aside to debate and develop legislation to provide further representation and influence for the people of the country. As Pirie and Worcester (2001: 21) noted, it was 'the new 1988 Education Act, steered through by the then Secretary of State Sir Kenneth Baker . . . [which] made the consumer agenda respectable'. Parliaments are important to ensure that any legislative output will have the intended effect and will work effectively, having the potential as it does to influence areas like education and health. They are also driven by political parties – hence the political marketing revolution link running through the system. This leads us onto the next chapter on marketing parliaments, which will analyse the extent to which they as individual institutions respond to their market demands in order to fulfil their traditional functions.

Notes

1 Education was first linked to political marketing by Lees-Marshment (2001a, 2001b) and by Brookes (2003).
2 The direct source of these quotations remains anonymous to protect individuals and institutions.

Bibliography

Allen, A. and T. Higgins (1994), *Higher Education: The International Student Experience*, HEIST, Leeds.

Baines, P. and R. Lynch (2003), 'Strategy Development in UK Higher Education: A Resource-Based Perspective', *Academy of Marketing Conference Proceedings* July.

Boxall, M. (1991), 'Positioning the Institution in the Marketplace', in *Universities in the Market Place*, CUA Corporate Planning Forum, Conference of University Administrators in Association with Touche Ross.

Brookes, M. (2003), 'Higher Education: Marketing in a Quasi-commercial Service Industry', special issue, *International Journal of Non-profit and Voluntary Sector Marketing* 8(2): 134–142.

Brown, P. (1992), 'Alternative Delivery Systems in the Provision of Social Services', *International Review of Administrative Sciences* 58: 201–214.

Christy, R. and J. Brown. (1999), 'Marketing in the Public Services', in S. Horton and D. Farnham (eds), *Public Management in Britain*, Macmillan, Basingstoke.

Collins, N. and P. Butler. (1998), 'Public Services in Ireland: A Marketing Perspective', Working Paper VII, Department of Public Administration, National University of Ireland, Cork, August.

Davies, B. and L. Ellison (1991), *Marketing the Secondary School*. Longman, Harlow.

Educational Marketer I (2003), Interview by J. Lees-Marshment with educational marketer at mainstream UK university, July.

Educational Marketer II (2003), Interview by J. Lees-Marshment with educational marketer at UK university, July.

Foskett, N., ed. (1992), *Managing External Relations in Schools: A Practical Guide*, Routledge, London.

Further Education Teacher (2002), Interview by J. Lees-Marshment with teacher at further education college, May.

Gadie, C. (2002), 'Marketing Aberdeen University', presentation at the political marketing conference, September.

Gammack, S. (2002), 'Catering Review Focus Groups', email to Aberdeen University staff, February.

Gibbs, P., D. Vrontis and W. Jones (2003), 'The Impact of Educational Marketing on what *is* Higher Education', *Academy of Marketing Conference Proceedings* July.

Grabowski, S.M. (1981), 'Marketing in Higher Education', AAHE ERIC Higher Education Research Report No. 5. AAHE, Washington, DC.

Graham, P. (1994), 'Marketing in the Public Sector: Inappropriate or Merely Difficult?', *Journal of Marketing Management* 10: 361–375.

Gray, L. (1991), *Marketing Education*, Open University Press, Buckingham.

Hanford, I. (1990), 'Secondary School Image', *Management in Education* 4(1): 4–8.

Hannagan, T. (1992), *Marketing for the Non-profit Sector*, Macmillan, London.

Harvey, J. and H. Busher (1996), 'Marketing Schools and Consumer Choice', *International Journal of Education Management* 4(10): 26–32.

HEIST (1995), *The Role of Marketing in the University and College Sector*, HEIST, Leeds.

Hesketh, A. and P. Knight (1998), 'Secondary School Prospectuses and Educational Markets', *Cambridge Journal of Education* 28(1): 21–36.

Holloway, D., S. Horton and D. Farnham (1999), 'Education', in S. Horton and D. Farnham (eds), *Public Management in Britain*, Macmillan, Basingstoke. pp. 194–212.

Hunt, M. and S. MacKay (2001), 'Service Quality and Customer Satisfaction in UK Higher Education (HE): A Conceptual Evaluation', paper presented at the Academy of Marketing Conference, Cardiff.

Jarratt, R. (1985), *Report of the Steering Committee for Efficiency Studies in Universities*. CVCP, London.

Keele University (2001), *Keele University: Annual Review 2001*, Keele University, Keele.

Keele University (2002), *Keele University: Annual Review 2002*, Keele University, Keele.

Kinnell, M. and J. MacDougall (1997), *Marketing in the Not-for-profit sector*, Butterworth Heinemann, Oxford.

Kotler, P. and K. Fox. (1985), *Strategic Marketing for Educational Institutions*, Prentice-Hall, Englewood Cliffs, NJ.

Laing, A. and J. Lees-Marshment (2002), 'Time to Deliver: Why Political Marketing Needs to Move Beyond the Campaign', paper presented at the PSA conference, Aberdeen, April.

Lees-Marshment, J. (2001a), 'Comprehensive Political Marketing: What, How and Why', *Proceedings of the Academy of Marketing Conference*, held at Cardiff University, 2–4 July.

Lees-Marshment, J. (2001b), 'Let's go Comprehensive: Reaching the Full Potential of Political Marketing', *Proceedings of the Political Marketing Conference*, held in Dublin, September.

Lovelock, C.H. and C.B. Weinberg (eds) (1990), *Public and Nonprofit Marketing: Readings and Cases*, Scientific Press, San Francisco, CA.

Macbeth, A. (1989), *Involving Parents*, Heinemann, London.

Manders, L. (2002), 'Marketing Education', Presentation by the director of marketing, University of Aberdeen, 18 March.

Marland, M. and R. Rogers (1991), *Marketing the School*, Heinemann, London.

McAuley, A. (2003), 'Scoping the Student Learning Experience: Drinking Deep or Tasting Little?', *Academy of Marketing Conference Proceedings* July.

McFarlane, E. (2003), 'Research and Market Intelligence', Presentation by the Research and intelligence officer at Keele University, 7 March.

Mitchell, S., A. Anson and E. Frith (2003), 'New Target Markets will Change the Future of Education', *Academy of Marketing Conference Proceedings* July.

Moore, P.G. (1989), 'Marketing Higher Education', *Higher Education Quarterly* 43(2): 108–124.

O'Fairchellaigh, P. and P. Graham (1991), 'Introduction', in C. O'Faircheallaigh, P. Graham and J. Warburton (eds), *Service Delivery and Public Sector Marketing*, Macmillan, Sydney. pp. ix–xiii.

Pagan, L. (1994) , 'Testing out Support', *Marketing* 12 May: 43.

Palfreyman, D. and D. Warner (1996), *Higher Education Management: The Key Elements*, Open University Press, Buckingham.

Pardy, D. (1991), *Marketing for Schools*, Kogan Page, London.

Parsuraman, A., V.A. Zeithaml and L.L. Berry (1988), 'SERVQUAL: A Multiple Item Scale for Measuring Consumer Perceptions of Service Quality', *Journal of Retailing* 64(1): 12–40.

Petch, A. (1986), 'Parental Choice at Entry to Primary School', *Research Papers in Education* 1(1): 26–47.

Petch, P. (1992), 'School Management: Theory and Practice', in T. Burgess, *Accountability in Schools*, Longman, Harlow.

Pirie, M. and R. Worcester (2001), *The Wrong Package*, report on a MORI poll by the Adam Smith Institute, London. Also at www.mori.com/polls/2001/asi.shtml or www.adamsmith.org.uk.

Sargeant, A. (1999), *Marketing Management for Nonprofit Organisations*, Oxford University Press, Oxford.

School Headteacher (2002), Interview by J. Lees-Marshment with headteacher of a school.

School Headteacher (2003), Interview by J. Lees-Marshment with headteacher of a school.

School Marketing Director (2002), Interview by J. Lees-Marshment with marketing director for Scottish independent school.

School Teacher I (2003), Interview by J. Lees-Marshment with teacher within an English secondary school.

School Teacher II (2003), Interview by J. Lees-Marshment with teacher within an English junior school.

Shumar, W. (1997), *College for Sale: A Critique of the Commodification of Higher Education*, Falmer Press, London.

Thorley, H. (2003), 'New Appointment: Directorate of Marketing', *University of Aberdeen Press Release* 28 November.

University of Aberdeen (2001), *Strategic Plan 2001–5*, Court and Planning Office, University of Aberdeen, Aberdeen.

University of Aberdeen (2002a), *Undergraduate Prospectus 2003*, University of Aberdeen, Aberdeen.

University of Aberdeen (2002b), 'Student Recruitment and Admissions Service: Presentation to New Staff', University of Aberdeen, 8 March.

University of Aberdeen (2002c), 'University of Aberdeen to Host Parents' Information Evenings across Scotland', University of Aberdeen Press Release, 8 March.

University of Essex (2003), *Prospectus for October 2004 Entry*, University of Essex, Colchester.

University of Stirling (2003), *CD-Rom Prospectus for October 2004 Entry*, University of Stirling, Stirling.

Wakeford, J. (2000), 'Dons in the Dock', *Guardian* 3 October.

Walsh, K. (1994), 'Marketing and Public Sector Management', *European Journal of Marketing* 28(3): 63–71.

8

Marketing parliaments

> The promotion or marketing of a parliament is not just an optional extra but can (and probably should) be a necessary activity. It is not simply a PR or public information exercise, but also enables a parliament to fulfil its real role and functions effectively. (Winetrobe 2003)

> The case with the Scottish Parliament [is that] expectations were quite high, but people sense that the Parliament has not yet come up with the goods. (Simon Braunholtz, in Scottish Parliamentary Corporate Body 2001: 922)

> Marketing a Parliament is not like marketing any other product. What is the product? Is it the parliament itself? Can you divorce the success of the Parliament from the success of its MSPs? Can you market the parliamentary process without getting into the politics? Should the Parliament spend public money on promoting itself? (Seaton 2002)

Marketing parliaments, especially established institutions such as Westminster, is a difficult challenge, because despite the basic premise of both marketing and democracy that they should be run to suit the people, any changes to the institutions will be directly determined by the elected politicians who work within them. History, tradition, the way the institutions are to begin with, and the interests of the dominant elite within them often prove almost insurmountable obstacles to bringing effective change when it is needed. Nevertheless, parliaments in the UK are changing and there is a strong desire amongst many for them to become more market oriented and responsive to their markets – not just those near Big Ben, but outside, including the media and the public.

This chapter will examine the state of marketing within Westminster and the new Scottish parliament. Analysis draws upon traditional political science texts on parliaments, papers by parliamentary practitioners and, with the new Scottish institution in particular, documentary analysis, visits and interviews with parliamentary staff. When I began this research, there was no existing literature on marketing parliaments: I had to follow my hunch all the way to Edinburgh to the warm reception of the newly founded Scottish parliament to confirm that I might not be completely mad in breaking yet more new ground.

A year later, in September 2002, Alex Salmond, former leader of the SNP and a key figure in the push for devolution, another MSP and a Scottish academic spoke at a public debate on 'Marketing the Scottish Parliament' at the University of Aberdeen. Together with sessions on parliaments at the 2002 Political Studies Conference, this meant parliamentary marketing had been put on the academic map. As very political institutions, subject to the same market forces as all the other organisations analysed in this book, parliaments are a prime if previously neglected area for political marketing. This chapter will set out a prescriptive theoretical framework for how parliaments might be marketed, and then set empirical reality against this. In doing so, it will show some of the obstacles to reforming and marketing parliaments as institutions, as well as make suggestions for future development.

Marketing Westminster: theoretical foundations

> Working on parliaments is not like any other work. This may seem a rather bold statement . . . but . . . parliaments are not like any other institution. They are truly unique. (Winetrobe 2003)

Importance of Westminster
Parliament plays a vital and important role within the political system. It is the next step in the process after parties have used political marketing to win office. All policy legislation must pass through parliament, thus influencing the ability of market-oriented political parties to deliver.

Nature of Westminster
The British parliament has two chambers. The lower House, the Commons, consists of over 650 MPs elected by voters at every general election; the upper House is the Lords, which was traditionally full of hereditary peers, most of whom the Labour government removed during 1997–2001. The Commons has an adversarial culture; the very architectural layout of the chamber places government against opposition. Party is very important and party unity high compared with other countries. If a government has a clear majority, it can be extremely easy to pass government bills and delivery legislation. The Lords is the second chamber and previously acted as a potential check on executive and party power as well as another scrutineer of legislation; the composition of the House is currently under review. The maximum life of one parliament is five years: the governing party has to call a general election within that time. The parliamentary session is from October to October with an adjournment in summer. Westminster is directly descended from the English parliament of the Middle Ages, and this history has produced many ancient rituals and traditions. It was not designed for the twenty-first century, and there are significant internal forces encouraging institutional inertia about the use of political marketing.

Goal

Parliament's main goal is to fulfil its functions to the satisfaction of its market. These functions can be gathered from general political science literature and are to:

- create government through elections to the Commons and votes of confidence in the House;
- carry out the business of government, assenting to government bills and requests for money supply;
- facilitate a significant opposition: the second largest party in the House forms an organised alternative government, with a Shadow Cabinet;
- scrutinise and hold to account government measures and actions on behalf of citizens, thus acting as a 'watch-dog' over the executive;
- safeguard the quality of legislation, exposing any mistakes or government errors before they become law and harm peoples' lives;
- debate, especially government policy;
- investigate maladminstration;
- ensure citizen voices are heard, both individually (including individual redress) and collectively;
- fulfil a symbolic, legitimising role;
- express and represent individual constituents' and constituencies' interests especially.

Market

Like other political organisations, parliament has several markets, each with different but important demands.

- *The public:* The Public need parliament to call the government to account, scrutinise legislation, and offer them a voice in government.
- *The governing party:* Parliament is the means by which parties deliver on their promises. The governing party therefore needs an institution that facilitates the garnering of support for the programme it has been elected on. There is little point, for example, in a major party undergoing the necessary change to become market oriented and succeeding in passing through the first seven stages of the political marketing process, only to fall down on Stage 8 because parliament blocks the implementation of its policy promises. However, if a party attracts enough electoral and internal support it can push legislation through, although it would be wiser to facilitate reasoned debate to ensure the policy will work once it is out of parliament, being implemented and affecting people's daily lives.
- *All parties:* The opposition, non-governing parties need parliament to provide them with an effective place for opposing the government and ensuring they themselves have some visibility to the electorate, to help them continue to have a chance of gaining government themselves in future elections.

- *Individual MPs:* Parliament should support and facilitate constituency work undertaken by individual MPs. MPs also want the institution to aid their own career and development through the House, and they all have their own demands as to what parliament should be like. Additionally, they may adopt a market orientation to their work in the House as individuals.
- *The media:* The media needs access to parliamentary work and behaviour. Like parties and the monarchy, Westminster needs to consider and facilitate the needs and demands of the media or it will bypass the institution to fulfil its own goals. As Winetrobe (2003) commented, 'any promotion or marketing of a parliament has to address [media] preconceptions and prejudices'.
- *Charities:* Charities are concerned with any policy change in parliament that affects them. Their demands will be for effective and fair access. As Chapter 5 showed, some charities have been given the opportunity to be involved in committees and investigations into their area and invited to contribute their specialised knowledge. Others may have engaged in lobbying and will want more particular influence on legislation.
- *Other parliaments:* Before devolution it could be said that Westminster had no competition, but since then, the highly visible Scottish parliament, with new means of operating and design, has made the older institution re-evaluate its own behaviour. The legal and constitutional implications of devolution mean that Westminster needs to work with the devolved institutions. The European Parliament is also a market, and possibly a competitor for power and influence.
- *The staff:* Staff working within the parliament are an important market and resource for MPs.

As with all political organisations, sometimes the demands of these different groups conflict. There may also be conflict between trying to make the hours of work for members better and the ability of the parliament to function effectively, although arguably if members have better working hours they themselves will perform better, which strengthens parliament overall. The interests of the governing party are different to those of parliament as a whole (Norton 2001: 7; see also Riddell 2001: 355).

Product

Parliament's chief product is legislation, but as with political parties, the organisational effectiveness can be influenced by many different aspects of the institution (see Winetrobe 2003). The product therefore includes a number of characteristics and components, such as those listed in Table 8.1. For example, whilst MPs are 'the front line of Westminster' (Fox and Lees-Marshment 2002: 5) and the most visible part of the product, the structure, processes and culture can have an important influence on behaviour in parliament; and although debates are more visible to the public, committees have influence on the final legislation.

Table 8.1 The Westminster product

	Details
MPs and Lords	Nature, characteristics (representation of society in terms of gender, race, class, occupational background), power, ability to represent constituents, character (deferential to government or of independent mind), relevant expertise, skill
Staff and resources	Parliamentary staff, resources (offices, equipment, research assistance) for MPs, resources for media, expert staff (academics, lawyers, scientists), training for members
Structure, processes and culture	
Debate and discussion	Can debate and discuss topical issues and government action as well as actual legislation
Legislation	Much debate in the legislative process; during the passage of a bill important amendments can be made
Committees	Design, powers, members, effectiveness, issues dealt with
Procedural representations of opinion	e.g. early day motions
Prime Minister's Questions	Chance for oral questions of the prime minister
Individual redress	MPs use parliament to deal with individual problems of their constituency met through their own surgeries
Timing, cycle and recess	
Events	e.g. state opening
Building	e.g. House of Commons Chamber, Palace of Westminster

Like all other political organisations, parliaments are increasingly criticised by both the public and the elites that work within them. Therefore, as Fox and Lees-Marshment (2002: 2) argued, '. . . political marketing has a worthwhile role to play in identifying ways in which Westminster can ensure its activities are relevant and important to those who need its services and policy output'. This chapter will outline the nature of a product-oriented parliament, a sales-oriented parliament and a market-oriented parliament in theory and then illustrate them empirically.

Product-oriented parliament

Definition
A product-oriented parliament would behave according to how it thinks best, passing legislation and meeting its functions in the way it thinks is best. It would assume that the public would be satisfied with its performance. Any criticism would be put down to lack of public knowledge, skills or expertise; parliamen-

---

Box 8.1 The process for a product-oriented parliament

Stage 1: Product design
Parliament designs its product, including MPs, Lords, committee structure and resources, to suit what it thinks is best. There is no regard for public opinion or demands, or the need to change behaviour to suit other bodies.

Stage 2: Communication
Parliament does what it does, and expects the media to cover it. It may convey factual information, but no thought is given as to how that might be done, or how best to convey it.

Stage 3: Delivery
Product-oriented parliaments do deliver by passing legislation. They will not, however, attempt to solicit feedback on whether they are seen to perform satisfactorily overall. They aim to deliver what they think is best.

---

tarians know best and parliament is there to decide how best to represent the people, not be told by the people what to do. See Box 8.1.

The British parliament has long been product-oriented, and only recently began to try to move beyond this to improve its communication. It is full of many traditions and practices dating back to an era long gone. As Winetrobe (2002: 2) commented, Westminster is 'the product of centuries of political and constitutional development' but 'is regarded nowadays as inefficient, ineffective and out-of-date, mired in archaic procedure and practice and divorced from those it is supposed to serve'.

There have been, and to a certain extent still are, many practices in Westminster that typify a product-oriented approach. The debating standard in the House of Commons is often juvenile and unpleasant, hostile and combative rather than reasoned and considerate (Garret 1992: 23). Fox and Lees-Marshment (2002: 12) noted that 'this way of debating issues can obviously soon become unappealing to the general public and those who desire to see an information rich environment' (see Hetherington et al. 1990: 73–74). A report by the Hansard Society noted how 'the style of procedures of the Commons are alien to most voters. Parliamentary debates are conducted in a manner that is, on occasion, difficult to understand. The Commons looks, for the most part, arcane and old-fashioned' (Hansard Society Commission on Parliamentary Scrutiny [hereafter 'Hansard Society'] 2001: 78).

Members of the Commons have also been traditionally unrepresentative socially: male, middle-class and white (a situation perhaps stemming from the history of the institution, as the job was not always paid). This problem was exacerbated by the working hours: the Commons started at 2.30 p.m. and went on until 10 p.m., and sometimes until the early hours of the morning, making it harder for parents, especially women, to be MPs. Obviously the nature of the

Lords before reform under the New Labour government was subject to elitism, as the lords were appointed mostly from the hereditary peerage.

Parliament's traditional recess during the summer is a problem when important events, even war as in September 2001, occur. The overall impression to the public remains that of an institution out of touch which neglects topical issues. Upon the reopening of parliament after the summer recess in 2000, Tony Benn MP (quoted in the Hansard Society 2001: 82) stated:

> We have been in recess since July, and during that time there has been a fuel crisis, a Danish no vote, the collapse of the Euro and a war in the middle east, but what is our business tomorrow? The Insolvency Bill (Lords). It ought to be called the Bankruptcy Bill (Commons), because we play no role.

Opposition and backbench MPs have the time to pick up on problems through their constituencies but do not have the power to move debates. For example, there was a crisis with the Passport Agency in 2000: the new computer system was not working and big delays in processing passport applications were occurring, meaning people were having to miss and cancel holidays. Problems first began to emerge in February of that year but parliament did not discuss it until the end of June; by this time the problem had developed into an actual crisis (Hansard Society 2001: 82).

Before the mid-1960s, parliamentary facilities were poor. MPs lacked resources to do a good job: space, secretarial assistance and research assistance. Norton (1994a: 322) explains that 'an MP was guaranteed only a locker in which to keep papers and received no allowance, either for hiring a secretary or even to cover the cost of telephone calls'. Even in the 1980s the demands on MPs increased tremendously but not the resources for them to meet them (Norton 1994b: 346). Surveys in the late 1980s and 1990s showed MPs themselves were dissatisfied with the working conditions and procedures (Norton 1994b: 346). There was also a degree of institutional inertia that made it very difficult to change anything; as a former staff member said (Seaton 2001), management reviews were conducted but nothing changed because of the institutional inertia.

In terms of communication, government publications from the Commons were highly statistical and complex and not easy to read. The House of Commons established an Information Office in 1978, which acted as a central answering point for enquiries from the public that relate to the work, publications, proceedings and history of the House of Commons, but simply supplied requested information. Until recent reforms in 2002/3, the hours of the Commons missed deadlines for newspapers and television (Hansard Society 2001: 79). Hansard commented that parliament needed to stop assuming broadcasters will cover what they do (Hansard Society 2001: 83) and think about how people receive communication: 'rightly or wrongly, the public is unused to simply listening to people speak, without any other aids or information, and it is regarded by many people as an outdated and ineffective form of communication' (Hansard Society 2001: 79).

Parliament was first televised in 1989, but did little to encourage coverage (Hansard Society 2001: 79). As Fox and Lees-Marshment (2002: 16) noted, committees were 'left to make their own press contacts'. Often committees publish reports on the same day, reducing potential media coverage (Hansard Society 2001: 81; Fox and Lees-Marshment 2001: 16). Until the turn of the century, there was no reception or visitors' centre at Westminster. (Fox and Lees-Marshment 2002: 1; Winetrobe 2002: 3). Robin Cook (2001: 9) noted how 'the public is herded around Westminster' when it does visit, and 'the information they receive tends to present Parliament in terms of its architecture and its history, not in terms of its role as an expression of democracy'. Until 2002, Westminster's website was full of information but was very old-fashioned. Indeed, the new site, which will be discussed later, states that: 'The old site was a comprehensive and detailed information resource, and it was ideal for users who knew what they wanted and where to find it. However, it became clear that for non-specialist users, the site was not organised in a way which was always easy to follow, and some people found this off-putting' (www.parliament.uk/site_information/about_this_site.cfm). The old site was designed to suit the producers, not the market – a product-oriented attitude. Overall there is strong evidence for a product-oriented approach in the British parliament. However, over time, debate about its role and performance has increased and with it the need for it to move towards a sales orientation, if not a market-oriented model.

Preaching better to the people? Sales-oriented parliament

The rows of empty green benches are not a convincing advert for the centrality of Parliament. (Hansard Society 2001: 82)

The House has come to eye up the Press Lobby as circling Apaches waiting to scalp us. In truth both the House and the Press Lobby need each other if we are both going to remain in business. It would be an admission of that symbiotic relationship if the House were to adopt working practices which gave the lobby a better chance to beat the competition for news coverage. (Cook, 2001: 4–5)

Causes of a move to a sales orientation
As Fox and Lees-Marshment (2002) observed, 'there has been a growing amount of concern regarding Parliament's ability to carry popular support amongst the British public and electorate' (see also Hazell 2001). The Hansard Society, Charter 88 and DEMOS have all criticised it. Research into public satisfaction with Westminster indicates a problem: 39 per cent (net total) feel 'satisfied' whilst 29 per cent feel 'dissatisfied' with the way in which parliament works (MORI 2001, cited by Fox and Lees-Marshment 2002).

Changes in the way political information is communicated in the political system also call for a move to a sales orientation. Norton (2000: 17) argued that although a 24-hour news service now exists, and 'there are now more diverse news media and they compete for viewers, listeners or readers on a continuous basis', the focus is on government itself, not parliament. Policy announcements by ministers are often conducted through the media rather than parliament. Parliament is often 'told of the policy only after the media has run the story and any parliamentary reaction may be ignored . . . by the time MPs get to question ministers the most salient political issues have already been discussed, and with the politics sucked out of an issue the parliamentary debate provides little that is newsworthy' (Hansard Society 2001: 80). Westminster has therefore begun to make changes to try to address this, by adopting a more persuasive, sales-oriented approach.

Definition

A *sales-oriented parliament* retains the same product design as a product-oriented one; it just attempts to sell it better. A sales-oriented parliament focuses on presenting the institution in the best light in order to achieve positive evaluations from the public. It concentrates on communicating the benefits of its behaviour. It conducts market intelligence to ascertain its weaknesses and strengths, and changes facilities and timings to suit the media, to ensure maximum coverage. It may change the focus of what it presents to the public in the light of market intelligence, but it does not change its actual behaviour. See Box 8.2.

Indeed, as will be discussed in the conclusion, Westminster appears to be responding to 'the competition', copying the Scottish parliament. It has made changes during the writing of this book, and may well make more by the time this book comes out, that move it more completely towards a sales orientation.

A new communications advisor to the House of Commons was appointed in the summer of 2000. Westminster sent a team up to the Scottish parliament to see how it ran communications (Lees-Marshment 2003). Parliament or bodies interested in it have conducted various market intelligence about its public standing and role, as already explored. There have been a number of debates and discussions about the public standing of parliament and suggestions for reform have been made. For example, the Hansard Society conducted several reports and commissions on how parliament should reform its communication system, and these have been responded to in changes in media provision. Parliament itself has run a select committee on the modernisation of the House of Commons, which began to meet in 1997 (www.parliament.uk/commons/selcom/modhome.htm).

Additionally, parliament has begun to alter the way it communicates in response to results from market intelligence. Major improvements have been made to the website, www.parliament.uk, responding to the Hansard Society (2001: 84) and the example set by the Scottish parliament. The site itself states:

Box 8.2 The process for a sales-oriented parliament

Stage 1: Product design
The product design will be the same as for a product-oriented parliament: parliament designs its product, including MPs, Lords, committee structure and resources, to suit what it thinks is best. There is no regard for public opinion or demands, or the need to change behaviour to suit other bodies.

Stage 2: Market intelligence
A sales-oriented parliament will conduct market intelligence (debate, discussion, commissions, focus groups, polls, reports) on the reaction of its market to its behaviour and performance, to find out where it is weak and where it is strong.

Stage 3: Communication
It will have an effective communications system enabling the best publicising of its work. Responding to the results of market intelligence, it may attempt to downplay its weaknesses and focus on its strengths. Communication is designed to improve the public standing of parliament. It necessitates the appointment of a communications director and potential changes in timing and facilities to suit the media, to ensure maximum communication. The style of communication is also geared to suit the audience.

Stage 4: Campaign
A sales-oriented parliament may undertake mini-campaigns to boost its profile, attract new members and publicise the work it is doing.

Stage 5: Delivery
Parliament will pass legislation and fulfil its functions, but still aims to deliver what it thinks is best.

Stage 6: Communication of delivery
It will also attempt to communicate the work it has done; for example, publicising the passing of important and interesting legislation, or a particularly significant committee investigation or commission.

What's new?

The main differences are:

A more modern and attractive design for the most widely used pages;
A better search engine, with an advanced search facility;
Improved navigation.

Other useful features include improved FAQs, a site map, index and Directory of MPs, Peers and Offices.

You can find more detailed information about the work, membership and remit of Parliamentary Committees, as well as new pages explaining the role and work of the House of Commons Commission. (www.parliament.uk/site_information/about_this_site.cfm, accessed 16 July 2003)

The site includes live coverage of committee meetings and the two chambers on www.parliamentlive.tv. Additionally, towards the end of the twentieth century, committees started using the internet and emailing interested parties about their work and the new site facilities. Interestingly, this section was run as a pilot project; a statement on the site read:

> during the first year all aspects of the service will be under constant review and a number of enhancements will be brought online over this period.
>
> Our aim is to make Parliamentary proceedings more transparent and accessible, and to this end we would welcome both general and specific feedback, as we are keen to alter the service in accordance with your observations. [i.e. further market intelligence]. (www.parliamentlive.tv/pilotnew.asp, accessed 16 July 2003)

There are panoramas for on-line visiting or viewing the building (www.parliament.uk/visiting/panoramas.cfm). The media has also been given easier access, with news reporters let in to broadcast directly from the central lobby area instead of being left outside on the lawn in front of Big Ben.

The Westminster parliament has some way to go before reaching a sales orientation and engaging in communication with maximum effectiveness, however. A report by the Liaison Committee, *Shifting the Balance*, criticised the layout of committee reports, saying it was poor; the chair, Robert Sheldon MP, described the design as 'an absurd situation' which 'relegates us to the also rans in the publicity stakes' (Hansard Society 2001: 85). Another means of communicating the work of the Commons is government publications. In recent years these have been redesigned to make them more presentable, but they 'still look like outdated mathematical textbooks' (Hansard Society 2001: 81). Parliament has some way to go in ensuring that the public is aware of its work. A report by the Hansard Society (2001: 78) argued that parliament needed not only to fulfil its functions but to be seen to do so: 'Parliament's task is to engage more fully with the public interest, highlighting and explaining issues . . . it must communicate more effectively with voters.' Overall, it has been slow to move towards a sales orientation, although plenty of commissions, organisations and think tanks argue that it needs to.

It is therefore unlikely that parliament will have moved beyond this to a market orientation by the time this book is published, yet there have been some signs of a move in this direction and there is increasing awareness of the need for it.

The market comes to Westminster – but not so fast: market-oriented parliament

> The Commission believes that the way that Parliament . . . consults with the public needs to be radically updated. (Hansard Society 2001: 82)

> Citizens need an effective Parliament . . . They need the security of knowing that, if there is a problem, there is a body to which they can turn to help, a body that can force public officials to listen. (Norton 2000: 5)

Need for a market orientation

Pressure is increasing on Westminster to become market oriented so it can play an important and effective role in the political system as a whole. The amount of work parliament has to do has vastly increased over the years; legislation has grown, but not the resources of the institution to scrutinise it. 'Parliament has been in danger of being overloaded with business' (Norton 2000: 12). Yet the demand for parliament to deliver what people want is greater than ever. Changes in society overall have rendered citizens more critical of their government and all institutions and organisations within it. As Robin Cook (2001: 4–5) noted, there has been an 'alarming trend' of 'disengagement from the process of parliamentary democracy by a growing proportion of the electorate'; there has also been a 'decline in deference in our society . . . We can no longer count on veneration for the antiquity of our institution to maintain its status. We have to win that respect by proving that we do something useful.'

Definition

A market-oriented parliament will design its product to suit what the public demand. It will conduct market intelligence to consider what the public most need and want, then design its product, including parliamentarians, power structure, committee system, staff, resources, rules and regulations, to suit the results from market intelligence. It aims to satisfy the public. See Box 8.3.

Box 8.3 The process for a market-oriented parliament

Stage 1: Market intelligence

A market-oriented parliament will conduct a wide range of market intelligence (debate, discussion, commissions, focus groups, polls, reports, from the public, related bodies and parliamentarians) about what parliament is good at and not good at, and think about how it might be improved. It is concerned with what the public need and want from it, not just what they think of it as it is. It will therefore include debates about the nature and role of parliament, involving related outside bodies and parliamentarians as well as the views of the public.

Stage 2: Product design

Parliament designs its product, including MPs, Lords, committee structure and resources, to suit the results from market intelligence. It therefore takes great heed of public opinion and the views of interested and related bodies. It changes its behaviour accordingly, being responsive to public opinion.

Stage 3: Product adjustment

- *Achievability:* It needs to ensure that the product design and promises can be achieved.
- *Competition analysis:* It will take into account the needs and views of the competition, such as the executive and the media, and adjust its behaviour to suit them.

continued on next page

Box 8.3 continued

- *Internal reaction analysis:* For the product design to be effective, it needs to be supported by those within the institution. Parliament must therefore ensure parliamentarians agree with the proposed changes, and that tradition is not completely thrown out but instead is integrated.
- *Support analysis:* Parliament may target some product changes, in particular areas where it is especially weak.

Stage 4: Implementation
For political marketing to work it has to be implemented effectively, using all the guidelines from marketing management literature. The findings from Stages 1–3 of the process must be implemented and a majority within the institution need to accept the new behaviour broadly and comply with it. The organisation must therefore proceed carefully, especially if major change is required. The major players must be got on board, above all the main parties and particularly the governing party.

Stage 5: Communication
Parliament will then communicate its work effectively and efficiently, responding to the needs of the media, the governing party and the executive. It will use all the techniques, tools and staff of a sales-oriented parliament. Communication is designed to ensure that the public is aware of the work of parliament, and also of how they may participate and what the institution offers them. The style of communication is geared to suit the audience.

Stage 6: Campaign
A market-oriented parliament may undertake mini-campaigns to boost its profile, attract new members and publicise the work it is doing

Stage 7: Delivery
Parliament will pass legislation and fulfil its functions in a way which meets public needs to the greatest extent.

Stage 8: Communication of delivery
It will also attempt to communicate the work it has done; for example, publicising the passing of important and interesting legislation, or a particularly significant committee investigation or commission. It will solicit feedback and user opinion on, for example, the effect of particular legislation in case amendment is necessary. This stage would be continual.

If parliament is really going to improve its public standing and fulfil its functions, and use political marketing to its full potential, it needs to pay more attention to its actual behaviour, or product, and adopt a market orientation. This analysis will deal with parliament's behaviour up until around 2001.

Stage 1: Market intelligence

Westminster is not short of market intelligence. A select committee on 'sittings of the house' advised different hours of sitting, better working conditions, better resources for MPs, better resources for the House and committees (e.g. in terms of staff), and more efficient and strengthened procedures (in the legislative process). The 1992 manifestos of all three parties were committed to reform to improve the effectiveness of the Commons. As mentioned above, there is also a select committee on the modernisation of the House of Commons that began to meet in 1997 (www.parliament.uk/commons/selcom/modhome.htm), which has considered and reported on issues such as sittings in Westminster Hall, facilities for the media, the parliamentary calendar and conduct in the chamber.

Committee consultation also provides a means of intelligence. Parliament needs to consult all interested bodies to be truly market oriented. Select committees do consult groups such as professional representative bodies, pressure groups and academics, but misses others. Those it misses can include those most affected by the issue being discussed, such as the disabled and blind, or those who live in remote areas and have linguistic barriers. The internet has been used to counteract this; for instance, the all-party parliamentary group on domestic violence used it to gain the views of women who had experienced domestic violence, and the Social Security Select Committee gained the views of low-income claimants through on-line consultation (Hansard Society 2001: 85). Petitions might be another means of channelling input from the people into the institution. Many more petitions are submitted to 10 Downing Street and the Scottish parliament than to Westminster. The Hansard Society (2001: 87; see also Norton 2000: 24) recommended that parliament create a petitions committee similar to that in the Scottish parliament.

Stage 2: Product design

There are some signs of a redesign of the product to respond to this. In terms of resources for MPs, every MP is now provided with an office; there is a new block of offices, Porticullis House, in Bridge Street opposite Westminster. In terms of members, the end of hereditary peers sitting in the Lords under the Labour government has made Westminster more reflective of society. In terms of representing society, the number of women MPs has increased, as major parties are becoming increasingly aware of the need to do something about this. Labour operated all-women shortlists for the 1997 general election, which greatly increased the number of women MPs elected, but this method was then outlawed.

Robin Cook was eventually successful in changing the hours of the Commons. The tradition of the parliamentary day beginning as late as 2.30 p.m. was ended in October 2002, in favour of starting at 11.30 a.m. on Tuesdays and Wednesdays instead. Cook was cited as seeing this as a more modern way of doing business and believing that the package would make the chamber more relevant (Jones 2002). Parliament also shortened the long summer recess and increased prelegislative scrutiny. The affects of this on participation will have to be seen – it is still some way from a professional 9–5 timetable – but it was an important and significant change. There remain, however, a number of weaknesses in the product, some of which will be highlighted here.

The media has been allowed into the central lobby rather than left outside on the green, but more can be done (see Norton 2000: 24). The media should be given much better resources and access, as with the Scottish parliament. Additionally, it can be argued that a market-oriented parliament would train its members, but this does not happen as yet (Norton 2000: 13). Norton (2000: 37) observed how, at present, 'The job of an MP is classed as a professional job but is remarkable for receiving no professional training. For newly elected members, there is little guidance as to what use can be made of the parliamentary process. Many have little grounding in government or in parliamentary procedure.' This really is remarkable when you consider that MPs are theoretically running the country. Business managers receive training; why not political managers, who are responsible for conveying citizen demands to the legislature and overseeing the design of policy legislation? A training unit should be created, with training provided by parliamentary staff and drawing on experts such as those within management and the law (Fox and Lees-Marshment 2002).

The timetable of debates and recess remains a barrier to relevant debate, as was shown vividly when a new war was waged at the beginning of September 2001 and parliament was not in operation. At a time when voters were demanding debate, when parliament was actually being wanted, it did not respond. Changes to the design of committees and the power of parliament could make important moves towards a more market-oriented parliament that fulfils its functions effectively. The difficulty is that these are contentious areas and debate ranges continually on how to ensure that parliament is market oriented and, indeed, what that would mean. As already noted, the demands of all Westminster's markets conflict. A market-oriented party in government needs to ensure it can deliver on its promises, and parliament is an important part of the process to achieve this. However, as Norton (2000: 5) noted, 'riding roughshod over Parliament achieves no benefit: it undermines the popular legitimacy of government as well as Parliament, it results in poor – and potentially unpopular – legislation at a later stage. Ultimately, no one – government, Parliament or citizen – benefits.'

Stage 3: Product adjustment
Internal reaction analysis was carried out during the debates on the reforms proposed by Robin Cook. However, the proposals for change to end most evening sittings met with a fierce debate and attracted opposition from cross-party backbenchers. Changing established institutions is not easy, and there is the same problem of balancing the need to appeal to the public market and the internal staff as with any organisation. In terms of competition, as already discussed, Westminster has responded to a more direct competitor, the Scottish parliament; but Westminster needs to respond more effectively to the media, which provides the better means of communication for MPs and the governing party.

Stage 4: Implementation

As Norton (2000: 9) observed, 'effective reform . . . requires also the support –
and sustenance – of all or most members. Changes to procedure have, in effect,
to be the property of the whole House.' There is arguably a need to change the
culture of parliament (see Norton 2000: 8) to one that is less product oriented,
and, for example, accepts the need to reach out to citizens and the media. The
changes to the hours of working initiated by Robin Cook were seen by his
shadow, Eric Forth, as 'the beginning of the end of the Commons' (quoted by
Jones 2002). The vote was only won by 311 votes to 234. The market-oriented
principle has not been fully implemented at Westminster.

Stage 5: Communication

The new website is a good means of conveying information. It even asks for
feedback on its live web-cast. However, despite the House's own recommenda-
tions (United Kingdom Parliament 2002), research by Jackson (2003: 135) suggests that MPs are not making the best use of website and email technology: 'the
vast majority of MPs view their website as primarily a one-way communication
tool, rather than creating two-way communication between MPs and constituents'. Much more needs to be done to convey the work of parliament to the
public.

Stage 6: Campaign

Westminster has not as yet engaged in any short-term campaign efforts.

Stage 7: Delivery; Stage 8: Communication of delivery

In terms of communicating delivery, Fox and Lees-Marshment (2002: 34–35)
noted that 'Commons Select Committees are beginning to co-ordinate publication of reports in order to ensure each receives maximum publicity and (hopefully) impact (author's interview with MPs) . . . General legislation currently is
communicated from Parliament to its markets predominantly through the
(often specialist) media but also through personal contacts and occasionally
through proactive Parliamentarians.' More co-ordinated communication is
needed.

Summary of marketing Westminster

Unfinished Business: Commons Reform. (Cook 2001: 3)

Overall, as Fox and Lees-Marshment (2002: 35) concluded, 'one of the most
evident aspects of our analysis is the lack of a unified all encompassing approach
to matching Westminster with its markets'. The marketing of Westminster is
hitherto extremely limited, especially in comparison with that of the new parliament in Scotland.

The Scottish parliament: a product designed to meet voter demands?

The Scottish parliament was formed in 1999. Unique amongst all other political organisations thus far studied, it was 'born' in an age when political marketing was already on the agenda. Unusually within the British political system, it was actually designed in response to voter demands. Unlike other institutions that grew out of history, the Scottish parliament started with a blank slate (Winetrobe 2002: 4). Winetrobe and Seaton (2000: 2) commented that 'this ensured that Scotland's new parliament was . . . tailored to suit the particular needs and culture of Scottish constitutional tradition and modern civic society'. It could therefore be designed with the modern demands of the current market and nature of the people in mind, rather than have to be brought up to date with a fight. In many ways the political marketing story of the Scottish parliament is therefore not of an institution first product oriented then sales oriented, then struggling to be market oriented, but of one whose founders and initial design-ers aimed for it to be market oriented and meet the needs of the Scottish people, and are now struggling to keep that approach.

In analysing the marketing of the Scottish parliament, it is important to understand the context from which it arose and in which it continues to operate.

Nature of the country and institutions
Scotland is a very distinctive country. Anyone who has lived there will know how important the unique identity, culture and organisations of Scotland are to its people. Scotland has its own church, law and courts, banking, education and media, including local mass circulation newspapers, which dominate reading in the big cities, and regional television. The BBC has always had a strong Scottish unit and autonomous council. Scotland had its own parliament many centuries ago, but this was merged with England by the 1707 Treaty of Union. The proce-dures and practices of the English parliament dominated the UK institution. Despite the creation of various Scottish offices and positions, this did not stop the demand for a truly Scottish parliament.

Demand for devolution
The call for devolution was due to a feeling or reasoning that the current system did not provide the Scottish people with enough influence over their government and therefore daily lives. There was a strong perception that Westminster did not show enough interest in Scottish affairs (Budge et al. 1998: 156). Discussions and debate took place at the elite political level through various commissions, reports and party proposals during the twentieth century. A referendum was held in March 1979 but failed to gain enough support. The Conservative party elected in 1979 was opposed to devolution, blocking change for 18 years. Campaigns for greater self-government continued. Following the 1987 general election, differ-ent strands of opinion united behind what eventually became the Scottish Constitutional Convention (SCC), set up in March 1989, composed of the polit-

Table 8.2 Results of the referendum on a Scottish Parliament, 1997

	Yes (%)	No (%)	Turnout (%)
There should be a Scottish Parliament	74.3	25.7	60.2
A Scottish Parliament should have tax-raising powers by up to 3p	63.5	36.5	60.2

ical parties in Scotland (except the Scottish Conservative and Unionist party and the Scottish National party [SNP]), local authorities, the churches and many voluntary and other public bodies and organisations. This produced *The Claim of Right for Scotland* in 1998, and published several documents arguing for devolution (see McFadden and Lazarowicz 1999: 2–3). The SCC produced in its final report in November 1995, *Scotland's Parliament, Scotland's Right*, containing proposals for the implementation of a devolution scheme.

The desire for devolution also manifested itself in electoral support. Paterson (1998: 229) noted how Conservative party support declined as the party's stance on devolution was to oppose it. Conversely, Labour was pro-devolution as it began to acquire support and then win in 1997; and the SNP's support increased as it continually argued for a change in the political system. In the 1997 election, both the Labour and Liberal parties committed themselves to a Scottish parliament in their manifesto, based on the SCC proposals. After Labour won the general election, it passed the 1997 Referendum Act through Westminster and a referendum of Scottish voters was held in September 1997. Voters were asked to say yes or no to two issues: see Table 8.2 for the results.

The introduction of devolution
The Scottish parliament was established by the 1998 Scotland Act, passed in the Westminster parliament. The secretary of state for Scotland had appointed a Consultative Steering Group (CSG) in November 1997. Its membership was representative of the major political parties in Scotland and other civic groups. After a period of detailed examination and consultation, the CSG produced a report in January 1999, *Shaping Scotland's Parliament*, which was used as the blueprint for the parliament's initial set of standing orders. The Scottish parliament was created following the Scottish parliament elections on Thursday 6 May 1999. It met for the first time on Wednesday 12 May 1999 and at various other times until its formal opening on 1 July, when its powers were officially transferred from Westminster.

Designing a market-oriented parliament and the Scottish parliament in 1999
In order to assess the marketing of the Scottish parliament it is important first to understand its market, functions and basic nature. The market is the Scottish counterpart of Westminster's – Scottish voters, media and MSPs – but also includes the central UK government, as in theory at least Westminster could

increase or reduce the power it devolves to Scotland. The Scottish parliamentary product is similar to Westminster's, including legislation, debates and information, albeit with different legislative powers. However, it was created within a political climate calling for a 'new Scotland' and post-Westminster politics, with a qualitative difference in terms of 'the way in which policy would be made' (Lynch 2001: 1). Where the Scottish parliament differs from Westminster is in its goals, which follow four key principles designed by the CSG:

- *Sharing the power*: The Scottish parliament should embody and reflect the sharing of power between the people of Scotland, the legislators and the Scottish executive.
- *Accountability*: The Scottish executive should be accountable to the Scottish parliament, and the parliament and executive should be accountable to the people of Scotland.
- *Access and participation*: the Scottish parliament should be accessible, open and responsive, and should develop procedures which make possible a participative approach to the development, consideration and scrutiny of policy and legislation.
- *Equal opportunities*: The Scottish parliament in its operation and its appointments should recognise the need to promote equal opportunities for all.

Applying the market-oriented parliament framework to Scotland

> The Scottish parliament is widely perceived as new and modern, lean and efficient, expressly designed for a particular purpose after much product research involving its future actors and potential consumers. (Winetrobe 2002: 3)

A market-oriented Scottish parliament provides an institution designed to meet the needs and wants of the public in a way that achieves its aims or functions. The Scottish parliament was set up with this basic orientation towards the Scottish people. The SCC's *Claim of Right for Scotland* (1989) declared:

> We, gathered as the Scottish Constitutional Convention, do hereby acknowledge **the sovereign right of the Scottish people to determine the form of Government best suited to their needs**, and do hereby declare and pledge that **in all our actions and deliberations their interests shall be paramount.**

Additionally, as Winetrobe and Seaton (2000: 8) pointed out, the first sentence of the Labour government's White Paper produced in July 1997 said 'the Government are determined that the people of Scotland should have a greater say over their own affairs'. Furthermore, 'even the CSG principle of sharing power may itself suggest that "the people" were not regarded as supreme but were to be allowed to become an equal player with the parliament and the executive in the system of governance'. In terms of how to achieve this, the Scottish parliament can go through a process and activities similar to those of the Westminster parliament: see Box 8.3 above.

Stage 1: Market intelligence

There was plenty of discussion and debate about the nature the Scottish parliament could have before its creation and during the first year. The CSG conducted a wide public consultation exercise, holding six public fora around Scotland and taking evidence. It commissioned expert evidence, e.g. an Expert Panel on Information and Communication Technologies, made up of people from government, civil service, academia and business. Staff were encouraged to make suggestions. They researched and visited models elsewhere: the Flemish parliament, Spain (Catalonia) and Germany (Bavaria), which have more modern parliaments, avoiding the model of Westminster (Lynch 2001: 1; Grice 2001). Building on the general principle of providing open and accessible government, several means were created by which the public could provide input into the parliament, such as through a strong petition system and consultations.

Stage 2: Product design

The Scottish parliament can make laws in the devolved areas such as health, education and training, local government, social work, housing, police and fire services, the environment and agriculture, forestry and fishing. Other issues are known as reserved matters and are still dealt with by the UK parliament at Westminster. The Scottish parliament is made up of 129 elected Members of the Scottish Parliament. There are also two deputy presiding officers. They influence the rules and meetings of parliament. The party, or parties, with the majority of seats in the parliament form(s) the Scottish government, known as the Scottish executive. The first minister, usually leader of the dominant party, is the counterpart of the UK prime minister. Constituency MSPs (73 in 1999) are directly elected as individuals to single-member constituencies using the first past the post system (FPTP), as used for UK general elections. Regional MSPs are elected by party, on a list system; voters vote for a party list on block (56 in 1999 divided across eight regions) using the Additional Member System. This form of proportional representation uses party lists, which ensures that each party's representation in the parliament reflects its overall share of the vote.

MSPs are socially and geographically mixed, and the gender balance of the MSPs is better than Westminster's. Of the 129 MSPs in the 1999–2003 parliament, 48 were women: 37 per cent of the total. Most MSPs were middle-aged, the average being in the forties, but a large section that made it into the Scottish executive and ministerial posts for the first parliament were 30-something.

Each MSP was given a welcome letter from the Chief Executive and an information pack (Grice 2001). They are supported by the Scottish Parliamentary Information Centre (SPICe) and a substantial intranet. Training on the use of information resources is available from the Scottish parliament's staff. However, like Westminster, the Scottish parliament does not provide more generic training in how to do the job of an MSP more effectively. Ben Wallace MSP (2002) noted that there is the potential to make too much work and too little work, and MSPs are not good at time management: 'no one trains the MSP in time management'. MSPs are therefore not all good at using resources and staff.

Hours   The dates for the recess are decided with regard to when schools in any part of Scotland are on holiday. The Scottish parliament's hours are much more sociable and professional than those at Westminster.

The building   Holyrood, the parliament's temporary home, is in and around the part of Edinburgh known as the Mound. A permanent home is being built at the foot of Edinburgh's historic Royal Mile. Rosemary Everett (2001), public information team leader, said she will get more space in the new building, which will make it more open and accessible. There will also be space for a crèche, a nursing mother room and a classroom for use by visiting school groups (see Scottish Parliamentary Corporate Body 2000e). However, the building has yet to be completed and the cost is a sore point in the parliament's relationship with its people. The chamber in the present and future parliament is horseshoe in design, to be less adversarial and promote more discussion than Westminster. MSPs have electronic voting, with an individual card, again a move away from Westminster's archaic system where members go past a teller through yea or nay booths and passages.

Staff   The Scottish Parliamentary Corporate Body (SPCB) was established to provide the Scottish parliament with the property, staff and services it needed, including staff who service committees, parliamentary researchers and librarians. As of the end of May 2000, there were 294 staff on the payroll (Scottish Parliamentary Corporate Body 2000b: 56). The Scottish parliament is managed more like a business than Westminster. The Scottish parliament is a corporate body with a corporate style and a management plan which staff work towards. Conversations with staff (see Seaton 2001; Everett 2001) suggested that the management plan makes work easier, providing impetus and a direction to their work. The culture encouraged ideas: staff are actively expected to innovate to progress. Although some staff came from Westminster, there are those such as Alan Smart, who became head of broadcasting from a media, non-civil service background, providing a strong impetus to think outside the box (Smart 2002).

Activities   The Parliament works in two main ways, through full meetings and committee meetings (smaller groups). Each committee has a web-page at www.scottish.parliament.uk/official_report/cttee.html. Committees can initiate legislation. Meetings are normally held in public, and can take place anywhere in Scotland. Some committees are mandatory, such as the Procedures Committee and the Public Petitions Committee. The parliament can establish subject committees to deal with a particular subject or area of public policy, e.g. the Health and Community Care Committee. Wallace (2002) noted that the institution is proud of its committees because they are run more to achieve their independent aims than for the good of the party. Committees have also been taken outside Edinburgh to provide better access to different regions within the nation.

Legislation   The Scottish Parliament has produced significant legislation in its devolved policy areas. Lynch (2001: 2) argues that 'without devolution, key legislative outputs simply would not have occurred in Scotland'. One example is legislation in the area of land reform, which was of particular importance to Scotland but which Westminster had neglected. Furthermore the Scottish parliament has produced policies on free care for the elderly and student tuition fees which are different from those imposed by Westminster on England. The new parliament has already made an important impact on people's lives in Scotland.

Stage 3: Product adjustment
In terms of product adjustment, some attempts at targeting have been made. Political targeting is problematic, however: when I tried to get my university students tickets to see the parliament when it visited Aberdeen, they were refused entry to the main chamber because the focus was on school children. Targeting could come from support and competition analysis further on in the institution's existence, when it can perhaps assess whether there are areas – socially, geographically etc. – that it is not reaching. Internal reaction analysis was carried out initially with the consultation. In terms of achievability, it did not perform this very effectively, arguably raising expectations too high during the process of campaigning for and opening the parliament, only to see public satisfaction then fall.

Stage 4: Implementation
Implementation of the product design was completed under considerable pressure, within a very short space of time (see Monteith 2002; Winetrobe and Seaton 2000: 7). The time period between the report issued by the CSG and the 'birth' of the parliament was only just over six months. Staff were left to create an immense number of practical rules. This time pressure may have had negative consequences. Winetrobe and Seaton (2000: 2) observed how just one year after the formation of the Scottish parliament there was 'talk in the media and elsewhere that the unique spirit of the Convention, referendum and CSG processes' was 'being lost in the everyday politics of the Parliament and the Executive'. This is a concern for those who wanted Scotland to have a different kind of parliamentary culture, and it needs to be monitored carefully.

Stage 5: Communication
The Parliament communicates its work reasonably effectively, at least within the organisation and to political elites.

Public information services   The Scottish Parliament Public Information Service provides information on parliamentary history, business and public access. It offers a Public Enquiry Service, information resources, an education service, a visitor centre and a shop. The visitor centre puts its work on show for the visiting public, using interactive computer displays. The education service offers a range of products: it is staffed by primary and secondary teachers and provides web resources and links, written material including fact sheets, video packs and teachers' guides. It also facilitates visits and, as Monteith (2002) observed, 'has a terrific outreach programme that ensures that every day there are at least half a dozen schools attending the Parliament watching us make serious decisions or make fools of ourselves'.

Website   The Scottish parliament has a substantial website full of information on its activities, in addition to a substantial intranet for those within the organisation. Web-casting – Scottish Parliament Live – is conducted because there is no dedicated TV channel, at www.scottishparliamentlive.com. This is extremely innovative in parliamentary participative terms. Viewers can even sometimes choose what they want to look at, seeing committees live as well as the chamber. Archives of previous activity are also available at www.scottishparliament-live.com/archive_historic.asp, which provides a permanent on-line history of the Scottish parliament, including items such as the opening ceremony and a visit by the prime minister. The web has evolved over time, with a new layout launched in summer 2001. Hazel Martin, webmaster, noted how it serves 'quite a variety of audiences with different information requirements . . . Parliamentarians, the media, lawyers, schools, citizens, visitors and people from overseas all have an interest and it is up to us to provide something that meets their needs' (*Holyrood Magazine* 2001b: 33).

Smart's previous work was as head of STV, and he has also televised Westminster, so he brought to the job an understanding of both the problems of Westminster and the needs of the media. He encountered some obstacles to communicating the work of the Scottish parliament. Some within the institution are still conservative about some aspects of this, being naturally protective of the parliament's public reputation and therefore not keen to encourage further criticism of its work (see Smart 2001b). Despite this, they created a section on the web called 'Interactive' that provided a sounding board for the public to raise issues of concern. It also enables on-line discussions on topics such as nursing.

The broadcasting unit and office   The Scottish parliament has its own broadcasting unit, which deals with the televising of all parliamentary proceedings and then makes them available to the media. The unit also web-casts all the proceedings, offers a picture still service and makes up videos that promote and explain the work of the parliament to the world (Smart 2001b). Coverage follows the rules of the web, which are more suited to television than those for Westminster; the rules are amongst the least restrictive in the world, allowing for the generous use of 'reaction shots' and the public gallery. As the gallery is more or less always full, this helps demonstrate to others that they can come and watch the parliament, an effective communication of the Scottish Parliament product. Smart (2001a) argued that the broadcasting office has made numerous achievements, including:

- 'a high level of satisfaction amongst the TV companies we serve';
- producing the world's first web-cast of a parliament's opening;
- web-casting of committee sessions which convene outside Edinburgh;
- providing 'direct internet-delivered promotion of it [the Scottish parliament] to the Scottish electorate and wider world', and targeted electronic communication of certain groups to inform them in advance of what is happening in parliament;
- 'a pictures still service for MSPs, the public and the press which extracts high quality colour j-pegs for print reproduction. This service has been widely promoted and is proving extremely popular.'

The media: access and facilities   Communication also occurs through media channels not controlled by the Parliament itself. In the beginning, the Scottish parliament lacked a separate media and press office, but the broadcasting unit facilitated reporting. Smart (2001b) held the attitude that if you give the media easy access, it is more likely to cover the parliament. In the chamber building itself there is a 'black and white corridor' (the floor is black and white chequered) just outside the chamber. Broadcasters come into the heart of the Scottish parliament's equivalent of Westminster's 'lobby' to speak and film. MSPs can just pop out of the chamber and speak in the black and white corridor. Interviews are conducted live, just doors away from the chamber. The Scottish parliament also has a Media Centre across the road from the chamber and provides the media with offices and television monitors. Media organisations with offices there include: the *Press and Journal*, the *Daily Record*, the *Scotsman*, the *Sun*, the *Herald* and Scottish FM radio. One floor is press; BBC radio and TV have another floor; and a third hosts television channels such as Sky, Scottish Grampian, ITV, SMG and Border TV.

Stage 6: Campaign
By late 2003, there have been four formal campaigns as such.

Delivery and communication of delivery
The Scottish parliament is extremely market oriented and businesslike in the way its reviews its own behaviour. It issues an annual report (Scottish Parliamentary Corporate Body 2000a, 2000b, 2000c, 2001e) and measures its performance against the CSG principles. However, the Scottish parliament perhaps neglected the communication of delivery: it did not ensure that the public was aware of the differences it has made in terms of policy and participatory structures. There is plenty of information on the web, but this relies on the public initiating communication with the Scottish parliament and going to find the information.

MSPs from all parties cite individual stories of a difference the Scottish parliament has made; for example, Nora Radcliffe (2002) noted how Kemnay Village Hall and other similar, non-central villages had been awarded parliamentary funding for a computer and internet access. A Tory MSP at the Scottish Party Conference in spring 2002 told the story of how she had helped to link people affected by a rare disease to form a support group that had helped them immensely. The wider public is not always aware of this, however.

The media is quick to pick out any weaknesses; for example, a story in the *Daily Telegraph* in January 2001 ran with the deadline 'Executive fails to meet half its targets' (Britten 2001). Whilst this is not the responsibility of parliamentary staff, it is in part a related function of the parliament, which is there to deliver legislation. Early communication has perhaps caused confusion between the behaviour of the Scottish government or executive and the parliament. As Winetrobe (2002: 4) noted, 'the language before 1999' failed to distinguish between the two, with comments such as 'the parliament will do this or that' referring in fact to what party politicians might do once in power, which even the most skilled parliamentary staff can never influence. Brian Monteith (2002) noted how 'the name "Scottish parliament" became mistakenly interchangeable with "Scottish executive"'. Perhaps one problem is the promotion of the executive's work: if this cannot be done by parliament staff, then the executive staff need to do it more clearly. The Scottish parliament website, for example, does not have a direct link from its front page to the executive: it should do, then it can make it clearer that a separate body is in charge of policy delivery.

From 2001 onwards: too much focus on sales rather than product delivery?

> This topic [marketing the Scottish Parliament] . . . [has] become one of the Parliament's strategic priorities. (Janet Seaton, head of Research and Information Services, Scottish parliament, 10 October 2001 email to author)

Stage 1: Market intelligence   There has been growing concern in the Scottish parliament that the public were increasingly disengaged from and dissatisfied with its performance. The public were sceptical about the effect of the parliament on their lives, and critical of high salaries for MSPs and the cost of building the new parliament. Ben Wallace (2002), a list MSP elected in 1999, noted that the electorate were disappointed because they did not feel it had changed their lives. They were 'glad they got it, but not glad what's in it'. In response, the Scottish parliament conducted its own formal internal and external market intelligence. The Parliament's Procedures Committee reviewed the extent to which the parliament met the four key CSG principles. Murray McVicar, staff member in the Scottish parliament and involved in the Procedures Committee, explained how they analysed existing research on the parliament (McVicar 2001) and then SPICe, on behalf of the committee, commissioned external research by MORI. This research was on different groups in Scotland – MSPs, parliament staff and the general public – and was both qualitative and quantitative. An initial report on this was made by MORI to the Procedures Committee on 23 October 2001 (see Scottish Parliamentary Corporate Body 2001c). Simon Braunholtz and Mark Diffley presented the results from MORI. Research into public awareness indicated concern. Recurrent themes (Scottish Parliamentary Corporate Body 2001b: 898–912) were, amongst others:

- 'There are very low levels of knowledge about and familiarity with the Parliament amongst the general public.'
- 'In some respects . . . the Parliament does not appear so far to have met the very high expectations that the public had of it when it was established.'
- The public 'know little or nothing about the committee system'.
- 'There was little awareness of the petitions system among the general public.'
- The public who actively seek information about the parliament find it; others feel there is little coverage.
- 'The public's perception is that the Parliament is not hugely open and accessible. The public do not know much about the travelling committees and there is a sense – even among people who know about them – that committees are closed.'

These were much more negative than those of MSPs, indicating a divergent opinion between the two groups: a concern because the politicians could simply continue blissfully unaware that the public had not grasped all the parliament had to offer. The issue arising from all this is that the Scottish parliament is perhaps product oriented with regard to its communication: it provides information and expects the public to come and get it, rather than trying to reach out to people in the way that they need to be communicated with. As Alan Smart (2002) said, 'the product has not been marketed. It has not been explained.'

Stage 5: Communication   The Scottish parliament responded in various ways. The head of Research and Information Services was asked to create a plan for promoting parliament and developing a communications strategy, involving MSPs, for the three months from October 2000 to January 2001. Parliament created a Media and Press Office to implement a media affairs strategy and take 'a more proactive approach to promoting the work of the Parliament and its Committees, (Seaton 2002: 10). The 2001 management plan had four strategic priorities, one of which was: 'Strategic Priority 3: Promoting the Parliament. This we see as being linked to a Scotland which is well informed about its Parliament, and also, where the people of Scotland are able to be involved with the Parliament.'

What the parliament needs to do is understand how to communicate with people, i.e. it is not enough to simply provide information, or to tell the public how good it is. Parliament needs to understand how people might access it, thinking from the public's point of view, in terms of where they might learn about it, how, what might interest them, and their time and capability to take an interest in it, rather as universities have designed prospectuses and widening participation posters to suit 17–18-year-olds, not professors.

Stage 8: Communication of delivery   The Scottish parliament is arguably still not doing enough to publicise occasions when it does deliver something new, or different to Westminster, and therefore demonstrate the difference it makes to people's lives. It is difficult to do this when the difference is a result of action by the executive, political parties or individual MSPs. The parliament produced a video of the first 1,000 days, including interviews with ordinary people in Scotland about the difference the parliament has made. The difficulty is that most people will not see these videos: they should perhaps have been broadcast on mainstream television instead. My students in Aberdeen also criticised them for being overly positive and therefore unbelievable. Another strategy has been to reduce public expectations: a form of demarketing similar to that in health care and local government. Even the queen's speech during her visit to the Scottish parliament when it sat in Aberdeen in May 2002 spoke of the need for time and more realistic expectations of what the parliament could do. Wallace (2002) argued that part of the problem of public dissatisfaction was false expectations that were not achievable.

From 2002 onwards

> As the novelty of the Parliament wears off, and it increasingly has to stand or fall on its own merits, dealing with its own growing baggage and distractions (such as the new Holyrood Complex), the challenge, both from an institutional and marketing perspective, will be to develop the product. (Winetrobe 2002: 5)

Overall, however, the initial response to the problems was sales oriented: focusing on communication rather than the product design. This approach has clear limitations. This is not to classify the Scottish parliament completely and conclusively as operating in that vein. Since my first assessment of the parliament, written in 2001, there have already been some signs of changes to the product in response to market intelligence. This is a quick-moving institution to analyse. For example, it was recognised that the parliament needed 'to reach out to those who are presently disengaged politically' (Scottish Parliament 2003a). The parliament has analysed its external visits (committee meetings, civic participation events, a partner library) since 1999 (Scottish Parliament 2003a): if this information is used, then it may lead to further product development and a move back to a market orientation. Research has also been conducted with the public as to why they have not accessed the parliament and what could be changed; for example, the Vale of Leven Elderly Forum 'warned against an over reliance on electronic means of communication' (Scottish Parliament 2003a), and written information sheets and videos were provided to suit that segment of society. Further developments in this direction may come in 2004, 2005 and so on.

Summary of marketing the Scottish parliament

The Scottish parliament has made a significant achievement in the way it was formed and created. It has moved rapidly under a pressured timetable; as Monteith (2002) noted, systems, a government, officials and a corporate body had to be set up in a very short space of time. The parliament has created communication systems and public access that its 'mother' Westminster is now seeking to emulate, and can therefore take credit for influencing the reform of that other parliament. As Monteith (2002) noted, the website and education services 'are the sort of quiet marketing approaches that can have great impact because of their contact with people rather than through other media'. This does not mean it can rest on its laurels, however. Market intelligence needs to be conducted on what voters really think of the parliament, and what they want out of it. There seems to have been little done on what voters think of it in detail – what should be done – even in the lead-up to devolution. There was a lot of debate at the elite level about the desire for a Scottish parliament but what is missing is an understanding of what the people want from it. The Scottish people wanted a parliament, an institution they could relate to and be involved in, that would above all make a difference to their lives. Whilst it is not easy to deliver this, the parliament must try or it risks alienating an entire political generation.

Conclusions

> Parliaments . . . are starting to appreciate how promotion and marketing is a major strategy in this area, in terms of their substantive work; in informing their public of who they are and what they do, and in creating and maintain their unique 'brand'. Parliaments should be regarded as essential areas of and for political marketing. (Winetrobe 2003)

> We are taking stock, assessing our performance, and questioning whether the Parliament is showing the signs of delivering on the promises, hopes and aspirations so evident during the 1997 referendum . . . the Parliament is, more and more, becoming the focal point in Scottish life – an institution which is delivering for, and with, the people of Scotland. (The presiding officer, Sir David Steele, in *Holyrood Magazine* 2001b: 10)

Parliaments do need marketing. All around the world, new and old parliamentary institutions seek to present and design themselves in a way that will respond to and engage the public, in an attempt to do what they were set up to do. The Scottish parliament and Westminster have undoubtedly utilised marketing to varying degrees and with different effect, and both are aware of the need to engage with and respond to the public.

The Scottish parliament is in a good position to be or become a market-oriented parliament. There is a systemic, institutionalised culture and attitude that are or are moving towards being market oriented; they are concerned with meeting the needs and wants of the people the parliament is intended to serve.

This will benefit the parliament and Scotland for years to come. It aids responsive political governance – and political marketing.

However, as has been found throughout this book, whilst political marketing
is undeniably important in the twenty-first-century British political system, it is
not an easy exercise. It requires not just ideas but full implementation, and therefore organisational factors come into play. There is a desire to change
Westminster, but as Jones and Moran (1994: 16) said, 'the problems of an institution such as the House of Commons cannot be solved by simply abolishing
that body and starting again'. As Winetrobe (2002: 5) contended, Westminster
'can certainly catch up with the Scottish Parliament and other public and private
institutions in terms of basic public engagement, through enhanced media,
public information and visitor services', but 'whether it can take that any deeper,
and can truly reform itself, both to make itself more effective and more market-
able, is problematic so long as the essential characteristics of government domination and insular focus remain'. As Fox and Lees-Marshment (2002: 36)
observed, 'Westminster is the poor marketing cousin in politics.' Westminster is
a very traditional and established institution. The staff ethos can also reinforce
this; Winetrobe (2002: 4) recalled that the officials or clerks 'operate almost as
high priests, with an instinctive obligation to preserve, and hand on to their suc-
cessors, the traditions and "mysteries" of Parliament from external dilution or
attack'. This therefore 'encourages an insular perspective . . . [and] hardly breeds
a sense of engagement with the wider public' (Winetrobe 2002: 4).

It will be much easier for the Scottish parliament to remain in contact with its
market, adapt to meet its changing needs and therefore maintain a market orientation over time than for Westminster, which has yet to even reach a market orientation. Indeed, the differences between the two institutions are marked. I recall
vividly when I went to Westminster and went into the central lobby area to meet
an MP I had arranged to interview. There was no reception desk, just an elderly
gentleman who barked at me for my name and insisted on writing down 'Janet'
in the visitors' book despite my protestations. I was left to sit on a bench and
after 20 minutes the MP did not turn up, so I gave up and left. This was in sharp
contrast to my visit to the Scottish parliament, where I have always been made
to feel welcome and given easy access to information, and where staff and
systems are generally more professional.

Westminster has, however, latterly responded to the 'competition'. It sent a
team of staff up to Holyrood to see how they were running communication
there, as well as other issues. Robin Cook also noted the higher number of
women MSPs in Scotland and said 'I don't believe we can do that without family-
friendly hours which can enable someone to be a member of the Parliament and
a member of the family at the same time' (cited in Peterkin 2001). Nevertheless,
it is not all plain sailing for the Scottish parliament either. The basic output from
parliament is policy, and the parliament is naturally perceived as close to the
executive: Wallace (2002) argued that 'when Labour fails, the Scottish Parliament
will fail'. The parliament was simply a means to an end. The public now want

the end to be delivered. Consumers don't buy a CD player: they buy something that plays music, with all the functions, sound quality and performance associated with it. The Scottish parliament has to deliver what voters want: the effect on their daily lives. As MacDonnell (2001) commented:

> Devolution was launched amid expectations that hospital waiting lists would be shorter, school standards would improve and transport would get better. Instead what has dominated this young parliament's first two years? The repeal of Section 28 and the bill to ban hunting, which is irrelevant to most Scots.

No amount of clever promotion will make a difference to satisfying Scottish voters' basic demand for good government. Comparative analysis of the Scottish parliament and Westminster aside, it could be argued that any parliament is difficult to market. The nature of legislation, debate and policy delivery connects back to the performance of political parties, and requires more in-depth but highly critical, yet cautious analysis, because of the overlap between the institution of parliament and the behaviour of politicians within it. Yet policy, the impact on people's lives, is really what it is all about. That is what concerns the average person. Parliaments are important, and so are parties, but so too is the coal-face of policy delivery: local government. Much of the legislation enacted by parliaments will eventually arrive at the door of local councils, and yes, they too use marketing in its various forms and guises; which is where we go for the next chapter.

Notes

The final form of this chapter draws on a first draft completed solely by the author in the summer of 2001 and on two conference papers, Fox and Lees-Marshment (2002) and Lees-Marshment (2003). Any material supplied particularly by Fox within Fox and Lees-Marshment (2002) is accordingly specifically referenced to that particular paper to ensure appropriate accreditation.

Bibliography

Britten, N. (2001), 'Executive Fails to Meet Half its Targets', *Daily Telegraph* 30 January.

Budge, I., I. Crewe, D. McKay and K. Newton (1998), *The New British Politics*, Addison Wesley Longman.

Coleman, S. (2001), Democracy Online: What do We Want from MP's Web Sites?', Hansard Society website, www.hansard-society.org.uk_publications/coleman.shtml.

Cook, R. (2001), 'A Modern Parliament in a Modern Democracy', State of the Union Annual Lecture by Rt Hon. Robin Cook MP, Leader of the House, Constitution Unit, London, December.

Everett, R. (2001), Interview by J. Lees-Marshment with Rosemary Everett, public information team leader, Scottish Parliament, Parliamentary Headquarters, George IV Bridge, Edinburgh, Thursday 25 October.

Fox, M. and J. Lees-Marshment (2002), 'Marketing Parliament: A 19th Century Institution in a 21st Century Political Market-place: Prospects for Marketing Political Institutions', *Political Marketing Conference Proceedings*.

Franklin, B., ed. (1992), *Televising Democracies*, Routledge, London.

Garret, J. (1992), *Westminster: Does Parliament Work?*, Victor Gollancz, London.

Grice, P. (2001), 'The Creation of a Devolved Parliament: An Overview of the Processes and Principles Involved in Establishing the Scottish Parliament', *Journal of Legislative Studies* 7(3): 1–12.

Hansard Society Commission on Parliamentary Scrutiny (2001), *The Challenge for Parliament: Making Government Accountable*, Vacher Dod, London.

Hazell, R. (2001), 'Reforming the Constitution', *Political Quarterly* 72(1), 39–48.

Hetherington, A., K. Weaver and M. Ryle (1990), *Cameras in the Commons*, Hansard Society, London.

Hill, P. (1998), 'The BBC Backs Away from Parliament', *British Journalism Review* 9(2): 16–22.

Holyrood Magazine (2001a), 53, 17 September.

Holyrood Magazine (2001b), 51, 2 July.

House of Commons Technology and Modernisation Committee (2002), 'Modernisation of the House of Commons: A Reform Programme', www.parliament.uk/commons/selcom/modhome.htmHC1168–I.

Jackson, N. (2003), 'MPs and Web Technologies: An Untapped Opportunity?', *Journal of Public Affairs* 3(2): 124–137.

Jones, B. and M. Moran (1994), 'Introduction: Explaining Politics', in B. Jones (ed.), *Politics UK*, Harvester Wheatsheaf, London. pp. 1–24.

Jones, G. (2002), 'MPs Vote for Switch to Daytime Working', *Daily Telegraph* 30 October.

Lane, E. and S. Ersson (2000), *The New Institutional Politics*, Routledge, London.

Lees-Marshment, J. (2001), *Political Marketing and British Political Parties*, Manchester University Press, Manchester.

Lees-Marshment, J. (2003), 'Marketing Political Institutions: Good in Theory but Problematic in Practice?', *Academy of Marketing Conference Proceedings*, University of Aston, 8–10 July.

Lees-Marshment, J. and D. Lilleker (2001), 'Political Marketing and Traditional Values: "Old Labour" for New Times?', *Contemporary Politics* 7(3): 205–216.

Lynch, P. (2001), *Scottish Government and Politics: An Introduction*, Edinburgh University Press, Edinburgh.

MacDonnell, H. (2001), 'What makes MSPs think they're worth it?', *Scotsman* 15 December: 9.

Marshall, E. (1982) *Parliament and the Public*, Macmillan, London.

McCallum, F. (2001), Interview by J. Lees-Marshment with Frazer McCallum, Justice and Europe Team Leader/Research Specialist, Scottish Parliament, Scottish Parliamentary Headquarters, Edinburgh, Thursday 25 October.

McFadden, J. and M. Lazarowicz (1999), *The Scottish Parliament: An Introduction*, T. and T. Clark, Edinburgh.

McKie, D. (1999) *Media Coverage of Parliament*, Hansard Society, London.

McVicar, M. (2001), Emails from Murray McVicar, research team leader, HELLF, and involved in the Procedures Committee, Scottish Parliament, correspondence with author, 29 October.

Monteith, B. (2002), MSP speech to debate on the Marketing of the Scottish Parliament, University of Aberdeen, September.

Mughan, A. and J. Swarts (1997), 'The Coming of Parliamentary Television: The Lords and Senate Compared', *Political Studies* 45: 36–48.

Norton, P. (1994a), *Does Parliament Matter?*, Harvester Wheatsheaf, London.

Norton, P. (1994b), 'Parliament I: The House of Commons', in B. Jones (ed.), *Politics UK*, Harvester Wheatsheaf, London. pp. 314–348.

Norton, P. (2000), *Strengthening Parliament: A Report to the Conservative Party*, The Conservative Party, London.

Norton, P. (2001), *The British Polity,* 4th edition, Longman, London.

Paterson, L., (1998), *A Diverse Assembly: The Debate on a Scottish Parliament*, Edinburgh University Press, Edinburgh.

Peterkin, T. (2001), 'Holyrood Inspires Moderniser Cook', *Daily Telegraph* 11 October.

Radcliffe, N. (2002), 'The Scottish Parliament and Democracy', presentation by MSP to the Deming Learning Network, Aberdeen.

Riddell, P. (2001), *Parliament Under Blair*, Politicos, London.

Rush, M. and P. Giddings (1998), 'Learning to Be a Member of Parliament', in G. Power (ed.), *Under Pressure: Are we Getting the Most from Our MPs?*, Hansard Society, London.

Scammell, M. (1995), *Designer Politics*, Macmillan, Basingstoke.

Scottish Parliament (2002), *Northern Light: Official Film of the Scottish Parliament's Week in Aberdeen*, Broadcasting Office, Edinburgh.

Scottish Parliamentary Corporate Body (2000a), *Annual Report of the Scottish Parliamentary Corporate Body*, Stationery Office, Edinburgh.

Scottish Parliamentary Corporate Body (2000b), *Scottish Parliament Statistics*, Stationery Office, Edinburgh.

Scottish Parliamentary Corporate Body (2000c), *Annual Report of the Scottish Parliamentary Committees*, Stationery Office, Edinburgh.

Scottish Parliamentary Corporate Body (2000d), *Principles of the Parliament: Overview of Relevant Research*, Stationery Office, Edinburgh, 13 October.

Scottish Parliamentary Corporate Body (2001a), 'How has the Parliament Embraced the CSG Principles? Have Your Say', Parliamentary news release, Tuesday 3 April.

Scottish Parliamentary Corporate Body (2001b), *Procedures Committee. The Scottish Parliament: Official Report*, Tuesday 26 June (morning). Stationery Office, Edinburgh, and www.scottish.parliament.uk/official_report?proced-01/pr01–0702

Scottish Parliamentary Corporate Body (2001c), *Procedures Committee. The Scottish Parliament: Official Report*, Tuesday 18 October (morning). Stationery Office, Edinburgh, and www.scottish.parliament.uk/official_report?proced-01/pr01–0602.

Scottish Parliamentary Corporate Body (2001d), *Procedures Committee. The Scottish Parliament: Official Report*, Tuesday 23 October (morning). Session 1. Stationery Office, Edinburgh.

Scottish Parliamentary Corporate Body (2001e), *Scottish Parliament Annual Report 2000–2001*, Stationery Office, Edinburgh, 23 October.

Scottish Parliamentary Corporate Body (2003a), *The Scottish Parliament 1999–2003: Working for You* www.scottish.parliament.uk.

Scottish Parliamentary Corporate Body (2003b), *Annual Report 2003*, www.scottish.parliament.uk/sp/annual/parlar03–01.htm#3.

Scottish Parliamentary Corporate Body (2003c), *The Founding Principles of the Scottish Parliament: The Application of Access and Participation, Equal Opportunities, Accountability and the Power Sharing in the work of the Parliament*, www.scottish.parliament.uk/official-report/cttee.

Seaton, J. (2001), Interview by J. Lees-Marshment with Janet Seaton, head of research and information services, Scottish Parliament, Scottish Parliamentary Headquarters, Edinburgh, Thursday 25 October.

Seaton, J. (2002), 'Marketing the Scottish Parliament: Whose Line Is It Anyway?', paper presented at the Political Marketing Conference, Aberdeen, September.

Smart, A. (2001a), *The Broadcasting Office*, Scottish Parliament, Edinburgh, March.

Smart, A. (2001b), Interview by J. Lees-Marshment with Alan Smart, head of broadcasting, Scottish Parliament, Scottish Parliamentary Headquarters, Edinburgh, Thursday 25 October.

Smart, A. (2002), presentation by the head of broadcasting, Scottish Parliament, as visiting speaker at Aberdeen University, 22 May.

United Kingdom Parliament (2002), *Second Report from the Select Committee on the Modernisation of the House of Commons*, www.publications.parliament.uk/pa/cm200102/cmselect/cmmodern/1168/116803.

Wallace, B. (2002), Interview by J. Lees-Marshment with Ben Wallace, MSP, Aberdeen University, during Scottish Parliament sitting at Aberdeen, 29 May.

Winetrobe, B. (2001), *Realising the Vision: A Parliament with a Purpose. An Audit of the First Year of the Scottish Parliament*, Constitution Unit, UCL, London.

Winetrobe, B. (2002), 'Political but Not Partisan: Marketing Parliaments and their Members', practitioner paper for Political Marketing Conference, Aberdeen, 20 September.

Winetrobe, B. (2003), 'Working In, With and For Parliaments', *Political Marketing Group Newsletter*, 5 March.

Winetrobe, B.K. and J. Seaton (2000), 'Creating a New Parliament in the UK: The First Year of the Scottish Parliament', paper delivered at the Annual Meeting of the American Political Science Association, 31 August–3 September.

9

Marketing local government

> Recent social, economic and political changes have brought pressures on local authorities towards a greater focus on the customer/citizen, and many users of public services now view themselves as consumers . . . The public is no longer deferential and accepting and often wishes to have the opportunity to make choices in service provision and to have some input into policy thinking and decision making. It's about the Council being responsive to need. (Campbell 2002)

Local government is the bottom line for delivery in political marketing. Despite all the efforts national party politicians make, or how carefully legislation is drafted, local services such as refuse collection, schools, transport can have significant impact on the political consumers' perception of overall delivery. Local councils are aware now that they need not just to communicate what they do with the money they get from local tax-payers, but to consult the public on local priorities and developments.

There is a dearth of research on local government marketing; some books (see, for example, Stoker 1991; Chandler 1991; Elcock 1982; and Kingdom 1991) are political science description, the only exceptions being Walsh (1989) and Beuret and Hall (1998: 2), the latter of which notes problems 'with many standard marketing approaches'. Local councils are 'nothing like a business' (Scofield 2003) and have very different goals and objectives. They are not the same as services marketing that includes financial services. However, one can see evidence of local government marketing everywhere: in council slogans, council newspapers delivered to every door, the increased on-line provision of information on services and contact numbers, and public consultation exercises on every issue from rubbish collection to the accessibility of public libraries by ethnic minorities. Local governments throughout the UK are using marketing not simply to inform but to consult with the public before deciding on policy or service design. This chapter will explore the different ways marketing can be used in local government, alongside discussing the limitations of marketing in practice, within the overall context of the entire political system.

Local government: the basics

Local government is generally responsible for local services – education, social services, police, fire, environment, libraries, leisure facilities, community care etc. The importance of local government has increased as the welfare state has grown. The cost provisions and numbers employed by local government are huge. However, local councils have no independent competence; all powers are granted by parliament, and councils cannot just do as they please (Peele 1995: 370).

Local government goals

The goals of local government can be drawn out of standard texts on local government that talk about its ideals and its functions (see Wilson and Game 1998: 31), and include provision of: a product (range of services) that local people need and want; representation on local issues; and a close-by, reachable system of government people can 'see', visit and give input into.

Local government markets

The market for a local council includes everyone within the local council catchment area plus externally related organisations, but more specifically:

- the local people within a council catchment area;
- internal and external staff – private sector contracting out (e.g. care homes for the elderly), staff within local schools, business;
- other product providers (e.g. private finance initiative funders, contracting-out organisations;
- elected councillors and their local parties;
- central government.

Some people may belong to more than one market, but equally others may not – someone who uses a local council product may never vote in a local election, for example. As with all political organisations, the demands of each market conflict, and there are not normally the resources to meet everyone's demands (Beuret and Hall 1998: 6).

Local government product

Below are just some examples of what the local government product can consist of, building on the Local Government Association guide to local authority services (www.lga.gov.uk/Documents/Briefing/laservices.pdf, accessed March 2003):

- services, e.g. housing department, education department, community care, elderly care, transport, planning, cemeteries, welfare and social services, trading standards, environmental health, emergency planning;
- leisure amenities, including parks, museums, art galleries, playing fields, swimming pools;

- libraries and general information provision about the local area;
- fire and rescue;
- waste regulation, disposal, recycling facilities;
- collection and spending of council tax;
- tourism;
- buildings;
- website, newsletter, brochures, annual report;
- staff, including their professional expertise, training, knowledge;
- elected councillors and potential candidates for office, as well as their respective local parties;
- local reputation;
- political orientation;
- symbols, including a logo or slogan.

Having outlined the basics of local government, we will now explore how councils can use marketing in theory and practice. We begin with the most recent evolution: towards market-oriented local government, outlining the theory first and then illustrating it with examples. There are hundreds of councils throughout the UK of varying nature, size, power and naturally equally varying use of marketing. This chapter therefore provides a discussion of how councils generally could and do use marketing, rather than an assessment of how individual councils have used it.

Responding to the citizen: Market-oriented local government

> The winds of change have been blowing through UK local government shaking it to its very foundations. (Gray and Jenkins 1994b: 471)

Marketing has been increasingly taken up by councils all over the nation, in the form of both communication with the public and consultation to identify their demands. Even if councils do not officially use the marketing terminology, many talk of the need to communicate with and 'get closer to' the public (Beuret and Hall 1998: 2). Moreover, the conversations I had with staff working in local councils suggested the focus is not so much on public relations as on local government forms of market intelligence: political marketing influencing the product design, not just promotion.

There are many reasons for this change in behaviour, which also support the overall argument that there is a political marketing revolution in the UK. The first is the rise of the political consumer, already noted for other areas of politics, and also true of local government, as evidenced by the quotation at the beginning of the chapter from Alan Campbell (2002).

As in health and education, pressures to become more responsive to citizens have come from party government; first from the Conservative governments under Thatcher and Major (see Walsh 1995: 29, 32; Birkinshaw 1987: 154–155; Prior 1995: 86) and most recently, the Labour government. Local government is now increasingly important in the delivery of services. In particular, New Labour encouraged greater public consultation in local government, introduced by the 1998 (Department of the Environment, Transport and the Regions [DETR]) White Paper *Modern Local Government: In Touch with the People*. The paper argued that this would 'ensure that local authorities are reflecting the priorities and wishes of the people they serve' (quoted by Leach and Wingfield 2000: 47; see also Campbell 2002).

Increasingly scarce resources and a demanding citizenry have stimulated a renewed interest in the role marketing might play in how to manage and respond to demand (Beuret and Hall 1998: 9). Another issue raised by the media and academics in the 1990s was concern about alienation and a loss of trust in local government in particular, reflecting the overall rise of the political consumer. There seemed to be increasing dissatisfaction with local democracy (Young 2000: 184) and therefore a desire to do something about it. There is another causal factor similar to that for health and education: the introduction of internal markets and competition (see Stoker 1991: 216; Walsh 1995: 28; Peele 1995: 350–366; see also Gray and Jenkins 1994b: 447).

Market-oriented local government: definition Market-oriented councils attempt to design their product, including a wide range of services, to provide the most benefit possible to the local community. These councils use a broad range of marketing intelligence to understand and anticipate local demands, designing a realistic product accordingly and ensuring they communicate the product on offer and deliver what they promise.

Market-oriented councils will go through several marketing activities in order to provide the service that their markets most need and want. This is outlined in Box 9.1. Each stage is then explored in greater detail, with empirical illustration.

Box 9.1 The process for a market-oriented local government

Stage 1: Market intelligence

Stage 2: Product design

Stage 3: Product refinement

Stage 4: Implementation

Stage 5: Communication

Stage 6: Campaign

Stage 7: Delivery and assessment

Stage 1: Market intelligence

Local government conducts market intelligence to identify needs, wants and other pertinent information to enable it to design its product to meet public demands. Market intelligence is used for several purposes:

- to identify demands: both wants and needs;
- to predict future behaviour and demands;
- to predict responses to proposed products;
- to pre-test policy and products;
- to focus resources;
- to counteract opposition to new products within and outside the council;
- to improve satisfaction with a current product by identifying reasons for low usage, or non-usage by particular groups in society.

The methods used vary but include citizen consultation, Planning for Real, (described under 'Stage 1. Market intelligence' below), publicly available polls (e.g. British Household Panel Survey), public meetings, citizens' juries, referenda, focus-groups, meetings and informal internal discussions with staff, surveys, results from local elections, and geodemographic data. Market segmentation can also be conducted to identify with particular needs groups, such as the elderly, disabled poor, juvenile offenders, children, ethnic minorities and single parents. It can also be used amongst non-users to find out whether, for example, a product is not good enough for them to use it. Segmentation can help focus resources where most needed, as often local government can't produce something to meet everyone's demands. This is also carried out in order to design communication activities. This can identify priorities, not just a wish list.

Local government uses a wide range of market intelligence (see Leach and Wingfield 2000). It has increasing access to a range of market intelligence, such as standard market research, consultation to identify public priorities, and databases. MORI is just one of the polling organisations used increasingly by local government to conduct surveys and focus groups into how it is performing. The Local Authorities Research and Intelligence Association (LARIA) exists 'to promote the role and practice of research within the field of local government and provide a supportive network for those conducting or commissioning research' (www.laria.gov.uk/index.htm, accessed March 2003).

Conducting market intelligence fits with the bottom-up strategy adopted by local governments to revitalise local democracy (Young 2000: 185). It can keep the council in touch with the people. It can be used to ensure decision-making is well informed of facts, not just opinions, and to help allocate scarce resources. It can also be used to help predict future behaviour and likely responses to potential policies. Pirie and Worcester (2001) observed that 'the consumer agenda . . . is a very practical one. People want their local authorities to concentrate on things which make a direct difference to their own lives.' Alan Campbell (2002), a senior council officer, noted that there are several benefits that consultation with citizens can bring, such as 'help in planning the development of new or improved services', and that 'it can be used to monitor attitudes and perceptions about how councils are performing [. . . and] help build closer links between organisations and citizens by involving them in decisions that affect them'. Aberdeenshire Council set one of its goals as aiming to 'seek new ways to directly involve local communities in making decisions that affect them' to 'continue to ensure that the Council focused on meeting the needs of its citizens and customers' (Aberdeenshire Council 2001: 4–5).

Newcastle-under-Lyme has two staff working on the People's Panel called 'Have Your Say', compiling reports from the ideas discussed there (Scofield 2003; Newcastle-under-Lyme Borough Council 2002c). The People's Panel survey was sent to 600 residents representative of the area's population, and it was used to identify spending priorities and areas in need of improvement. Birmingham City Council runs a People's Panel as part of its consultation methods. Birmingham runs consultation on a wide variety issues, including its libraries. It appointed a consultation and involvement officer 'to talk and listen to people across the city about the proposed Library of Birmingham' (www.birmingham.gov.uk, accessed March 2003). Stafford Borough Council commissioned MORI to do a survey of residents in 2000 (Stafford Borough Council 2000).

Aberdeen City Council, which I studied in more detail, uses a variety of methods, all with the aim of finding out from people what they most need. For the Office of the Chief Executive, Community Development Section, these are: public meetings; a citizens' panel; a citizens jury; focus groups; surveys; the 'Open Space' and 'Pathway' projects; a video voxpop; and community contacts (Kilgour and Valentine 2002a). This city council office also conducts an exercise called 'Planning for Real', something developed and used in England too (Kilgour 2001; Kilgour and Valentine 2002a). The office has an open meeting, with maps made of a whole neighbourhood. The Arts and Development Department get children to make a three-dimensional model, through schools, of where they live. People are given cards which are prompts for issues, e.g. vandalism, and then asked to place them on the map to show where they think they are most a problem. Children bring parents along. It is then sold as a fun day, with free food and other events for the children, rather than directly as consultation – the council thinks hard about how to reach people. 'Planning for Real' gets more people to come than a normal general public meeting would. 300 people came to one in the deprived area of Maastrit. Kilgour (2001) noted how this type of market intelligence works better than normal meetings in part because a lot of people do not like speaking in public.

Many councils, particularly larger city councils, have a statement about consultation: see Box 9.2.

Intelligence can be used to identify why people do not use a product on offer and to see if something is not working effectively. Hounslow Council in West London conducted research to understand why Asian citizens were not using leisure facilities. The council found that cultural differences made some of these citizens reluctant, therefore dialogue was created between the council and the

---

Box 9.2 Statement by Manchester City Council on consultation

Consulting our Customers

So that we can make sure that your views are always taken into account by the people who make the decisions, the Council has a consultation strategy. This makes sure that when the plans are made, what you think is considered. When we do consultation projects like surveys we try to plan them ahead so that we can make sure that we have enough information at the right times to make informed decisions.

Consultation is an important part of the best value process. The Council is committed to consulting people who use the services (and often those who don't use them) as part of every best value review. In addition to this, every year the Council carries out the city wide *Best Value Survey*.

During the survey, thousands of residents and businesses are asked what they think about different Council services and about how they feel about the city and their local area.

We are interested in what everyone who might want to use our services has to say. This means that we try to consult a broad variety of people across the city. If our consultation shows that we are not collecting the views of groups like disabled people, women, black and ethnic minority people, lesbians and gay men, older or younger people we will try to do extra work to make sure these groups are not left out. We won't only listen to the views of the majority, the views of just a few people (or one person with a good idea) matter too. You can find out *more on equality*.

We always try to make sure that we tell the people who have been consulted what we have done with the results. We always try to tell you when services have been improved because of what you have told us. If we have not been able to put your ideas into practice we will do our best to tell you why. We may do this on the web, or through newsletters, the city newspaper *Manchester People*, or sometimes through a personal mailing.

Source: www.manchester.gov.uk/bestvalue/consult/intro.htm, accessed 18 March 2003

Asian community, and a new self-help exercise programme for Asian elders was initiated (quoted in Beuret and Hall 1998: 74). Birmingham City Council designed its consultation on its library to focus on key communities, both those that had a particular vested interest in the library and 'those which do not currently make much use of library and archive services', such as children and young people, lesbians and gay men, and people with disabilities (www.birmingham. gov.uk / GenerateContent?CONTENT_ITEM_ID=16738&CONTENT_ITEM _TYPE=0&MENU_ID=5384, accessed March 2003).

Citizens' juries are another effective means of obtaining market intelligence. They consist of local people representative of the area who discuss a policy issue in detail, hearing evidence from different people and then making a final decision. It enables greater and more detailed discussion than a simple survey, and encourages political consumers to think more broadly about the public rather than their individual interest (see Beuret and Hall 1998: 100–102; Young 2000:

194 for further details). Aberdeen City Council have used citizens' juries (the Great Northern Partnership, a programme of co-operation between councils in the north of Scotland, with funding from the Scottish executive), holding one on drugs, for example. Twelve people were selected to represent different groups in society, came together for a week, and listened to submissions from witnesses, including drug users and those running drug services (Kilgour 2001).

Stage 2: Product design

The next stage is for the council to design the product – all aspects of the council's behaviour, including staff, symbols, websites and services – according to the results of market intelligence. This can mean developing new products or improving existing behaviour.

Market intelligence is used by councils to inform product design as well as prioritise areas for improvement to the existing product. This can be as simple as using intelligence to inform the development of housing in a variety of areas, including aspects such as rents, security, noise and shared gardens (Beuret and Hall 1998: 92), but any area of council work can be considered. Councils can introduce a new service in response to market intelligence that asks for a new playground or bus route, for example.

Market intelligence is also used to develop goals and strategic plans. Many councils develop mission statements and strategic plans which are used as guides for product design and performance measurement. The existence of a mission statement does not mean that the council has adopted a market orientation (Beuret and Hall 1998: 4), but it is at least some indication this has been considered (see, for example, Aberdeenshire City Council 2001; Campbell 2002; Newcastle-under-Lyme Borough Council 2002b). Aberdeen City Council identified 14 city challenges from its 'Imagine Aberdeen' consultation exercise (see Aberdeen City Council 2001: 5ff for further detail) and produced an overall plan to meet such challenges with targets and goals, called *Aberdeen Futures* (Aberdeen City Council 2001). New products planned included an interactive website and a customer care centre (Aberdeen City Council 2001: 22).

One example of the general responsiveness of councils to public opinion is their reaction to environmental issues. As Young (2000: 181) observed, public concern about the environment rose from the late 1980s onwards: it was clearly evident from market intelligence in the form of public opinion polls. Local government responded to this by focusing on a wide range of products it could produce which would help the environment. This included:

- recycling facilities;
- tree-planting;
- protection of wildlife;
- pollution control;
- cycle paths;

- leisure facilities to allow people to enjoy the environment, such as paths, walks and forests;
- reclaiming and redeveloping land used by industry;
- sustainable disposal of waste;
- promotion of public transport not cars;
- inner-city or urban suburb regeneration, including aspects such as housing and building planning and road-building.

Stage 3: Product refinement
This has four main aspects

- *Achievability*: Ensure the product is achievable in terms of cost, time and other constraints. Avoid promising what the council can not deliver.
- *Reallocation of resources*: Consider altering the budget in order to provide maximum output from resources, so that time and money are spent on areas that most need new products, for example.
- *De-marketing*: Reduce or manage demand where needed and manage expectations.
- *Target marketing*: Target new products or resources on certain areas or sections of community in most need.

Achievability   Marketers often point out to critics that marketing does not mean promising everyone everything they want – and in political marketing we argue that indeed this would be foolish, because in politics no one can ever have everything she or he wants. That is the nature of politics, and why it exists: to allocate scare resources in a demanding world market. As Beuret and Hall (1998: 6) observed, local councils are increasingly 'being franker about what they can and cannot do'. Product refinement means ensuring that the product design is really achievable, and being honest about it. It is important to let people know if what they want cannot be produced. A more realistic approach helps to maintain public support for local government as a whole. If people have an explanation, then they are far more likely to accept the results.

Reallocation of resources   Market-oriented behaviour includes reallocation of existing resources to suit changing demand and needs. Councils have responded to results from consultation in terms of reallocating existing resources to match public priorities identified during market intelligence (Beuret and Hall 1998: 7). Following market intelligence and consultation on public priorities, in 2002 Aberdeen City Council cut back expenditure in those areas which the public did not see as most important and put more money into areas such as safety and security, for example, expanding CCTV. The research conducted by Newcastle-under-Lyme Borough Council (2002c: 9–10) specifically asked respondents where they thought there could be a reduction in spending, obtaining demands for reduction in areas such as mayoral services and costs, council tax collection costs, and providing allotments, providing additional street signs. Overall the survey resulted in a list of priorities for increased spending, but also areas where there could be a reduction in spending, which is potentially of more practical use than a simple wish list.

Demarketing   Demarketing is needed where there are scarce resources and limited budgets. Beuret and Hall (1998: 93) cite the case of council grants for home insulation, and how in the past grants had been claimed by more affluent areas; so with limited funding available, one council only distributed information about the scheme in the most deprived areas, which resulted in the end in grants going to those most in need.

Target marketing   Target marketing is used by local councils to help prioritise and allocate limited resources most effectively. As Hannagan (1992: 30) observed, although this is a political decision, 'factual information from the market can ease the decision-making process'. Targeting can be used in several stages of the political marketing process, including market intelligence, to consult with particular sections of society; product design, to develop products to suit certain market segments or reallocate resources to give more to one group or product; and communication, to ensure those who are most in need are also aware of what is on offer. Kilgour (2001) reported that Aberdeen City Council targets resources on regeneration, developing poorer areas.

In terms of targeted communication, Beuret and Hall (1998: 17) cite a councillor who noted how the council did not have enough minibuses to transport all children who would want to use them to the summer play schemes, so it only advertised the transport to the two most deprived wards. This form of target marketing isn't about maximising customers to make the most money, or targeting swing voters to obtain the most votes to win, but focusing on those who most need the service. It is quite a different form of marketing.

Price is important, in terms of how much money goes into a particular product or how much is charged. As Beuret and Hall (1998: 7) observed, this can include 'withdrawing uneconomic services, cross-subsidising, charging, taking a profit or breaking even'. Barry Scofield, head of policy review and communication at Newcastle-under-Lyme Borough Council, noted that local government, because it has different goals and objectives, does not operate pricing in the same way as businesses. For example, when running the local swimming baths the objective is not so much to make money by charging a good price as to encourage children from a wide range of backgrounds to swim (Scofield 2003; see also Beuret and Hall 1998: 22).

Indeed, different prices may be charged to different groups, responding to different market segments (Beuret and Hall 1998: 23). For example, councils may offer a leisure ticket to those on unemployment benefit that entitles them to lower-cost or free use of council services. Local councils employ accountants to understand cost-benefit analysis and track expenditure. However, cost-benefit analysis should not always be done in economic terms. Certainly not all pricing levels need to be determined by income; for example, Beuret and Hall (1998: 95) noted that 'encouraging young people to use leisure centres may have a beneficial effect in reducing crime or vandalism', and encouraging the elderly may help promote good health. There are other goals here that are not financial or about cost.

Stage 4: Implementation

Councils then need to implement the refined product design, ensuring there is internal acceptance and understanding of any proposed changes in behaviour, and that staff are trained and supported. Local councils can be big bureaucratic organisations and internal change requires effective management, especially for creating a market-oriented culture within the organisation.

Implementation is a key part of marketing in local government, and requires careful organisation and management to ensure that all those who work for and with the public understand the behaviour expected of them. Some council staff report departmental organisation or budget lines being obstacles to developing a market-oriented organisation that can respond effectively to emerging needs (see Kilgour 2001, for example). However, using marketing – even the word, let alone the activity – in local government can be problematic. As one staff member reported (to remain anonymous for ethical reasons), often staff are seen as being like spin-doctors, with all the negativity associated with that. They need to be apolitical because their work continues past local elections and any change in partisan power those may bring. Leach and Wingfield (2000: 52–53) found from their case studies that there was some opposition to consulting public opinion in councils, which hindered the adoption of more innovative methods. General management and leadership are therefore very important factors in marketing local government.

Stage 5: Communication

Local councils need to communicate their product, without raising expectations; they should deal respectfully with local people and any complaints, and also engage in two-way communication to obtain both input and feedback from the public. Information should be made readily available to the public in a way that people can understand and access. Communication can use a variety of vehicles, including regular newspapers, the council's website, annual reports and leaflets. Communication can also be used to demarket a product to reduce demand, or targeted on specific social groups or geographical areas.

Beuret and Hall (1998: 5) observed that there is increasing interest 'in the provision of advice, publicising information, performance indicators and monitoring'. Communication efforts by councils have expanded in recent years, and include better information, leaflets, communication officers, use of local media and remote access to rural areas (Beuret and Hall 1998: 24). Councils often produce regular newspapers which contain useful information and publicise the work of the council, particularly new products. Newcastle-under-Lyme produces one entitled *Reporter: Your Newspaper Working With You*

(Newcastle-under-Lyme Borough Council 2002a, 2003) and Aberdeen City Council's newspaper is called *Bon-Accord*, the traditional name for and 'spirit' of the city (Aberdeen City Council 2002). Newcastle-under-Lyme Borough Council's December 2002 edition of its newspaper was headlined 'Click Here for Service', with the lead story advertising a new service that enabled reception staff at community locations to report residents' concerns via the web directly to the organisation provider, therefore hopefully speeding up the response process.

Symbols and brand identities can also be developed by councils. Scofield (2003) recalled how one of his first jobs was to introduce a corporate identity and logo for Newcastle-under-Lyme. Hitherto every department had had separate colours and styles of writing, which prevented a recognisable, uniform symbol for the council from emerging. This was replaced with a green and turquoise colour scheme and the slogan 'You'll notice the difference.' The council produces a number of publications beside its newspaper, for both internal and external markets, including:

- *Grapevine*, a staff magazine which ensures staff within the organisation understand what is going on;
- *Know Your Councillor*, a guide to how to contact councillors and what they do;
- an A–Z of council services, with contact numbers;
- *How to Make a Complaint*, a leaflet on how and to whom to complain if the product provided by the council is not good enough;
- *Information Pack*, a short booklet on what the council does and how people can have their say in it.

Responding to the 2000 Freedom of Information Act, Bradford City Council produced a new booklet, *Freedom of Information*, to give people better access to information about the council. The booklet described how the council worked and how to obtain information from and contact different departments, with details about plans, policies and reports, as well as explaining the public's rights and how people could complain. The booklet was made available in the town hall, libraries and council information centres (council's website www.bradford.gov.uk; press release 5 March 2003).

Websites are increasingly important for councils. They can contain a wide variety of information for local citizens and be updated regularly without the cost of printing and sending out leaflets. One example is Birmingham City Council's website, www.birmingham.gov.uk. This was established in 1994, and by 2002 had received 12 million page hits. It contains a very wide range of information about the council and the city as a whole. It was recently rated one of the top ten UK local authority websites by the Society of Information Technology Management (Socitm), which visited all the websites managed by 467 Councils throughout the UK (for further information see www.birmingham.gov.uk press release, 6 March 2003).

Websites can also be used to provide information to help local residents to enjoy the local area. The headline buttons on the website for Kent County Council, for example, are 'Caring', 'Living', 'Working', 'Enjoying', 'Learning' and 'Travelling'. These are all very positive links to information; 'Enjoying' includes substantial information on walking and riding, parks, tourism centres and cycling, and has a separate linked website for 'access to the countryside'.

Certain councils with large ethnic minorities supply important information in different languages: Liverpool and Glasgow city councils are examples of this. Communication can help make different pricing of council services effective, especially where concessions are targeted on particular groups, because all the pricing efforts and strategies will go to waste and have no effect if people do not know they are available (Beuret and Hall 1998: 95). If the product and price of it are targeted, so must the communication be.

Stage 6: Campaign
Councils can also engage in one-off, short-term communication to promote a new or underused product they provide, with possibly targeted communication to increase awareness and use that benefits the local community. A campaign should be a short-term communication activity, highly focused and given a high profile.

Campaigns can be undertaken on a variety of issues, such as to promote a new leisure centre or an after-school club, to increase awareness of a product already in existence, to increase public use of a product or to launch a new development. They can also be used to reduce behaviour which has a negative impact on local residents. Birmingham City Council launched a campaign called 'You Are Your City' to encourage people to stop dropping litter, and introduced a £30 one-off fine for anyone caught dropping rubbish (www.birmingham.gov.uk, accessed March 2003). Market-oriented councils do not use campaigns to 'sell' themselves as such, but to increase the benefit to the local community of what they are already doing. Campaigns differ from general ongoing communication because they are carried out for a short period only.

One example of a campaign by local government is Bruce Strachan's (2001) campaign on the environment for Aberdeen City Council. A summary of the plan for this is in Box 9.3.

Box 9.3 Aberdeen City Council's campaign on the environment

Overall aim: To encourage the participation of other local authorities in the 'North of Scotland' area, develop a set of key themes and investigate mechanisms for the delivery of the envisaged two-year campaign.

Goals of the campaign
To:

• increase public awareness of the environmental facilities provided by, and actions to protect the environment taken by, local authorities;

continued on next page

Box 9.3 continued

- increase public involvement in the environment and environmental facilities pro-vided by local authorities;
- change public attitudes and behaviour, e.g. greater use of public transport.

Results of research conducted to understand the market
These explored:

- perceived levels of current knowledge;
- issues regarded as important by the public;
- what could be done to facilitate greater awareness;
- whether greater awareness led to behavioural change.

Market segments
These were identified as:

- pro-environment;
- those who were vaguely interested but had not taken much action to date;
- those who were unlikely ever to respond to this campaign.

The needs of each were perceived as different. The first group might simply have needed information about environmental facilities and activities. The second might have needed not just information but some persuasion as to the benefits of using and being involved in such facilities and activities.

Demographic markets
These were identified as:

- those whose opinions were not yet formed, such as school children;
- those with more time to participate or who were predisposed to participate, such as university students and middle-class, educated professionals;
- those the campaign needed to target, such as car users;
- those already involved, such as members of environmental interest groups like the RSPB.

Proposed campaign
The themes were waste; recycling; traffic; transport air pollution; climate change; biodiversity loss; opportunities; pollution; energy efficiency; renewables; health; agriculture and chemicals; buying; sustainable rural living (access); incineration; housing; supporting communities; sustainable buildings; tourism; marine environ-ment; population decline; and agricultural and non-agricultural business.

Mechanisms were school projects; newspaper articles; local radio; leaflets; internet; local groups; meetings; television; bus advertising; posters; an events programme; a roving panel display; fact sheets; a campaign newsletter; seminars; badging of build-ings and vehicles; billboards; a roadshow or staffed display; awareness raising events; beer mats; pens etc.

Source: summarised from Strachan (2001)

Such plans take significant effort and resources to put into action, but this indicates the type of thinking that a market-oriented council will undertake in trying to improve its product and achieve its goals. Councils all over the UK engage in similar campaigns, perhaps focused on improving security in a neighbourhood or promoting new youth clubs or waste management. Campaigns in this instance are a valuable part of marketing because they help to ensure that the product the council delivers has the maximum impact possible. Although the product is the most important part of political marketing, it will have only limited impact if no one knows about it.

Stage 7: Delivery and assessment

The last stage is delivery, which includes assessment – seeing how the delivered product is received. This involves enabling and responding to public grievances and complaints. Independent organisations such as the Audit Commission may also assess performance. The council needs to analyse how its products are received, especially as demand can alter over time as society changes – compare the product lifecycle concept in business, which predicts that organisations go through stages of quick growth, maturity, slow decline and then quick decline. From this, the council can then return to market intelligence and use marketing continually, going back to improve existing products and develop new ones once again.

More detailed research is needed to assess delivery in local councils, but it is clearly an important aspect of political marketing. One of the difficulties is that political delivery for all organisations is complex and difficult; it is not easy to ensure citizens are satisfied with the product they receive. People are often quicker to complain than report a positive experience, and there is always room for improvement. Councils also need to spend time communicating delivery and assessing it, before feeding the results back into the beginning of the marketing process.

Councils have recently provided better means of consumers' raising complaints. For example, as well as providing clear information about how people can register a complaint, Manchester City Council make a 'promise' to citizens about how it will deal with complaints:

> *This is the Council's promise to you*
> - We will answer all complaints within 15 working days or explain why a reply may take longer.
> - We will acknowledge receipt of your complaint within 5 working days.
> - We will use plain language.
> - We will give you a contact name and telephone number.
>
> We also promise to deal with all complaints in confidence, fairly, efficiently and to provide a full reply at the very earliest opportunity. Your views will help us to provide a better quality service to which all have equal access'. www.manchester.gov.uk/bestvalue/perform/complain, accessed March 2003)

The performance of local councils is assessed externally by organisations such as the Audit Commission or the independent District Auditor Service. For example, in 2002 Birmingham City Council had a corporate assessment conducted by the Audit Commission. The report was pasted on its website, with assessments of its performance so far and how it could improve in the future. Manchester City Council sent a copy of the summary of its Performance Plan 2003/4 to every household in Manchester and placed it on the website (www.manchester.gov.uk/bestvalue/perform/plan03/index.htm, accessed March 2003).

Indeed, delivery can lead to cyclical marketing. It provides the opportunity to report what has been achieved so far and then ask for further input into what more needs to be done, linking back to Stage 1, 'market intelligence', again. For example, Aberdeen City Council produced reports on its progress in the areas that the public were most concerned about, and made them available in the form of leaflets that were distributed in the council's newspaper and other venues such as community centres, universities and GP's surgeries. It also asked for feedback from the public on how it might improve further.

There is significant evidence that the vast majority of councils are at least trying to become market oriented, or considering adopting that approach, even if they have not all achieved such a status in all of their activities. However, it certainly used to be the case that, like many political organisations when they first start to use marketing, councils looked more to a sales-oriented approach in order to respond to growing dissatisfaction and increasing criticism from the public. We will therefore highlight how such an approach would work.

Marketing as promotion: sales-oriented local government

Definition of a sales-oriented council   A council that is sales-oriented focuses on presenting its work in the best possible lights, ensuring it presents it activities effectively, and promotes its work wherever possible. Energy is centred on communication activities to sell the council, rather than improving the actual product or service offered.

Sales-oriented councils use marketing in a less complex way, which focuses on communications activities: see Box 9.4. Again, the stages are then explored in more detail, with empirical examples.

Box 9.4 The process for a sales-oriented local government

Stage 1: Product design

Stage 2: Market intelligence

Stage 3: Communication

Stage 4: Campaign

Stage 5: Delivery and managing response

Stage 1: Product design

The council designs its product, including all aspects of its behaviour, according to what it thinks is best.

Stage 2: Market intelligence

The council conducts limited market intelligence, not to identify demands but to assess support for that it has already decided to do and to enable targeted communication to reduce public opposition if necessary. The council may also undertake consultation to justify what it has already decided it wants do do, or to buy time to diffuse a strong public outcry.

One distinction between a sales and market orientation is that with a market-oriented approach the council 'ensures that there is plenty of scope to change its position after the participation process is over . . . the participation process comes at the start of the policy-making process and is not grafted on to a process that is already well advanced' (Young 2000: 185). For example, a public meeting I attended in March 2003 about what was going to happen to an old railway line was criticised by people for taking place too near to the date when the work would start for their opinions to have any influence.

Often consultation is not taken seriously. One local government communication officer (to remain anonymous for ethical reasons) whom I interviewed talked about the latest consultation as being used simply to gain support for what the council had already decided it wanted to do. Young (2000: 186) also observed this type of attitude amongst many councils. Market intelligence is used merely to help communicate product benefits, or if there is disagreement, then communication is designed to downplay elements that market intelligence has shown that the public will not like.

Stage 3: Communication

The next stage is to create an effective, strong communication strategy to promote the council's product, but also to persuade people if necessary that what the council proposes to do is the right way ahead. Communication includes methods such as developing corporate logos, slogans, flashy websites, glossy brochures and nice reception areas – the focus being on the presentation of the product not the product itself.

As Temple (2000: 131) noted, local government has clearly paid attention to the presentational side of its behaviour:

> Local authorities increasingly have Press and Public Relations departments, just as companies do. They operate expensive reception desks modelled on Bank or Building Society high street premises with staff in smart corporate costumer. The function of these is chiefly to confirm the (artificial) status of their clients as customers as this confirmation is required as much by the organisation itself as it is to make a signal to the citizen.

Temple's use of the word 'artificial' is significant. Not all local councils pay as much attention to changing their actual product; the approach to marketing is sales oriented. Many local councils have adopted new logos, indicating at the very least a movement towards a sales orientation. Examples are:

- *Manchester* – 'We're up and going'
- *Glasgow* – 'The friendly city'
- *Merseyside* – 'a pool of talent'
- *Dudley* – 'in the heart of England'
- *Newham* – 'in the heart of East London'
- *Havant* – 'at the heart of the South Coast of England'
- *Bromsgrove* – 'the gateway to rural Worcestershire'
- *Christchurch* – 'where time is pleasant'
- *Corby* – 'in the middle of everywhere'
- *Bradford* – 'one landscape many views'
- *Newcastle-under-Lyme* – 'You'll notice the difference'
- *Surrey County Council* – 'putting people first'
- *Stone Town Council* – 'your progressive local council'. (building on Beuret and Hall 1998: 3)

Stage 4: Campaign

Campaigns can be used, for example, to increase public support for a new product the council wants to initiate, or to publicise a product to ensure the public think favourably of the council. They could include the issue of a positive annual report prior to an increase in council tax, for example. They may also include social marketing that aims to change behaviour.

Campaigns can be undertaken to promote council work or increase support for proposed action such as the building of new housing estate in green belt land. A more positive aspect of sales-oriented marketing in local government is campaigns to change behaviour, or social marketing. This takes a product-oriented approach to design, but does so in the interest of society at large. One example is 'Safer Routes to School', a campaign whereby councils tried to encourage children to walk to school and get exercise as well as reduce congestion from parents driving them. In order to ensure children were safe, councils worked with schools and parents to create safe routes with safe houses on the way (see also Beuret and Hall 1998: 109). Other examples include safety campaigns with speed cameras, educational campaigns about the environment in schools, and those against drink-driving often launched at Christmas. Trying to change behaviour is often very difficult, however, and meets with limited success. It is a well-meaning use of marketing, but not necessarily effective.

Stage 5: Delivery and managing response

Sales-oriented councils do deliver a product, but because it is not driven by market demand, it may not always be received well; therefore communication techniques and public relations need to be in place to manage the response and deal with any problems, as well as to highlight anything that works and goes well.

Clearly some councils continue to adopt a sales orientation in part if not in total, and although research needs to be conducted to be sure, it is possible that elected councillors may also prefer to use marketing to justify their party policy decisions – to promote the party line. On the whole, though, the evidence suggests that councils are more likely to attempt to be market oriented.

We now move on to outline what councils used to be like: more traditional, product-oriented organisations.

The past: product-oriented councils

> Many local government services were cosy monopolies protected from market forces and the harsh winds of competition. (Gray and Jenkins 1994b: 472)

Although most councils would not try to be product oriented now, it is still useful to outline what we mean by this so that if it is present, it can be identified and understood. Certainly in the past councils traditionally held a product-oriented attitude. As Gray and Jenkins (1994b: 461) observed, the traditional local government structure was run in 'a paternalistic way'. The marketing process used was therefore very simple, from product design through communication to delivery.

Indeed, Birkinshaw (1987: 154) commented how before 1979 and the election of the Thatcher government, local councils 'had made little effort to be either accountable or accessible'. Local government communication was 'indifferent' and not open to complaints, let alone responding to public demand (see also Birkinshaw, 1987: 155; Beuret and Hall 1998: 16, 21). The product-oriented attitude is still to be found within some local councils, or some departments within them. Beuret and Hall (1998: 90) noted how the provision of council housing, for example, is an area where often the attitude is that the recipients have to be grateful for whatever they get. However, even if citizens are receiving a 'free' service, being market oriented is still more appropriate for councils if good, positive relationships are to be built up between government and the governed. Those receiving services now will be voting, or paying taxes later, and the council will benefit from creating a feeling of good will and responsiveness rather than being dogmatic and unhelpful.

Nevertheless, there are many potential criticisms of a market-oriented approach to local government.

Issues of market-oriented marketing in local government

Market intelligence raises expectations
A concern often expressed not just by academics but by councillors is that if people are asked what they'd like in the course of market intelligence, they will ask for a brand new swimming pool every time, or things that are just not practical or affordable. Kilgour (2001) said that in his experience the community did not actually expect that much; and furthermore it was more about the structure and service delivery, not just money (see also Beuret and Hall 1998: 6).

Certainly, consultation exercises need to be handled carefully. The meeting I went to in March 2003, where the council talked us through what they were going to do to the old railway line at the back of some houses, was a clear reminder of this. As soon as the council started seeking our views, the meeting became somewhat tense and fractious, as each household – and we're only talking about 15 – had individual requests and demands for the two-metre stretch of land at the back of their house. People also started talking about non-council-related matters, such as floods from land beyond the council control. It was useful and did give us the opportunity for input, but certainly people did not give the council an easy ride. Perhaps as the political marketing revolution evolves, we will learn more effective ways of both conducting and participating in such consultation meetings. This has to be partly the responsibility of the political consumer, the citizen, as it is for the elite, the government, to be responsive.

Costs of consultation

Market intelligence is expensive. Leach and Wingfield (2000: 55) noted how participation 'adds to the cost of providing a service'. Consultation can also hinder decision-making, as it takes a long time to design, conduct and compile the results. This is difficult when the council is under pressure to do something (see Campbell 2002).

Limited impact of market intelligence due to lack of public expertise

Market intelligence does not always empower people: the general public are limited by their own knowledge and expertise, as Murdoch et al. (2000: 207) observed in their study of planning for housing. They found that although there was some scepticism and doubts about the central government figures used, the public and associated groups did not have the political power to challenge the statistics (Murdoch et al. 2000: 209–10). Stoker (1991: 85) questions 'whether the activists involved in user organisations really are well-equipped to make informed, "good" decisions'.

Market intelligence is always biased to affluent, educated, middle-class groups

Kilgour (2001) noted how a lot of people do not like speaking in public, so traditional means of market intelligence such as public meetings can lead to biased results. Leach and Wingfield (2000: 56) found from their research that 'patterns of social exclusion are invariably reproduced' in public participation, and 'young people and ethnic minority groups are particularly hard to reach'. Barnes (2000) evaluates different methods; they have different values and disadvantages. This needs to be taken into account when councils decide what methods to use.

Market-oriented councils: the potential

Although there are significant arguments against marketing, and certainly these issues need to be explored and discussed further, there are still benefits of the idea that councils should consult local people when developing their product. Some arguments counteract the criticisms above. For example, Beuret and Hall (1998: 98) observe 'growing evidence to suggest that people are capable and ready to make distinctions between their individual needs and what is best for meeting the broader needs of local citizens'. Young (2000: 192), however, observes that the effectiveness of consultation is not clear: 'looking more widely across British local government in the 1990s, it is not possible to draw clear conclusions about the impact of the participatory experiments', and views are varied and divided.

Some research has indicated the positive uses of marketing. The study by Clapham et al. (2000: 232) of community-based housing organisations (CBHOs) in Scotland found one such. They concluded that CBHOs did 'deliver accountability . . . [and] are open to the influence, in practice not just in principle, of most of the people they serve. Moreover, they seem to be successful in delivering services which satisfy most people', and have done so for ten years. It has also been suggested that marketing may be good for democracy. Young (2000: 195) argues that a move 'away from bureaucratic, paternalistic, welfare provision' towards a bottom-up approach can even help reduce 'social exclusion, alienation, and loss of faith in the capacity of local government to deliver'. Marketing could potentially help politics regain people's trust. Kilgour and Valentine (2002a), both working in local government, suggested that the use of market intelligence could help address the democratic deficit and strengthen local democracy, by 'bringing decision making closer to citizens'. Leach and Wingfield (2000: 52) make an important and significant link between market intelligence (though they call it participation or consultation) and participatory democracy. As they point out, there is an argument that such participation can strengthen the institution of representative democracy. More detailed research is needed to explore whether using market intelligence to design services in local government does produce a better product.

Conclusion

In summary, it is clear that local government is also being permeated by marketing. Although the extent to which it is used may remain limited in some cases, there is no doubt that the use of market intelligence is widespread and councils at least desire to be market oriented and responsive to local people where possible. Marketing can help councils allocate scarce resources, target their products, and communicate effectively with local people to help provide the best service possible.

Local government is important not just in itself but because of its links to other areas of the political system. As we said at the beginning of this chapter, it is an important part of the national government's delivery in areas such as education and health. Indeed, the theme running through the entire book is that all parts of the political system are integral to the success of marketing by political parties. Although party marketing remains undeniably important and worthy of

further research, the delivery aspect of marketing is so complex and so significant – it is after all what can make a different to people's daily lives – that political marketing now needs to extend to all other areas of politics. Without this,
the overall marketing revolution in politics will be incomplete and ineffective –
if not extremely troublesome. This may be why the Labour government set up a
new delivery unit after the 2001 general election, to oversee delivery and the
achievement of goals in a wide range of government activity.

Certainly, the empirical overview of marketing in these other areas presented
in this book indicates that marketing is permeating institutions like the monarchy, the BBC and Westminster, and that both the concepts and techniques of
marketing have been implemented in the education and health care sectors, even
if the acceptance of masrketing's utility is limited. The implications of the political marketing revolution spread wider than most people are perhaps aware of.
The next chapter will therefore be devoted to exploring the potential consequences of this change in behaviour for the UK political system as a whole.

Bibliography

Aberdeen City Council (2001), *Aberdeen Futures: A Social, Economic and Environmental Design for Our City*, Aberdeen City Council, Aberdeen.

Aberdeen City Council (2002), *Bon-Accord* (Aberdeen City Council newspaper), August.

Aberdeenshire Council (2001), *Aberdeenshire Strategic Plan*, Aberdeenshire Council, Aberdeen.

Barnes, M. (2000), 'Researching Public Participation', in L. Pratchett (ed.), *Renewing Local Democracy? The Modernisation Agenda in British Local Government*, Frank Cass, London. pp. 60–75.

Beuret, K. and R. Hall (1998), *Marketing in Local Government*, Financial Times, Pitman, Trowbridge.

Birkinshaw, P. (1987), 'Consumers and Ratepayers', M. Parkinson (ed.), *Reshaping Local Government*, Transaction Books, Oxford. pp. 154–164.

Campbell, A. (2002), 'Consultation Costs! The Aberdeenshire Experience', presentation to the Political Marketing Conference, Aberdeen, September.

Chandler, J.A. (1991), *Local Government Today*, Manchester University Press, Manchester.

Clapham, D., K. Kintrea and H. Kay (2000), 'User participation on Community Housing: Is Small Really Beautiful?' in G. Stoker (ed.), *The New Politics of British Local Governance*, Macmillan, Basingstoke and London. pp. 215–233.

Elcock, H. (1982), *Local Government: Politicians, Professionals and the Public in Local Authorities*, Methuen, London.

Gray, A. and B. Jenkins (1994a), 'The Management of Central Government Services', in B. Jones (ed.), *Politics UK*, Harvester Wheatsheaf, London. pp. 426–446.

Gray, A. and B. Jenkins (1994b), 'Local Government', in B. Jones (ed.), *Politics UK*, Harvester Wheatsheaf, London. pp. 447–477.

Hannagan, T. (1992), *Marketing for the Non-profit Sector*, Macmillan, London.

Kilgour, D. (2001), Interview by J. Lees-Marshment with the principal development officer, Aberdeen City Council, Aberdeen, 13 November.

Kilgour, D. and D. Valentine (2002a), presentation about the Community Development Section, Aberdeen City Council, Aberdeen University.

Kilgour, D. and D. Valentine (2002b), presentation about the Community Development Section, Aberdeen City Council, Political Marketing Conference, Aberdeen, September.

Kingdom, J. (1991), *Local Government and Politics in Britain*, Philip Allan, Hemel Hempstead.

Leach, S. and M. Wingfield (2000), 'Public Participation and the Democratic Renewal Agenda: Prioritisation or Marginalisation', in L. Pratchett (ed.), *Renewing Local Democracy? The Modernisation Agenda in British Local Government*, Frank Cass, London. pp. 46–59.

Murdoch, J., S. Abram and T. Marsden (2000), 'Technical Expertise and Public Participation in Planning for Housing: Playing the Numbers Game', in G. Stoker (ed.), *The New Politics of British Local Governance*, Macmillan, Basingstoke and London. pp. 198–214.

Newcastle-under-Lyme Borough Council (2002a), *Reporter: Your Newspaper Working With You*. Newcastle-under-Lyme Borough Council, Newcastle-under-Lyme, December.

Newcastle-under-Lyme Borough Council (2002b), *Performance Plan 2002–2003*. Newcastle-under-Lyme Borough Council, Newcastle-under-Lyme.

Newcastle-under-Lyme Borough Council (2002c), *Have Your Say: The Newcastle People's Panel; 'Setting council priorities' Consultation, via the People's Panel and Newcastle Borough Councillors*, Newcastle-under-Lyme Borough Council, Policy Review and Communications Department, Newcastle-under-Lyme, November.

Newcastle-under-Lyme Borough Council (2003), *Reporter: Your Newspaper Working With You*, Newcastle-under-Lyme Borough Council, Newcastle-under-Lyme, February.

Peele, G. (1995), *Governing the UK*, Blackwell, Oxford.

Pirie, M. and R. Worcester (2001), *The Wrong Package*, report on a MORI poll by the Adam Smith Institute, London. Also at www.mori.com/polls/2001/asi.shtml or www.adamsmith.org.uk, accessed March 2003.

Pratchett, L. (2000), *Renewing Local Democracy? The Modernisation Agenda in British Local Governance*, Frank Cass, London.

Pratchett, L. and D. Wilson (1996), *Local Democracy and Local Government*, Macmillan, Basingstoke.

Prior, D. (1995), 'Citizen's Charters', in J. Stewart and G. Stoker (eds), *Local Government in the 1990s*, Macmillan, Basingstoke. pp. 86–103.

Rees, P. and H. Gardner (2003), 'Best Value, Partnerships and Relationship Marketing in Local Government', *International Journal of Non-profit and Voluntary Sector Marketing*, 8(2): 143–152.

Scofield, B. (2003), Interview by J. Lees-Marshment with Barry Scofield, head of policy review and communication at Newcastle-under-Lyme Council, January.

Stafford Borough Council (2000), Stafford residents survey 2000, conducted by MORI. www.staffordbc.gov.uk/live/welcome.asp?id=1025, accessed March 2003.

Stewart, J. (1995), 'A Future for Local Authorities as Community Government', in J. Stewart and G. Stoker (eds), *Local Government in the 1990s*, Macmillan, Basingstoke. pp. 249–267.

Stoker, G. (1991), *The Politics of Local Government*, 2nd edition, Macmillan, Basingstoke and London.

Stoker, G. (ed.), (2000), *The New Politics of British Local Governance*, Macmillan, Basingstoke and London.

Strachan, B. (2001), Meeting by J. Lees-Marshment with Bruce Strachan, Environment Awareness Project, Planning and Strategic Development, Aberdeen City Council, University of Aberdeen, 4 October.

Temple, M. (2000), *How Britain Works: From Ideology to Output Politics*, Macmillan, London.

Walsh, K. (1989), *Marketing in Local Government*, Longman, Harlow.

Walsh, K. (1991a), 'Citizens and Consumers: Marketing and Public Sector Management', *Public Money and Management* 11(2): 9.

Walsh, K. (1991b), 'Quality in Public Services', *Public administration* 69: 503–514.

Walsh, K. (1995), 'Competition and Public Service Delivery', in J. Stewart and G. Stoker (eds), *Local Government in the 1990s*, Macmillan, Basingstoke. pp. 28–48.

Wilson, D. and C. Game (1998), *Local Government in the United Kingdom*, Macmillan, Basingstoke.

Young, S.C., (2000), 'Participation Strategies and Environmental Politics: Local Agenda 21', in G. Stoker (ed.), *The New Politics of British Local Governance*, Macmillan, Basingstoke and London. pp. 181–197.

10

The political marketing revolution

> Consumption is the sole end and purpose of production; and the interest of the producer ought to be attended to only so far as it may be necessary for promoting that of the consumer. (Adam Smith, *The Wealth of Nations*, Book 4, Chapter 8, quoted by Laing et al. 2002: vii)

> Society has become more demanding. Consumers expect ever-higher levels of service and better value for money . . . Three trends highlight the rise of the demanding, sceptical citizen-consumer. First, confidence in the institutions of government and politics has tumbled. Second, expectations of service quality and convenience have risen. (Department of Society Security, 1998, quoted by Newman 2001: 49)

Loathe it or love it, political marketing is being used throughout the UK political system, challenging predetermined notions as to political behaviour and organisation, raising the spectre of the political consumer, and transforming the way that the UK is governed. The revolution may have gone unnoticed by some, partially recognised by others, but this book makes it clear that no political organisation or actor is immune from the forces of the market. With it, the political marketing revolution brings fresh perspectives on old questions, such as what democracy is, how it is best achieved, how political actors organise themselves, what the relationship between mass and elites is, and how this might be improved.

This is not going to be the definitive work on political marketing, or the last world. Further testing, conceptual exploration, refinement and discussion, drawing on literature not just within marketing or political science, but in education, health, sociology, economics, criminology and psychology, will doubtless come in the same way as new work has already been conducted following my *Political Marketing and British Political Parties* (see, for example, McGough 2002; Rudd 2002; Ormrod 2003; Lilleker and Lees-Marshment forthcoming). This book set out to show that political marketing is not just about parties. It has, at the very least, fulfilled this objective. Clearly, not all political organisations have moved towards implementing a full market orientation. There are empirical inconsistencies with the model; Westminster, for example, has a long way to go before achieving a full sales orientation, let alone a market orientation. Universities are beginning to design aspects of their product in line with market demand, but few if any have yet developed their entire educational provision in response to student as opposed to academic views. Parties such as the Tories have attempted to become market oriented but failed. Indeed, as each chapter has shown, there are many obstacles that work against political entities achieving a market orientation. Nevertheless, the trend is towards a market orientation, and the potential remains for this approach to restore trust in political and professional elites, as well as contributing to the survival of organisations such as the monarchy and the electoral success of parties such as New Labour.

A new empirical study in ten or twenty years time may find further movement in all of these areas towards a market-oriented approach. However, even if all practical obstacles are removed, there are and always will be normative questions about the spread of marketing to all areas of politics. At this stage there cannot really be a conclusion to these questions, but this chapter will at least discuss the rise of the political consumer, reassert the broader definition of political marketing, examine the link between party marketing and others areas of the political system, and discuss the potential link between political marketing and governance in the UK. Lastly, it explores how we can reah the full potential of political marketing, suggesting the need to rebalance the political marketing elite – mass relationship and discussing the difference between citizen and consumer.

Rise of the political consumer

All of the staff and politicians I spoke to noted how their 'consumers' were more critical of their work and behaviour in their particular organisation and area. However, such criticism is not unique to the institutions this book deals with. The rise of the political consumer is likely to be true of all political organisations. Voters are more critical of parties, tax-payers more questioning of councils, society less deferential towards the monarchy and viewers more demanding of the BBC. As Simon Lewis, former communications secretary to the queen, said (Lewis 2001), '18- to 24-year-olds . . . are much more ambivalent about institutions than other generations. It doesn't just refer to the monarchy, it refers to the BBC, it refers to the church, any of the established institutions.'

The rise of the political consumer can be viewed as part of the overall trend towards commodification or consumerism within western society. There is a significant literature within management and sociology about the rise of consumerism (see, for example, Abercrombie 1994; Campbell 1989; Gabriel and Lang 1995; Du Gray and Salaman 1992; Lury 1996; Lee 2000; Firat and Dholakia 1998; Belk 1995; Laing et al. 2002: 101). This literature could be explored further to understand better how political consumers might act in relation to marketed political organisations and actors, as much to inform the empirical practice of political marketing as any academic study. (The literature on postmodern consumerism could also be utilised.) This aspect can also be linked to the decline in voting and trust that has become a focus of debate for academic political scientists and political marketers, politicians, local councils and organisations such as the Electoral Commission (see, for example, Dermody and Hammer-Lloyd 2003; Bannon 2003), although some suggest that political marketing itself may be the cause of the discontent (see Lilleker 2003). Alternatively it could be the result of the imperfect or problematic use of political marketing currently. There remain, of course, sections of society still willing to trust professionals or officials, and other sections that may not exercise their rights at all, but the broad movement is away from a deferential, trusting relationship of elites to one much more critical and sceptical. Further research is needed to explore this. Politics is not like a business and there is no safety in assuming that consumers of commercial products will act in the same way as citizens of public organisations.

After the party is over . . .: political marketing redefined

> The reasonable man adapts himself to the world; the unreasonable man persists in trying to adapt the world to himself. Therefore all progress depends on the unreasonable man. (George Bernard Shaw, *Man and Superman*, 1903)

As the above quotation suggests, the central thesis of this book – that marketing is permeating all areas of politics – is likely to cause objections from some, but is nevertheless necessary in order to enable effective discussion of an empirical phenomenon. Political marketing is not just about campaigning, but it is not just about parties either. It extends way beyond the marketing of party politics to the head of state, parliament, local government, charities or interest groups, the media, health and education. In short, all areas of politics are subject to and using marketing in some form (see Lees-Marshment 2001, 2003a, 2003b). Political marketing equals, quite simply, the marketing of politics. Everything that is deemed political and uses marketing can be included.

Political marketing includes areas not covered in this book, such as police marketing (see, for example, Mawby and Worthington 2002; Granik 2000), marketing and the courts (the US Supreme Court, for instance, is often argued to be influenced by public opinion), marketing and central government or government departments (see Gelders and Walrave 2003, for example), social services marketing, the civil service, the government marketing of whole countries (see, for example, Rose 2003) and all legislatures (including the UN, the European parliament and the Welsh asssembly). Even the army started using adverts in cinemas in 2002 intended to appeal to young people in order to recruit new soldiers. Political marketing therefore includes but is not limited to:

- the courts;
- the police;
- the army and navy;
- social security and welfare provision;
- government departments;

- the head of state or monarchy;
- the media;
- local government;
- health;
- education;
- unemployment agencies;
- central government and No. 10;
- the civil service;
- political Parties;
- parliaments: the US Congress, the European parliament, the UN, Westminster, the Welsh assembly, the Scottish parliament.

Politics: is it really different to business?
The difficulty with doing cross-disciplinary research is that you end up being exposed to such an array of different ideas that you never satisfy anyone and always get questioned about something. The advantage is that it makes you think harder about explaining what might be obvious to some but not clear to others. One question that marketers ask me is why politics is different to a business. Why lump parties with health, when health is normally kept within the services marketing area? In other words, what makes political organisations different to businesses, or, on an even more fundamental level, what makes politics politics?

Politics is politics because it is about conflict and representation, and in countries like the UK it is linked to the election of a government that can then influence other parts of society. Whilst government may have general influence over individual business, it is not generally held directly responsible for success or failure in business in the same way as it is for any problems with the provision of health and education. The view of the market – the people – is that all of the areas listed above within the redefinition of political marketing are political. The difference is also clear from listening to those working within the wide range of political organisations studied in this book, especially those who have worked in both business and politics. For example, a university marketer noted that universities are not free as a business is to offer more places on a course, even when the demand is there, because the targets are set by government (Educational Marketer). A director of health for the Primary Care Trusts (to remain anonymous for ethical reasons) noted how 'resources are limited: parliament sets [the budget]', emphasising the link to government. A Labour MP (also to remain anonymous) said 'in politics you have to lead and make hard choices that won't appeal to people', and the queen's second communications secretary noted that 'dealing with the media at Buckingham Palace is a very different job to working with them at British Airways, or in any PR consultancy' (Walker 2003).

Additionally, a number of difficulties were mentioned as common to all political organisations studied, such as:

- lack of resources – funds, staff, time;
- misunderstanding of the nature of marketing;
- ideological opposition to marketing;
- the need for professional autonomy;
- lack of freedom;
- the need to lead, not just follow;
- a long-term perspective;
- the difficulty of just changing the product to suit changes in market demands.

To sum up, there are several main differences that mark politics as distinct from business. Political organisations:

- have a distinct ideology and value within them;
- do not hold making money as their main goal;
- have an obligation to serve the entire market;
- are linked to the election and influence of a government;
- are not free to act – they are constrained by government policy, which can be changed by election;
- are, and are expected to be, somewhat elite or distinct from society;
- possess a form of leadership or professional skill the rest of society does not have.

There are, naturally, overlaps and similarities with business, and I fully accept there is much to be learnt from that area. There are also overlaps with the arts or the church, for example, which are not businesses but are also not political, because they are not linked to the government and elections (see Shapiro 1973: 132).

The political marketing revolution: the link between the marketing of parties and other political organisations

When I completed *Political Marketing and British Political Parties* I was aware I was charting a change in party behaviour that could have profound implications for the political system and the workings of democracy. This change impacted not only on parties but on the rest of politics as a whole. This book upholds this view as, stepping back to analyse the system as a whole, we can see how changes in party behaviour have added further pressure for political marketing to be used in other aspects of the system. The development of the Labour party into a market-oriented party to win the 1997 election created pressure for the rest of the political system to become more responsive to its market. Not only are political organisations facing pressures from the development of the political consumer, but the government itself is encouraging movement towards more market-oriented forms of behaviour. Responding to Scottish public demand meant that the 1997 Labour government introduced devolution; the Scottish parliament was formed in the twenty-first century and was therefore much more market oriented than Westminster; then Westminster copied Scotland. A market-oriented party in government needs to deliver, and therefore put pressure upon health and education services to use marketing. Additionally, the range of interviews conducted for this book indicated that often staff involved in marketing move from one area to another, encouraging the spread of the use of marketing. Overall, therefore, we may be seeing a transformation in the way that Britain works, which will challenge the traditional notions of UK government.

Transforming the government of the UK: political marketing and governance

As is usual in Britain, the revolution may be occurring quietly, never completely overthrowing the system because elites respond in time as they have before in the nation's history,[1] but having significant implications for the overall way in which the political system works. If, as this books argues, all political organisations are using marketing – conducting market intelligence, designing their product and behaviour to suit public demands – then this suggests that the overall governance of the UK is also changing. Winetrobe and Seaton (2000: 17) noted that the creation of the new Scottish parliament was conducted by some with the hope that it would result in 'a new form of governance, distinct from, and an improvement on, the forms hitherto familiar in the UK'. Governance is a somewhat nebulous concept, hotly debated, but refers to the overall process of government within society, or 'the processes and mechanisms through which social co-ordination or order is established within a society' (Kooiman 1993, quoted by Laing et al. 2002: 53). It is discussed by many (see, for example, Rhodes 1996; Newman 2001; Kooiman 1993a; Wilson 1976; Rhodes 1997; Rose 1980) from different perspectives. Political marketing, by changing the relationship and decision-making process between elites and the masses, may affect the overall governance of the UK.

It will affect, for example, the 'way of delivering services' (Rhodes 1996: 653). It may also strengthen or weaken but will undoubtedly alter networks between organisations involved in delivering services (Rhodes 1996: 658), as organisations need to form networks not with each other but with people as a whole. It is unlikely to lead to a further hollowing out of the state (Rhodes 1996: 661), much as the politicians may like to see this, simply because it is not what the market – the public – want. It may just make it harder for politicians to control delivery when they need to because the public demand that delivery takes place. Political marketing is about the relationship between citizens and the state, between the people and the politicians, between the masses and the elite, and so the idea that 'governance defined as self-organizing inter-organizational networks does help us to understand change in British government' (Rhodes 1996: 666) is missing something: there is little reference to the market or the people. As Kooiman (1993a: 5) noted, 'more traditional policy models or arrangements seem to be either too government-oriented or too limited in scope'. The notion instead of a 'self-governing state', where 'the citizens . . . take part in the production process itself, not only as co-producers but also as citizens deciding what is to be produced and under what circumstances' (Beck Jorgensen 1993: 223), holds more potential to capture the development of political marketing. Newman (2001: 179) talks about 'a modern governance' with 'responsive institutions'.

The relationship between the political marketing revolution and governance remains to be explored fully, but there is a clear potential implication from the development of the former on the assumptions of existing analysis of the latter. It calls for the classical questions of representative and deliberative democracy, political authority and legitimacy, consent, balancing resources, and civic behaviour (Rose 1980: 6–26; see also Haaland Matlary 1995) to be revisited with the acknowledgement of the existence of political marketing in mind.

The development of the political consumer: blending the citizen and consumer

As a child of Thatcherism, who attended a comprehensive school, who became an academic in a rather long act of rebellion against society's proclamation that coming from a single-parent family I would develop into a crime-ridden delinquent, I am predisposed to favour the idea of the political system being run to suit the demands of the people. However, over the past six years, as I have watched the world from a political marketing perspective whilst working as a professional in a university, I have become nervous about the idea of a market-oriented political system which does not place responsibilities as well as rights on its consumers, and offer rights as well as demanding responsiveness from those who are under pressure to serve us all under difficult circumstances. There needs to be a rebalancing of the relationship between the elites and masses, and a redefinition of the consumer as a political consumer that incorporates some notion of citizenship.

Rebalancing the political marketing elite–mass relationship

Patients have the right to be treated well, but nurses also have the right not be physically and verbally abused when offering health care. Students have the right to a good degree, but not without recognising that their own efforts play a part in the result. And the most elitist of them all, the royal family, should be there to serve us, but the media hounding of Princess Diana was heavily criticised by the public after her death.

Indeed, if we want the best people at the top, consulting us, designing the best possible political product, then we need to ensure they will want to be there. Elitism in its purest form is not a nice concept, but to ensure those in elitist positions will give us what we want, it is partly our responsibility to support them and attract the best. When living in Scotland, I watched the selection of Jack MacConnell to be Scotland's third first minister in November 2001. It didn't start with a speech about Scottish politics, or what he would do for the people, but with a press conference where he and his wife gave statements about the affair he had seven years ago. Is this really the political product people wanted delivered?

I do not in any form suggest a return to deference. But we must create the best working practices and environment if we want the best people to be serving us.

Need for leadership: the consumer is not always right

> The message is simple. Political marketing is important and is certainly no threat to the democratic process. It is simply that it will not prove effective unless it is founded on substance . . . Political parties cannot just become marketing exercises even if they wish to. Ultimately it will fail because the public won't wear it . . . *there will always be a market for conviction in politics.* (McLetchie 2002)

There is always the need for some leadership and professional input into decision-making, and the *political* consumer is not always right. One area which may illustrate this is war. Can war be subject to marketing and public opinion? Tony Blair, one of the champions of party marketing, who took Britain into war on Iraq in the autumn of 2002, seemed to think not. At the time of deciding, potentially apparently against the will of most in his party and the majority of public opinion, he spoke of his belief, his certainty, his conviction that it was the right thing to do, adopting a more traditional, product-oriented attitude. Aside from whether the war was right or wrong, it can be argued that at times politics and society need unpopular decisions to be taken by elites. This has been discussed in areas such as health and education, where there is a value in professional, trained judgement. It is also true of party politics.

The true political consumer: blending consumerism with the citizen

Democracy and political marketing are related and not necessarily different in their goals and outcomes. Political marketing, by focusing discussion on the masses rather than the elites, holds the potential to improve democracy and give greater voice to the majority rather than the minority. But does it? Throughout this book it has been clear that there are potential weaknesses in making the entire political design subject to the people's demands. Students do not know as much as academics; doctors know more about health care than patients; politicians could at least in theory rise above individual demand and choose what is best for society as a whole. Marketing focuses on the individual, on more selfish wants, for each person, not everybody. Walsh (1994: 67) argued that consumer sovereignty perhaps 'does not express the fullness of citizenship, with its basis in community as well as individual rights'. Sturdivant (1981) also criticises marketing itself, because of its focus on the individual, consumer sovereignty and satisfying needs or whims.

Arguably, political consumers perhaps need to embrace elements of citizenship. Politics exists precisely because resources cannot simply be allocated according to need and demand. Marketing and management also contain those who doubt or challenge the notion of the consumer, even for business products. Gabriel and Lang (1995: 174) noted how citizens differ from consumers. Citizens are active members of communities, listened to but also prepared to defer to the will of the majority. They have to argue their views and engage with the views of others, and choosing as a citizen leads to a very different evaluation of alternatives from choosing as a consumer. Consumers need not be members of a community, and do not have to act on its behalf. They operate in impersonal markets, where they can make choices unburdened by guilt or social obligations. The idea of the consumer comes from 'economic man, who seeks the good life in markets'; the idea of the citizen comes from politics and philosophy (Gabriel and Lang 1995: 174–175). This brings us back to the usual dilemma of studying and practising political marketing: it is a blend of two worlds, of two disciplines, of two aspects, of two ways of doing things. The notions of citizen and consumer, when brought into the political sphere, need to be blended as political science and marketing tenets are blended by the emerging paradigm of political marketing theory, which takes some direct from each discipline but adapts others to create new theories.

Indications of the need for such a blend are already in existing analysis. For example, the World Health Organisation notes the responsibility of people, not just health professionals: 'Health for all will be achieved by the people themselves (World Health Organisation, Alma Ata Declaration, 1977, quoted by Hogg 1999: 138; see also Hogg 1999: 45–46). When local councils offer consultation about the path behind your house, if you do not go to the meeting, how can you expect your demands to be met? For political marketing to work, political consumers need to be active to a degree, otherwise there is little chance that political organisations will get it right. For this new political marketing relationship to work in health care, patients need to take their rights and responsibilities seriously. Laing et al. (2002: 101) contend that they need to exercise their rights but also 'accept the responsibilities given to them'. This may include not only complaining and voicing their opinion, but also participating in health programmes such as exercise or reducing alcohol intake in order for medical treatment to be effective. As Laing et al. (2002: 102) argued, 'well-being is more than simply the outcome of health care, it is a partnership between the individual and professional that requires both to play a part'.

This is true for all areas. Political consumers may need to act in a certain way for the market-oriented political marketing relationship to work. In moving towards a market-oriented model, Britain needs to be careful not to overbalance the rights of the political consumer relative to the political producer. It is not necessarily in the interest of society for us to dictate the personal lives of the royal family, any more than it would be the other way round. Students should not be able to buy their degree, even though they should receive the best service possible that academics can provide with the resources they are given and obtain. Political organisations are identifying the needs and wants of those they seek to serve and attempting to meet these demands. Political marketing has the potential to improve the representative function of a political system and democracy as a whole. But for this to happen, the political consumer needs to play as much of a role as the political producer. Political marketing focuses attention on the people, the market, the consumer, the citizen; so it makes sense that for it to reach its potential, not just the political elite but the political market make it work. Ultimately it is up to political consumers to ensure that their political organisations work to the maximum benefit of both the individual and society. It is, after all, only when a change is brought about by the masses that a revolution is enacted, and revolution will always be more of a political phenomenon than a business concept any day.

Notes

1 History suggests Britain had the potential for a number of revolutions in the nineteenth century, for example, but avoided the fate of countries such as France because the elites responded in time. For instance, the Conservative party responded to the need for greater democracy with the 1867 Great Reform Act.

Bibliography

Abercrombie, N. (1994), 'Authority and Consumer Society', in R. Keat, N. Whitely and N. Abercrombie (eds), *The Authority of the Consumer*, Routledge, London.

Bannon, D. (2003), 'Electoral Participation and Non-Voter Segmentation', paper presented at the PMG panels at the Political Studies Association Conference, April, Leicester.

Beck Jorgensen, T. (1993), 'Modes of Governance and Administrative Change', in J. Kooiman (ed.), *Modern Governance: New Government–Society Interactions*, Sage, London. pp. 219–232.

Belk, R.W. (1995), *Collecting in a Consumer Society*, Routledge, London.

Campbell, C. (1989), *The Romantic Ethic and the Spirit of Modern Consumerism*, Blackwell, Oxford.

Cotrim Maciera, J. (2002), 'Marketing Irish Political Parties: The Case of Fianna Fáil', *Political Marketing Conference Proceedings*, University of Aberdeen, September.

Dermody, J. and S. Hammer-Lloyd (2003), 'Exploring Young People's Trust in Politicians and Political Parties: Towards a Research Framework', *Academy of Marketing Conference Proceedings*.

Du Gray, P. and G. Salaman (1992), 'The Culture of the Customer', *Journal of Management Studies* 29(5): 616–633.

Educational Marketer (2003), Interview by J. Lees-Marshment with educational marketer at mainstream UK university, July.

Firat, A.F. and N. Dholakia (1998), *Consuming People: From Political Economy to Theaters of Consumption*, Routledge, London.

Gabriel, Y. and T. Lang (1995), *The Unmanageable Consumer*, Sage, London.

Gelders, D. and M. Walrave (2003), 'The Flemish Customer Contact Centre for Public Information from a Marketing and Management Perspective', *International Journal of Non-Profit and Voluntary Sector Marketing* 8(2): 166–180.

Granik, S. (2000), 'The Thames Valley Police and Restorative Justice', Class Discussion Document.

Haaland Matlary, J. (1995), 'New Forms of Governance in Europe? The Decline of the State as the Source of Political Legitimation', *Cooperation and Conflict* 30(2): 99–123.

Hogg, C. (1999), *Patients, Power and Politics: From Patients to Citizens*, Sage, London.

Kooiman, J. (ed.) (1993a), *Modern Governance: New Government–Society Interactions*, Sage: London.

Kooiman, J. (1993b), 'Social-Political Governance: Introduction', in J. Kooiman (ed.), *Modern Governance: New Government–Society Interactions*, Sage, London. pp. 1–8.

Laing, A., M. Fischbacher, G. Hogg and A. Smith (2002), *Managing and Marketing Health Services*, Thomson, London.

Lee, M.J. (ed.) (2000), *The Consumer Society Reader*, Blackwell, London.

Lees-Marshment, J. (2001), 'Comprehensive Political Marketing: What, How and Why', *Proceedings of the Academy of Marketing Conference*, Cardiff University, 2–4 July.

Lees-Marshment, J. (2003a), 'Marketing Political Institutions: Good in Theory but Problematic in Practice?', *Academy of Marketing Conference Proceedings*, University of Aston, 8–10 July.

Lees-Marshment, J. (2003b), 'Political Marketing: How to Reach that Pot of Gold', *Journal of Political Marketing* 2(1): 1–32.

Lewis, S. (2001), 'Communicating the Modern Monarchy,' Rolls-Royce Lecture, http://www.cf.ac.uk/jomec/reporters2001/lewismain.html, accessed February 2003.

Lilleker, D. (2003), 'Is There an Emergent Democratic Deficit in Britain? And Is Political Marketing the Cause?', paper presented at the PMG panels at the Political Studies Association Conference, April.

Lilleker, D. and J. Lees-Marshment, eds (forthcoming), *Political Marketing in Comparative Perspective*, Manchester University Press, Manchester.

Lury, C. (1996), *Consumer Culture*, Polity, Cambridge.

Mawby, R.C. and S. Worthington (2002), 'Marketing the Police: From a Force to a Service, *Journal of Marketing Management* 18: 857–876.

McGough, S. (2002), 'Selling Sinn Fein: The Political Marketing of a Party in Conflict Resolution', *Political Marketing Conference Proceedings*, University of Aberdeen, September.

McLetchie, D. (2002), 'Political Marketing and Democracy', speech at debate at the Political Marketing Conference, Aberdeen Town Hall, September.

Mochrie, R. (2003), 'Niche Marketing as an Entry Strategy: Formation and Growth of the Scottish Socialist Party', paper presented at the Political Studies Association Conference, Leicester.

Newman, J. (2001), *Modernising Governance: New Labour, Policy and Society*, Sage, London.

Ormrod, R. (2003), 'An Empirical Test of a Conceptual Model of Political Market Orientation', paper presented at the Political Studies Association Conference, Leicester.

Rhodes, R.A.W. (1996), 'The New Governance: Governing without Government', *Political Studies* 44(4): 652–667.

Rhodes, R.A.W. (1997), *Understanding Governance: Policy Networks, Governance, Reflexivity and Accountability*, Open University Press, Buckingham.

Rose, J. (2003), 'Government Advertising and the Creation of National Myths: The Canadian Case', special issue on *Broadening the Concept of Political Marketing*, ed. J. Lees-Marshment, *International Journal of Non-profit and Voluntary Sector Marketing* 8(2): 153–165.

Rose, R. (ed.) (1980), *Challenge to Governance: Studies in Overloaded Politics*, Sage, London.

Rothschild, M. (1979), 'Marketing Communications in Non Business Situations: Or Why it's So Hard to Sell Brotherhood Like Soap', *Journal of Marketing* 43: 11–20.

Rudd, C. (2002), 'Marketing the Message or the Messenger? The New Zealand Labour Party 1990–2002', *Political Marketing Conference Proceedings*, held at University of Aberdeen, September.

Shapiro, B. (1973), 'Marketing for Non-profit Organisations', *Harvard Business Review* 51: 123–132.

Shumar, W. (1997), *College for Sale: A Critique of the Commodification of Higher Education*, Falmer Press, London.

Sturdivant, F.D. (1981), 'Marketing, the State, and Legitimacy', in M.P. Mokwa and S.E. Permut (eds), *Government Marketing: Theory and Practice*, Praeger, New York.

Walker, S. (2003), Interview by J. Lees-Marshment with Simon Walker, former communications secretary to the queen, 19 February.

Walsh, K. (1994), 'Marketing and Public Sector Management', *European Journal of Marketing* 28(3): 63–71.

Wilson, H. (1976), *The Governance of Britain*, Sphere, London.

Winetrobe, B.K. and J. Seaton (2000), 'Creating a New Parliament in the UK: The First Year of the Scottish Parliament', paper presented at the Annual Meeting of the American Political Science Association, 31 August–3 September.

Index